Palgrave Studies in the History of Finance

The study of the history of financial institutions, markets, instruments and concepts is vital if we are to understand the role played by finance today. At the same time, the methodologies developed by finance academics can provide a new perspective for historical studies. Palgrave Studies in the History of Finance is a multi-disciplinary effort to emphasise the role played by finance in the past, and what lessons historical experiences have for us. It presents original research, in both authored monographs and edited collections, from historians, finance academics and economists, as well as financial practitioners.

More information about this series at
http://www.springer.com/series/14583

William A. Pettigrew · David Chan Smith
Editors

A History of Socially Responsible Business, c.1600–1950

palgrave
macmillan

Editors
William A. Pettigrew
School of History
University of Kent
Canterbury, UK

David Chan Smith
Department of History
Wilfrid Laurier University
Waterloo, ON, Canada

Palgrave Studies in the History of Finance
ISBN 978-3-319-60145-8   ISBN 978-3-319-60146-5 (eBook)
DOI 10.1007/978-3-319-60146-5

Library of Congress Control Number: 2017952819

Cover credit: Mo Peerbacus/Alamy Stock Photo

Printed on acid-free paper

This Palgrave Macmillan imprint is published by Springer Nature
The registered company is Springer International Publishing AG
The registered company address is: Gewerbestrasse 11, 6330 Cham, Switzerland

In memory of Chris Kobrak

Contents

Editors and Contributors

About the Editors

William A. Pettigrew is Reader in History at the University of Kent, the Founding Director of the Centre for the Political Economies of International Commerce (PEIC) and the Lead Investigator of a Leverhulme Trust grant project on England's seventeenth-century overseas trading companies. His first book was *Freedom's Debt: The Royal African Company and the Politics of the Atlantic Slave Trade, 1672–1752* (2013).

David Chan Smith is an Associate Professor at Wilfrid Laurier University who is researching the history of corporate social responsibility and beginning his next project on Matthew Boulton, innovation in the Industrial Revolution and the emergence of global carbon networks. His first book, a study of early modern common law, was *Sir Edward Coke and the Reformation of the Laws* (2014).

Contributors

Aske Laursen Brock is Research Assistant in the Centre for the Political Economies of International Commerce (PEIC) at the University of Kent. His Ph.D. dissertation investigated the role of company directors in early modern English society. His research examines the relationship between directors, global expansion and state formation in England.

Emily Buchnea is a researcher at Newcastle University Business School. Her research pertains to historical business networks, in particular the British corporate network and networks of early Anglo-American multinational enterprises.

Leslie Hannah is a Visiting Professor at the London School of Economics and divides his time between there and Tokyo. His latest article (with Makoto Kasuya) is "Twentieth-Century Enterprise Forms: Japan in Comparative Perspective", *Enterprise & Society* (March 2016).

Rod Lohin is Executive Director of the Lee-Chin Institute at the Rotman School of Management, where he oversees the Institute's research, grants and initiatives to reach business leaders and engage students in corporate sustainability. Formerly a management consultant specialising in corporate sustainability strategy, his clients have included RBC Financial Group, SunLife, BlackBerry, Ericsson, Kellogg and others.

Jon Mackay has degrees in management, economics and philosophy from the University of Waterloo, Canada. His research deals with corporate governance, often using the theoretical and analytical tools of social network analysis.

Jason Russell is an Assistant Professor of History and Labour Studies at Empire State College—State University of New York. His monograph was published by Athabasca University Press, and he has also published in *Management & Organizational History* and *Labour/Le Travail.*

Janette Rutterford is Professor of Financial Management at the Open University, UK. Her research interests include the history of investors and corporate governance as well as institutional investment. She is the author of *Stock Exchange Investment* and co-editor (with A. Laurence and J. Maltby) of *Women and their Money, 1700–1950* (2009).

Philip Scranton is University Board of Governors Professor, History of Industry and Technology, at Rutgers University.

Andrew Smith is Senior Lecturer in International Business at the University of Liverpool.

Edmond J. Smith is Research Associate at the Centre for the Political Economies of International Commerce (PEIC) at the University of Kent. He completed his Ph.D. at the University of Cambridge in 2015 and specialises in the history of trading companies in early modern England.

Kevin D. Tennent is Lecturer in Management at the University of York.

Michael Wagner obtained his M.B.A. from Concordia University in Montreal and worked in the telecommunications and energy industries in Canada, New Zealand, the UK and Portugal. He obtained his doctorate in history at the University of Oxford, where he teaches courses in eighteenth-century British history in the Department for Continuing Education.

Robert E. Wright is the Nef Family Chair in Political Economy at Augustana University.

List of Figures

List of Tables

1

The History of Corporate Social Responsibility: Towards a Comparative and Institutional Contribution

David Chan Smith and William A. Pettigrew

The common-law joint-stock corporation was born social. The drafters of the charter of the Muscovy Company (1555), the first English joint-stock company, had as much in mind when they explained that the company was intended to expand the "general wealth" of the kingdom. Though this was a commercial corporation trading for the private benefit of its members, the drafters also described the company as a "society" of merchants, and so the governor and his assistants were granted authority to make by-laws "for the government, good condition and laudable rule of the said fellowship and community of Merchants".[1] Charters of the period conventionally included similar expectations that companies should contribute to the public good through self-government and by providing wider social benefits. This

D.C. Smith (✉)
Department of History, Wilfrid Laurier University, Waterloo, Canada
e-mail: dasmith@wlu.ca

W.A. Pettigrew
School of History, University of Kent, Canterbury, UK
e-mail: W.Pettigrew@kent.ac.uk

W.A. Pettigrew and D.C. Smith (eds.), *A History of Socially Responsible Business, c.1600–1950*, Palgrave Studies in the History of Finance,
DOI 10.1007/978-3-319-60146-5_1

language operated to legitimize corporations whose grants and privileges reflected concessions by the crown in aid of governing markets, people and eventually territories. Though the twentieth century is assumed to be the heyday of the corporate entity, incorporated bodies proved useful for many purposes throughout the early modern period. Alongside universities, charities and religious institutions pursuing more recognizably public missions, incorporated towns and guilds kept markets in good order, trading companies pursued England's mercantilist ambitions overseas, and colonial corporations planted settlers with the aim of expanding national influence.[2]

This volume and its essays investigate this long history of national and multinational business across a wide geographical range. Their shared historical perspective illuminates the diversity of corporate forms and the very different social terms upon which companies have operated in the past and among varied cultures. By emphasizing diversity, such a comparative analysis questions the normative position of the joint-stock, for-profit corporation. Instead, these essays direct attention to the larger institutional influences on how people have conceived, regulated and operated corporations. Douglass North's definition of institutions is particularly apt, as "the rules of the game in a society or, more formally, are the humanly devised constraints that shape human interaction".[3] These institutions might take formal shape, as in the legal system, or instead as norms of behaviour, such as those influencing executive pay. The essays in this volume explore these institutional contexts and contribute alternative ways of thinking about the terms upon which business have been embedded within them socially and responsibly.

The link between how societies choose to organize their corporate existences, and the larger political and social effects of these decisions, has been a longstanding historical theme. F. W. Maitland was among the earliest English legal historians to examine the linkages between state formation and the forms of corporate life, pointing to a dynamic exchange between the two.[4] Translating and building on the insights of the German jurist Otto von Gierke, Maitland observed the rapid expansion of corporate law in England in his own time and sought to explicate the underlying, and poorly understood, theory. His contribution highlighted the changing organization of associational groups over time and their relationship with institutional transformation, especially the emergence of a strong, centralized state in England. Maitland's investigations participated in three important debates of his time. The first was an energetic discussion in Europe and America about the nature of corporate personality that continues to the present day.[5] Second, historians and legal scholars of his time were particularly keen to trace the idea of the corporation back in time, variously ascribing conceptual origins to Romano-canonical law, Italian joint-stock trading practices and Germanic patterns of collective association. Third, historians explored the causes of the quickening of formal incorporation in Europe. Among the most important of these theses was the argument that the central government extended the privilege of incorporation as part of a deliberate programme to create and expand national markets.[6]

The narrative of corporate change over time, however, is still incomplete. Few comprehensive accounts of the early modern and nineteenth-century corporate economy have been written.[7] For example, although there have been detailed studies of individual companies, there has been no general survey of early modern English commercial companies since Percival Griffiths's study in 1974.[8] Associational life also appears more complex than a top-down concession from the state. Recent literature has examined the autonomy and political self-interestedness of corporate boroughs and even trading corporations.[9] Furthermore, revisionist accounts have stressed that corporate change in England was often an expedient and pragmatic response to changing governmental and organizational practices rather than the application of clear policy or theory.[10] Corporate development was frequently ad hoc, and the legal theory represented subsequent rationalizations. Tracing the history of corporate development over time illuminates these changes, and situates present-day ideas about business and society within a longer term pattern. This introduction provides a brief example of this approach by examining the development of the business corporation at the common law and its relationship to the emergence of corporate social responsibility (CSR). By doing so, this analysis suggests how institutional analysis can strengthen the understanding of why the social responsibilities of business change over time.

The fifteenth century marks the first major locus of activity in English legal sources as groups of individuals sought formal letters patent from the crown using the language of incorporation.[11] J. H. Baker has observed that many corporations, such as colleges and religious houses, had not received formal grants of incorporation prior to the fifteenth century, and later, lawyers had to make claims of implied grants, custom or prescription.[12] The term "corporate" appears in the medieval *Year Books* (the serial report of legal cases) by 1408, though "corporation" is absent until 1429.[13] Susan Reynolds notes that in her study of cases for the years 1446–1452; there was yet no consistency in the corporate characteristics granted by these charters.[14] Grants were also being given to new corporate forms: in the early sixteenth-century professional associations such as the College of Physicians (1518) and later in the century to colonizing ventures.[15] The need for legal systematization was apparent in the humorous observation of one early sixteenth-century lawyer that "Defining the qualities of a corporation" could take weeks on account that "there are various kinds of corporation, and their qualities are different".[16] Even as lawyers debated the nature of legal personality over the next century, a clear consensus may have been elusive, despite Sir Edward Coke's oft-cited definition in 1612 that a corporation was an artificial construct of the law, "invisible, immortal, and resteth only in intendment and consideration of the Law".[17]

Business companies were rarely mentioned in legal treatises about corporate entities. Instead, the discussion focused on the paradigmatic corporations of the time, towns or guilds or charities and religious associations such as dean and chapter. It is therefore fitting that the leading corporate law case from the period, the *Case of Sutton's Hospital* (1612), in which Coke's famous dictum appears, was about a charity for the poor and indigent. When William Sheppard published the first common-law treatise on corporations (1659), the trading corporation is mentioned only infrequently.[18] Instead, the evolution of corporate law often took place in the context of cases about boroughs, charities and guilds. In turn, these ideas about "non-profit" corporates influenced the conceptualization of commercial companies. The relationship remains to be worked out, but has been observed: a modern commentator remarked that the similarities in the charter language of for and non-profit corporates "reveal the development of national commerce along lines which were familiar in municipal life".[19] The drafters of the charters of early business corporations described these entities as societies of individuals or "bodies politic" organized to govern their markets in the public interest. This conceptualization was distinctly political, as Tim Alborn for the nineteenth century and Phil Stern for the earlier period have ably demonstrated.[20] The political remit of the company often extended beyond the care of its immediate society. In the case of the East India Company, some corporations expanded to include territorial domination, and the corporate form was also used for companies of settlement, first in Ireland, and then the Virginia Company.

The specific social expectations of these commercial companies responded to the economic and political circumstances of the time. Early grants to groups of merchants in the fourteenth century included the privilege of self-government to maintain the challenges of long-distance markets and to keep merchants abroad in good order to prevent disruptions in trade.[21] Similar challenges confronted the earliest incorporated overseas trading companies, many of which were established or formally chartered during the sixteenth century, such as the Muscovy Company (1555), the Levant Company (1581) and the East India Company (1600). Incorporation solved problems of risk, capitalization and especially co-ordination in foreign markets. Similar to towns and guilds, they were granted by-law making power to enforce trade restrictions and to discipline traders in their markets. Their social responsibilities were sometimes radically different from modern expectations of corporate purpose. Corporate government of a commercial society was intended to regulate markets and to pursue the goals of a nascent mercantilism, or the belief that commerce or colonies, or both, and a positive balance of trade were essential to securing the wealth necessary to compete with other European nations.[22] The promoters of early modern corporations never tired of declaring the many new commodities, jobs and political influence that accrued to their country due to their company's efforts.

They were responding to these social expectations in order to protect their legitimacy and licence to operate. While commercial corporations were seldom the object of sustained jurisprudential analysis, they were often debated in political forums such as parliament and in public discussions about the regulation of commerce. Their exclusive trading privileges, in particular, made corporations controversial and were a magnet for complaint.[23] Already by the 1610s, writers were questioning whether the East Indies trade should be opened to independent traders or even managed by a regulated company. With the chartering of a new wave of companies for overseas trade in the later seventeenth century, such as the Royal African Company and the Hudson's Bay Company, the debate over monopoly powers intensified in leading cases, such as *The East India Company v. Sandys* (1683) and *Nightingale v. Brydges* (1689).[24] Throughout, defenders of corporate trade and advocates of open markets used the language of the public good, identifying the benefits or harm of corporate government of distant markets. Corporations promoted their control over markets with appeals to the public interest, claiming that free traders placed their own interests ahead of the commonwealth.[25] But even as these monopolies were weakened or removed, frenzies of corporate speculation broke out in the 1690s and then in the 1710s as new corporations were formed or advertised. Corporations such as the Bank of England (1694) and the South Sea Company (1711) added a further public service—the management of the increasing public debt and its transformation into a relatively liquid market.[26] But as speculation intensified and promoters sought to attract capital through fraudulent or ill-conceived incorporation schemes, rapid rises in share prices gave way to collapse in the Bubble year of 1720. The Bubble Act (1720) emerged first to dampen a runaway stock market and then to regulate strictly the corporate form.[27] Subsequent historians assumed that the act retarded further development in the corporate law, placing the corporate entity under "bureaucratic lock and key".[28] The partnership and sole proprietorship continued to be the dominant business forms throughout the eighteenth century, suggesting to many historians that the Bubble Act had held up a natural progression to general incorporation. The needs of society had decoupled from the legal and political willingness to meet them.[29]

Those who lived through the Industrial Revolution did not see things this way. Criticism of the business corporation was sharp.[30] Adam Smith is only the best-known spokesperson of a widely articulated set of assumptions: that corporations were not as efficient as partnerships; that they tended towards monopolies which harmed the public interest; that they promoted speculation and frauds; and that they were only suitable for very limited contexts that served the public good. Smith, with characteristic insight, articulated the agency problem:

> The directors of such [joint-stock] companies, however, being the managers rather of other people's money than of their own, it cannot well be expected, that they should watch over it with the same anxious vigilance with which the partners in a private copartnery frequently watch over their own.[31]

Others warned that the expansion of limited liability, often associated with incorporation, would produce reckless and irresponsible trading.[32] These fears were confirmed in the minds of many contemporaries during another bubble year, 1824–1825, leading the *Monthly Review* to declare in disgust that "the age of companies is passed".[33] In a sense, it was because with the passing of general incorporation statutes in 1844, 1855 and 1856 a new institutional regime finally emerged in Britain—behind both Continental and American law.[34] This prompted the attachment to corporations of a new and shifting set of social expectations and obligations. During the debates over general incorporation in the British Parliament, and before committees of inquiry and Royal Commissions, it was repeatedly asserted that general incorporation was not intended to solve a problem of lack of capital.[35] Instead, advocates of general incorporation argued for the need to expand the range of investments for the middle class and to facilitate the combination of working-class entrepreneurs. Incorporation would permit them to compete against established capitalist interests at lower cost and reduced risk, and especially to develop alternative, co-operative ventures.[36] Even proponents of liberalism such as John Stuart Mill and Richard Cobden pursued this line of reasoning, explaining that allowing capital to flow unhindered to talented working-class inventors and entrepreneurs would help to reduce the tension between capital and labour that the Industrial Revolution had made acute.[37]

General incorporation marked a trend towards the relaxation of corporate restrictions, especially in the USA, and it raised new issues about the social obligations and impact of these entities. Through instruments such as the trust and holding company, and the removal of interstate trading restrictions, large-scale entities such as Standard Oil emerged.[38] So too did new legal theories, which had formerly often conceptualized the corporation as an artificial person created through the operation of law by a gracious legislature or sovereign. The corporate person was increasingly theorized as either a "real entity" or an aggregate of shareholders acting in concert and contracting among themselves.[39] Thus, the corporate person should be entitled to similar rights as a natural one, as Holdsworth long ago observed: "This idea that the corporation is to be treated as far as possible like a natural man is the only theory about the personality of corporations that the common law has ever possessed".[40] In the USA, the Supreme Court has recognized the adherence of due process rights under the fourteenth amendment as well as free speech rights in *Citizens United*.[41]

The growing size of corporate entities made the agency problem particularly pressing, and this issue has preoccupied modern corporate law. As the shareholding public increased, its membership deepened to expand beyond those who took an active role in managing the company. Passive shareholders increasingly relied on the judgement and expertise of professional managers. How then to control the decision-making of these managers in such a way as to make them responsive to shareholder interests? Adolf Berle addressed this problem of separation and control by asserting that the authority granted to managers and directors was "necessarily and at all times exercisable only for the ratable benefit of all the shareholders as their interest appears".[42] This argument was of a piece with the decision by the Michigan Supreme Court in *Dodge v. Ford* (1919) that insisted directors should prefer the interest of the company's shareholders.[43] New theories of the firm, especially by Ronald Coase, and Michael Jensen and William Meckling, interpreted the development of the firm within the context of economic efficiency.[44] Socially responsible decision-making, it was argued, imposed unnecessary and inefficient transaction costs on shareholders. Milton Friedman gave these arguments point in his well-known article when he asserted that managers were not qualified to distinguish and pursue social ends, nor was it even ethical to allocate corporate assets in this way.[45] The social responsibility of business people was "value maximization", or as Friedman put it, "to increase its profits".

But the concentration of power and wealth represented by large corporations also prompted new critiques and eventually the beginnings of the distinct field of corporate social responsibility. The establishment of general incorporation and the removal of specific, socially conceived obligations in charters, left absent a justification for managers to pursue social ends. Advocates of CSR have continued to attempt to solve this problem.

E. Merrick Dodd was among the earliest and most influential proponents of social responsibility within the new corporate economy. Social responsibility, he claimed, emerged from the concentration of corporate influence: "Power over the lives of others tends to create on the part of those most worthy to exercise it a sense of responsibility".[46] Moreover, Dodd reinterpreted the entity theory of corporate personality to argue that because the corporation was a legal person distinct from its stockholders, it was consequently "affected not only by the laws which regulate business but by the attitude of public and business opinion as to the social obligations of business".[47] The managers of the corporation were therefore responsible to the institution as a fictive person or real entity, rather than simply to the owner-shareholders. The corporate person, like any other person in society, had a social existence and was therefore responsible for contributing to the wider society.

As the field began to coalesce in the 1950s, early CSR writers were adept at describing the social responsibilities of business, but less so at explaining why managers might be incentivized to fulfil them. Howard Bowen's seminal work, *The Social Responsibilities of the Businessman*, explained that CSR "refers to the obligations of businessmen to pursue those policies, to make those decisions, or to follow those lines of action which are desirable in terms of the objectives and values of our society".[48] Bowen argued that the attitudes of American businesspeople had changed under the influence of the Great Depression and World War II. On the one hand, the economic collapse of the 1930s brought forth sceptical attitudes towards laissez-faire that might spur increased regulation, such as the New Deal. Critical scrutiny brought pressure on business from other interest groups, especially organized labour and government regulators. The war, however, made manifest the productive potential of capitalist enterprise and often involved businesspeople in government service, "broadening" their perspectives.[49] Moreover, the businessperson was embedded in society, and society had changed: "the most basic explanation of the new business ethos has been the marked evolution in the underlying social ideals of the American people. In the last fifty or seventy-five years, humanitarian concern for the individual human being has been widespread".[50] Bowen pointed to the institutional context of business as the underlying motivation for social responsibility: "the businessman has been subjected to pressures originating from the new social climate in which he operates, and at the same time he himself has assimilated many of the values and attitudes that are characteristic of this new social climate".[51]

Keith Davis linked the concept of legitimacy to this association between corporate power and responsibility. Formulating the so-called iron law of responsibility, he warned that "Whoever does not use his social power responsibly will lose it. In the long run those who do not use power in a manner which society considers responsible will tend to lose it because other groups eventually will step into assume those responsibilities".[52] Nor was such responsibility exhausted by simply fulfilling the obligations imposed by the law on corporate managers. CSR involved going beyond the law in a voluntary capacity: "A firm is not being socially responsible if it merely complies with the minimum requirements of the law, because this is what any good citizen would do".[53]

These analyses were particularly telling of the New Deal and Cold War environment in which they were written. On the one hand, there might be a sense of patriotic or social duty, especially during the Cold War. Post-war corporatism laid heavy emphasis on the professional and civic duty of executives, and their social duty was often interpreted within the context of resistance to communism and maintaining the virtuous circle of consumption.[54] Moreover, substantial challenges to business existed in the form of labour unions, consumer advocacy groups, and government regulators that might influence managers to at least consider stakeholder and public interests. But especially during the late 1970s, and the growth of the shareholder capitalism and deregulation movements, the influence of those forces on managerial decision-making was weakened.

Increasingly, therefore, CSR became associated with claims for improved bottom-line performance. In this way, social responsibility was aligned in the literature with shareholder interests and the newer institutional context that privileged value maximization. Conscientious decisions would make the companies more profitable in the long run, a notion examined by early CSR pioneers such as Johnson, and popularized by the management writings of Peter Drucker.[55] CSR could be operationalized as part of business strategies in various forms, including as a means to bolster reputation and brand value, the instrumental pursuit of corporate philanthropy, cost savings through sustainability practice, and improved retention through conscientious human resources policies. These strategies enabled managers to pursue the "triple bottom line" (profit, planet and people), and Michael Porter and Mark Kramer's "shared value".[56] The relationship between CSR and innovation has also been explored.[57] These ideas have stimulated a significant literature on CSR and corporate results, a literature that has not yet established a clear correlation across sectors.[58]

They also explicitly emphasized the larger institutional context within which firms operate, even beginning to suggest institutional reform in the law and economic theory, and focusing on the process of legitimation. S. Prakash Sethi was one of the earliest to formalize this analysis, writing against the backdrop of Japanese competition in 1975.[59] Sethi observed the "humane" organizational structure and wage and human resource policies of leading Japanese corporations. But these businesses' practices, according to Sethi, were not the consequence of altruism, but rather responded to the expectations of Japanese society. In order to preserve their legitimacy within that society, managers pursued these policies and constantly strove to pattern their activities in order to be "in congruence with the goals of the overall social system".[60] Thus, institutional context operated to define and shape the processes that provided legitimacy, and in turn affected managerial decision-making. Sethi argued that legitimacy flowed from a company's "social performance", attained in three broad ways. Managers responded to social obligations imposed on them by market or legal constraints. They engaged in social responsibility to align with "the prevailing social norms, values, and expectations of performance".[61] Finally, companies were socially responsive insofar as they anticipated and prevented future adverse consequences of their behaviours. But the benchmark of social performance, Sethi insisted, was institutional and "must be to a great extent culturally and temporally determined".[62] Similarly, in his influential elaboration of the CSR concept in 1979, Archie Carroll emphasized the wider context: "the social responsibility of business encompasses the economic, legal, ethical, and discretionary expectations that society has of organizations at a given point in time".[63]

Researchers in stakeholder theory, and allied concepts of corporate citizenship, corporate philanthropy and corporate social accountability, have also interrogated the influence of the larger institutional context.[64] These developments suggest an evolving debate over the relationship between corporations and society, and the need to restructure the institutional context within which managerial decisions are made. They also point to the imperative to move the analysis of social responsibility beyond the firm, especially by reshaping the legal framework within which companies operate. John Parkinson's exhaustive study of English company law argues, for example, that "From the standpoint of advocates of social responsibility, therefore, it should be a function of company law to facilitate the reception and proper weighting of third-party interests in corporate decision-making, even though this may require the adoption of policies which are not privately profit-maximizing".[65] The subsequent literature on legal mechanisms to promote corporate social accountability has suggested the need for a renewed understanding of the indirect influence of the legal system on corporate decision-making.[66] On this account, the law provides more than a minimum standard of behaviour and can be shaped to push managers in socially desirable directions through direct and indirect compliance requirements.

Institutional approaches have prompted interest in comparative work across national boundaries and cultures on the varieties of corporate social responsibility.[67] Geoffrey Jones and Bryan Husted have demonstrated the potential of a comparative examination of social responsibility by examining its manifestation in both a global and chronologically broad context.[68] Their investigations suggest the value of such comparative work, placing CSR as a specific and recent manifestation of a debate about associational life that has been ongoing across cultures and time. The significant attention by researchers to *gappon-shugi* or Japanese ideas of ethical capitalism is particularly well explored. The literature on Shibusawa Eiichi (1840–1931), a serial entrepreneur and founding advocate of *gappon-shugi*, and Japanese business practices that are socially responsible have highlighted the unique cultural contexts that gave rise to these ideas, as well as their similarities to European and American CSR.[69]

The historical understanding of these institutional contexts and their impact on corporate evolution is still developing. Morrell Heald provided an early example of such an analysis, stressing the prevalence of corporate philanthropy in the nineteenth century, reflected in the paternalism of George Pullman and corporate contributions to charities.[70] W. Randy Evans and his co-authors have sketched a longer term story, tracing the discussion over the business and its relationship to society back to the Code of Hammurabi (1750s BCE).[71] Likewise, Christian religious thought, Owenism, and attempts by businesspeople to ameliorate factory conditions and improve employee living standards during the Industrial Revolution have also been identified as precursors to CSR.[72] Nicholas Eberstadt has offered a broad historical thesis connected to the Industrial Revolution to explain the evolving relationship between business and society, arguing that "Business traditionally has been a tightly regulated instrument of social development".[73] The concentration of capital during the Industrial Revolution enabled businesses to "circumvent checks on power". CSR therefore reflects a return to "the social contract of power with responsibility".[74] Husted has also noted that the "most interesting antecedents" occurred as a consequence of the Industrial Revolution. Industrialization confronted business people with a series of problems, including labour unrest, poor working conditions and environmental impact.[75] The "pressures for legitimacy" as well as genuine concern about inequality, social order and the human condition, led businesspeople to respond in socially responsible ways, though these reactions differed among countries.[76]

These explorations into the deep past have, however, been glancing. Early reconstructions assume that previous manifestations of the business and society connection reflect a prelude to the formal expression of this problem in CSR. The path-breaking historical studies of CSR by Archie Carroll, W. Randy Evans and Ken Lipartito have been focused on identifying the roots of the field and reconstructing its formation.[77] Thus, while Carroll observes it is "possible to trace evidences of the business community's concern for society for centuries", only during the past century has social responsibility been an object of "formal writing".[78]

The essays in this volume continue the work of comparative CSR in both the temporal and cultural senses. They adopt the methodological perspective that through comparative work on institutions as well as firms, many different manifestations of social responsibility can be detected. By doing so, they make three key contributions to the established literature. First, their cultural and chronological breadth emphasizes how corporations have been conceptualized differently across time and space, and the manifold ways in which their social connections can be understood. This perspective directs attention to the institutional factors that shape corporate behaviour and their change over time and contests the normative status of the publicly traded, for-profit corporation by examining the social obligations of a variety of corporate forms, including non-profits and regulated corporations. The essays actively identify connections among these different corporate forms, rather than distinguishing them along separate paths of development.

Second, the long-term perspective illuminates the evolution of the corporate form over time, a transformation that continues today. This evolution is not necessarily progressive, but rather demonstrates how corporations develop or fail to develop according to their institutional environments. The primacy of non-profit corporates in the early modern period, for example, reveals characteristics of the society and economic organization of the time radically different from the present day. There are also continuities that a long-term perspective can reveal: just as writers on the early modern period have highlighted the political functions of the corporate form, so too has recent literature noticed the political behaviour of corporations, many of which are assuming formerly "public" functions.[79]

Finally, these perspectives can contribute to the comparative CSR conversation. CSR's history as a formal field began in the 1950s, but the constellation of issues and problems that CSR writers engage have been subject to debate since laws in different jurisdictions recognized the corporate entity. CSR is thus one manifestation of a much larger phenomenon. Placing CSR within this context underscores the many different ways that societies have interpreted the social existence of corporations in their midst, and chosen to regulate them or imposed social obligations. Conceptualizing CSR within a larger conversation about the social responsibilities of corporations also questions the exportability of CSR and its limitations as a field developed within a specific temporal and institutional context. But a comparative perspective also suggests very different approaches across cultures and time—a seedbed—to the same problems tackled by the present manifestation of CSR. By doing so, the past may point to the possibility of a different future.

***

The chapters in this volume assess the social responsibilities of business across the seventeenth, eighteenth, nineteenth, and much of the twentieth centuries. This long-timeframe allows us to focus on a wide variety of businesses: from joint-stock and regulated trading companies to modern multinational corporations, from non-profit corporations to family partnerships. Although these various forms operated, for the most part, in Anglo-North American contexts (with the important exception of the communist companies that Philip Scranton analyses), these organizations operated around the world and responded to the different social contexts they encountered. An overarching theme of the volume is how businesses struggled to uphold their social responsibilities as their operations became more international. The chapters assess the full range of social obligations with which corporations interacted across the period: their responsiveness to state directives; their contribution to state policy and to the public purse, philanthropy and civil society; their embodiment of broader cultural norms that compelled corporate activity to advance the public good; and the ways in which networks structured the relationships between corporations and their social obligations. The chapters move beyond firm-level analyses of the corporation and investigate the social life of the corporation from three key perspectives: from the leadership of the corporations; from their investors; and from their broader stakeholders (including government and representatives of their social constituencies). A persistent concern among several chapters is how businesses structured complex social networks and how these networks encouraged socially responsible activity as well as helping to facilitate commercial success. In this way, corporations resemble processes of negotiation with external social constituencies rather than hierarchical institutions managing from centralizing boards of directors to often distant supply chains.

The second and third chapters focus on English early modern trading corporations. They depict early multinational businesses as instinctively social concerns—sensitive to long-established cultural prescriptions that expected commercial gain to be justified by provisions for society. In their opening chapter, *Leadership and the Social Agendas of the Early Modern English Trading Corporations*, William A. Pettigrew and Aske Laursen Brock analyse the significance of the trading corporations' social obligations (at home and abroad) to the seventeenth-century English understanding of what constituted good corporate leadership. They explore the theories and practice of socially determined leadership styles as well as the prosopography of corporate leaders in this period. Their chapter stresses that leadership in early modern trading corporations was principally about forging positive relationships with constituencies typically characterized as external to the corporation: the labour force, the state, suppliers, the needy and the public. Pettigrew and Brock also note (as do other contributors to the volume) how satisfying social obligations often helped to cement commercial relationships. Through engagement in corporate projects such as "the Stock for putting Poor French protestants to work", directors of multinational companies were instrumental in improving society while aiding sociability that facilitated strategic network-building.

In the second chapter focusing on seventeenth-century English trading corporations, *Socially Responsible and Responsive Business in*

Seventeenth-Century England, Edmond Smith concentrates on the petition as a mechanism that allowed the broader constituents of corporations to hold directors to account and ensure they upheld their social obligations. The chapter examines the petitioning culture of the 1620s in detail before briefly examining the later 1670s and 1680s to show how social responsibility became an ingrained part of the governance of corporations, with sophisticated mechanisms in place to ensure businesses kept the end of the social bargain that made their existence possible. Echoing Pettigrew and Brock's chapter, Smith suggests the corporations were responsive to a broader corporate constituency whose breadth confirms that, despite their exclusivity, corporations depicted themselves as inseparable from the social basis that supplied their labour force, customer base and social environment.

In the third chapter, *Profit and Surety: The British Chartered Trading Companies and the State Before the Nineteenth Century*, which connects the seventeenth-century English context for trading corporate activity with the eighteenth century, Michael Wagner concentrates on perhaps the most important social contribution of business—tax. Wagner examines the changed relationship between trading corporations and the state authorities that chartered them. The chapter concentrates on the public funds used to support the companies' operations and the tax contributions the companies made to the state. From the beginning of their existence, trading companies celebrated their social role as the providers of employment and as a syphons for legitimate (as opposed to smuggled) trade that could be taxed. Similarly, the state protected the companies through tariffs that also helped finance the naval convoys that offered protection in a different form. Wagner also assesses the alliances and lobbies formed between the state and corporate interests that allowed this collaboration to function until its logical endpoint—global commercial predominance allowed private corporations to concentrate on profit as trading companies entered a long slow decline through the nineteenth century.

Robert Wright's chapter, *Corporate Social Responsibility and the Rise of the Non-profit Sector in America*, pushes the analysis of socially responsible business into the early period of US history and shifts institutional focus from trading companies to non-profit corporations. Wright shows that the emergence of the non-profit sector helped to clarify the profit-seeking role of private corporations and to end the public and financial appeal of chartered companies as well as the limits of the state's social field of view. Since the nation's early years, business corporations were to sell goods to customers and provide employment for the sole purpose of generating profits for stockholders. As Wright makes clear, aside from obeying the law, they had no direct social responsibility to employees, including corporate officers, or other elements of society. At the same time, non-profits provided public services that government would not provide at all or could not provide as efficiently.

Emily Buchnea's chapter, *Local Concerns, Global Impact: The Social Structures and Influence of Early Anglo-American Firms at Home and Abroad, 1815–1840*, tests the developing insights about the social constituencies of corporate bodies on the businesses that operated as transatlantic partnerships. Her chapter examines the transnational networks of early Anglo-American "multinational" merchant firms and the variegated social impact they had upon England, the USA, Canada, the Caribbean and Central and South America: from the financial sector and transportation networks to mining and land acquisition in distant locations. These firms succeeded across national borders because of their ability to develop networks of agents in different societies. As unchartered entities, they enjoyed some freedom from state regulations during the first half of the nineteenth century, a crucial period for multinational enterprises. But they remained subject to the cultural expectation that they act sensitively towards the local communities with which they interacted. While they were careful to nurture a socially responsible profile locally, beyond the need to cultivate overseas agents for their businesses, they neglected the social constituencies of their overseas trading hinterlands. Buchnea's chapter is the first to point out the ways in which the development of increasingly global businesses dissolved the local social ties that had sustained the socially responsible expectations of, for example, trading corporations. Buchnea's partnerships pioneered structures for unregulated, unchartered multinational enterprise, and in doing so began to expose the challenges of acting socially in their global as well as local constituencies.

Janette Rutterford's chapter, *The Distant Shareholder: Attenuated Investment and the Diffusion of Social Concerns*, sustains this theme for the late nineteenth and early twentieth centuries. Focusing on British investors, this chapter concentrates on the relationship between distance, shareholding and supply and demand for securities, both domestic and overseas, and the effects of these patterns of corporate ownership on the social implications of business activity. Rutterford examines how the democratization of shareholding influenced the social obligations of companies and how the increasing tendency to invest in international firms further dissolved corporations' relationships to local stakeholders. As Rutterford makes clear, while the owner of capital in local firms could derive some social status and often invested funds philanthropically, the increasingly distant investor cared more about returns and—on the whole—less about ethics.

Jon Mackay's chapter, *Canadian Regional and National Business Elites in 1912: Local and Social Connections*, returns the volume to the social networks of businesses and how these facilitated—in particular circumstances—socially beneficial outcomes. Mackay's chapter recreates the national network of business elites and their ties to one another. It finds that most growing urban centres throughout Canada generally maintained business connections with executives in Montreal or Toronto—the major financial and business centres of the country. Mackay focuses on a fascinating exception: the ethnically German city of Berlin in Waterloo County, Ontario. In Berlin, the regional elites looked inward. They chose to work together and align the city of Berlin's public policies in ways to aid regional businesses, instead of accessing resources through the existing network of Anglo-Canadian business elites. Over time, business elites and the city also invested in public goods in the form of public utilities. As Mackay summarizes, the Berlin business community offers an instructive look at the social assumptions often underlying private business relationships and the ways in which the interests of different publics were served by these relationships. Berlin distinguished itself as a community—based on ethnicties—that prospered because its business leaders served in public office and invested in public infrastructure out of a collective social conscience facilitated by cultural and ethnic cohesion.

Leslie Hannah's chapter, *Trust, Reputation, and Regulation: Securities Markets in Europe, the US, and Japan before 1914*, offers a new understanding of the importance of regulatory mechanisms designed to uphold socially responsible agendas in explaining the size of early twentieth-century stock markets. Hannah's chapter also shows how local networks of trust between investors and enterprises often assisted stock-market size as well as legal protections for investors and the state's attention to particular corporate governance provisions.

In the chapter by Jason Russell, Andrew Smith and Kevin D. Tennent, *Adolf Berle's "Good Neighbour" Critique of US Corporate Interests in the Caribbean Basin*, the focus shifts from investors to state policy—in this case, in the USA in the 1930s and 1940s. Focusing on Adolf Berle, who served as Assistant Secretary of State for Latin American Affairs from 1938 to 1944, the chapter argues that, while Berle was critical of the excesses of some US corporations in the region, he was neither anti-capitalist nor an opponent of US overseas economic expansion. Instead, the policies Berle promoted ultimately served to strengthen the long-term well-being of US business interests overseas by reining in the worst abuses of US business imperialism in Latin America. Berle's belief that the long-term interests of US business in the western hemisphere could be served by sometimes siding with Latin American governments in disputes with particular US firms contributed to his strong support for Franklin Roosevelt's "Good Neighbour" policy. The chapter demonstrates how US foreign policy began to appreciate that prioritizing the overseas social basis for US corporate expansion offered a surer means to uphold the longer term interests of those corporations and their domicile nation.

In the final full chapter, *Social(ist) Responsibility and Communist Management in Postwar Central Europe*, Philip Scranton introduces an entirely different context—that of the communist economies of Central Europe in the 1950s. Scranton uses this context to demonstrate how prioritizing social concerns proved just as difficult for businesses operating in a socialist setting as it did for those in profit-maximizing cultures. As Scranton puts it: "Building a better society ran a distant second to getting the goods out the door and the operation to the planning year's end". Scranton also uses his analysis to challenge the view that commercial success was predetermined in capitalist countries and impossible in communist countries. He ends by suggesting that his comparison with communist enterprises implies that regulation holds the key to proposing a "centre that will hold" between planned economies and those led by the market. Rod Lohin, the Executive Director of the Michael Lee-Chin Family Institute for Corporate Citizenship at the Rotman School of Management in Toronto, offers an afterword, *The History (and Future History) of Socially Responsible Business*, which places the conclusions of each essay into the context of the ongoing policy work of the Institute.

The volume therefore offers a range of examples over time to demonstrate how businesses have defined and responded to their social expectations. Overall, the volume's long-term perspective demonstrates the oscillation between cultural norms that encouraged socially responsible business and states that tried to force businesses to behave responsibly. It suggests that corporations have been both socially and financially constructive when cultural and regulatory mechanisms have operated interdependently.

Notes

1. Richard Hakluyt, *The Principal Navigations, Voyages, Traffiques and Discoveries of the English Nation* (London, 1589), 268, 270.
2. Recent contributions to the early modern historiography include Anna Winterbottom, *Hybrid Knowledge in the Early East India Company World* (Basingstoke: Palgrave Macmillan, 2016); William A. Pettigrew, "Corporate Constitutionalism and the Dialogue between the Global and Local in Seventeenth-Century English History", *Itinerario* 39, no. 3 (2015): 487–501; Germain Sicard, *The Origins of Corporations: The Mills of Toulouse in the Middle Ages*, ed. William N. Goetzmann, trans. Matthew Landry (New Haven: Yale University Press, 2015); Jonathan Eacott, *Selling Empire: India in the Making of Britain and America, 1600–1830* (Chapel Hill: University of North Carolina Press, 2015); Theodore Binnema, *Enlightened Zeal: The Hudson's Bay Company and Scientific Networks, 1670–1870* (Toronto: University of Toronto Press, 2014); William A. Pettigrew, *Freedom's Debt: The Royal*

African Company and the Politics of the Atlantic Slave Trade, 1672–1752 (Chapel Hill: University of North Carolina Press, 2014); Emily Erikson, *Between Monopoly and Free Trade: The English East India Company, 1600–1757* (Princeton: Princeton University Press, 2014); Philip J. Stern, "Corporate Virtue: The Languages of Empire in Early Modern British Asia", *Renaissance Studies* 26, no. 4 (2012): 510–30; Philip J. Stern, *The Company-State: Corporate Sovereignty and the Early Modern Foundations of the British Empire in India* (New York: Oxford University Press, 2012); H. V. Bowen, *The Business of Empire: The East India Company and Imperial Britain, 1756–1833* (Cambridge: Cambridge University Press, 2008); David Chan Smith, "Empire, the Political Economy of Cooperation, and the Social Life of the Hudson's Bay Company", *William and Mary Quarterly*, forthcoming.

3. Douglass C. North, *Institutions, Institutional Change, and Economic Performance* (Cambridge: Cambridge University Press, 1990), 3; see also John Searle, *The Making of the Social World: The Structure of Human Civilization* (Oxford: Oxford University Press, 2010), and the exploration of organizational and institutional co-evolution in Marcelo Bucheli and R. Daniel Wadhwani, eds., *Organizations in Time: History, Theory, Methods* (Oxford: Oxford University Press, 2013).
4. F. W. Maitland, *State, Trust, and Corporation*, eds. David Runciman and Magnus Ryan (Cambridge: Cambridge University Press, 2003).
5. Paul Vinogradoff, "Juridical Persons", *Columbia Law Review* 24, no. 6 (1924): 594–604; George F. Canfield, "The Scope and Limits of the Corporate Entity Theory", *Columbia Law Review* 17, no. 2 (1917): 128–43; Samuel Williston, "History of the Law of Business Corporations before 1800. I", *Harvard Law Review* 2, no. 3 (1888): 105–24; Arthur W. Machen, "Corporate Personality", *Harvard Law Review* 24, no. 4 (1911): 253–67; Harold J. Laski, "The Early History of the Corporation in England", *Harvard Law Review* 30, no. 6 (1917): 561–88; W. S. Holdsworth, "English Corporation Law in the 16th and 17th Centuries", *Yale Law Journal* 31, no. 4 (1922): 382–407; Ronald Ralph Formoy, *The Historical Foundations of Modern Company Law* (London: Sweet and Maxwell, 1923); John Dewey, "The Historic Background of Corporate Legal Personality", *Yale Law Journal* 35, no. 6 (1926): 655–73; Franklin D. Jones, "Historical Development of the Law of Business Competition", *Yale Law Journal* 35, no. 8 (1926): 905–38.

6. William Cunningham, *The Growth of English Industry and Commerce* (Cambridge: Cambridge University Press, 1925); George Unwin, *The Gilds and Companies of London* (London: Methuen, 1925); Charles Gross, *The Gild Merchant: A Contribution to British Municipal History* (Oxford, 1890); Maitland, *State, Trust and Corporation*, 66; This thesis can be seen to inform the analysis of Karl Polanyi, for example, *The Great Transformation: The Political and Economic Origins of Our Time* (Boston, MA: Beacon Press, 2001), 66–70.
7. The most recent is Ron Harris, *Industrializing English Law: Entrepreneurship and Business Organization, 1720–1844* (Cambridge: Cambridge University Press, 2011). Older works are still cited as authoritative, such as W. R. Scott, *The Constitution and Finance of English, Scottish and Irish Joint-Stock Companies to 1720* (Cambridge: Cambridge University Press, 1910–12); A. B. Dubois, *The English Business Company after the Bubble Act, 1720–1800* (Oxford: Oxford University Press, 1938); Bishop Hunt, *The Development of the Business Corporation in England, 1800–1867* (Cambridge, MA: Harvard University Press, 1936); W. S. Holdsworth, *A History of English Law* (Boston, MA: Little, Brown, 1924), vol. 8, 192–220; Cecil T. Carr, *Select Charters of Trading Companies, 1530–1707* (London: Bernard Quaritch, 1913).
8. Percival Joseph Griffiths, *A Licence to Trade: The History of English Chartered Companies* (London: E. Benn, 1974); a short, recent survey is John Micklethwait and Adrian Wooldridge, *The Company: A Short History of a Revolutionary Idea* (New York: Modern Library, 2005). Leading surveys of the development of the early US corporate economy include James Willard Hurst, *The Legitimacy of the Business Corporation in the Law of the United States, 1780–1970* (Clark, NJ: The Lawbook Exchange, 2010) and Glenn Porter, *The Rise of Big Business, 1860–1920* (Wheeling, IL: Wiley–Blackwell, 2005); and in France, Charles E. Freedeman, *The Triumph of Corporate Capitalism in France 1867–1914* (Rochester, NY: University of Rochester Press, 1993); Charles E. Freedeman, *Joint-Stock Enterprise in France, 1807–1867: From Privileged Company to Modern Corporation* (Charlottesville: University of North Carolina Press, 1979).
9. Paul D. Halliday, *Dismembering the Body Politic: Partisan Politics in England's Towns, 1650–1730*, Cambridge Studies in Early Modern British History (Cambridge: Cambridge University Press, 1998);

Phil Withington, *The Politics of Commonwealth: Citizens and Freemen in Early Modern England* (Cambridge: Cambridge University Press, 2009); Phil Withington, "Company and Sociability in Early Modern England", *Social History* 32, no. 3 (2007): 291–307.

10. Heinz Lubasz, "The Corporate Borough in the Common Law of the Late Yearbook Period", *Law Quarterly Review* 80 (1964), 228–43 (229, 231), and Susan Reynolds, "The History of the Idea of Incorporation or Legal Personality: A Case of Fallacious Teleology", in *Ideas and Solidarities of the Medieval Laity: England and Western Europe*, ed. Susan Reynolds (Aldershot: Variorum, 1995), 1–20, and literature cited at 21n.
11. Reynolds, "Idea of Incorporation", 12.
12. J. H. Baker, *The Oxford History of the Laws of England: Volume VI: 1483–1558* (Oxford: Oxford University Press, 2003), 622.
13. David Seipp, "Formalism and Realism in Fifteenth-Century English Law: Bodies Corporate and Bodies Natural", in *Judges and Judging in the History of the Common Law and Civil Law: From Antiquity to Modern Times*, eds. J. Getzler and P. Brand (Cambridge: Cambridge University Press, 2012), 40.
14. Reynolds, "Idea of Incorporation", 12–13.
15. Baker, *The Oxford History of the Laws of England*, 622–23.
16. John Spelman, *John Spelman's Reading on "Quo Warranto": Delivered in Gray's Inn, Lent 1519*, ed. J. Baker (London: Selden Society, 1998), 154.
17. *Case of Sutton's Hospital*, 10 Coke Reports 32 b, 77 *English Reports* 973. Compare John Marshall's definition of the corporation as an "artificial being, invisible, intangible, and existing only in contemplation of law": *Trustees of Dartmouth College v. Woodward*, 17 US 4 Wheat. 518 (1819), 636. The absence of agreement on the nature of corporate personality was the case in the fifteenth century, see Seipp, "Formalism and Realism in Fifteenth-Century English Law," 39. Theories of corporate personality seem to have been privileged at different points in time, Reuven Avi-Yonah, "Cyclical Transformations of the Corporate Form: A Historical Perspective on Corporate Social Responsibility", *Delaware Journal of Corporate Law*, 30 (2005): 767; the conceptual separation of members and their company at law may not have been until the nineteenth century, Paddy Ireland, "The Conceptual Foundations of Modern Company Law", *Journal of Law and Society* 14, no. 1 (1987): 149–65 (150).

18. William Sheppard, *Of Corporations, Fraternities, and Guilds* (London, 1659).
19. Carr, *Select Charters*, xii.
20. Tim Alborn, *Conceiving Companies: Joint Stock Politics in Victorian England* (London: Routledge, 1998); Stern, *Company-State* and, more recently, "'Bundles of Hyphens': Corporations as Legal Communities in the Early Modern British Empire", in *Legal Pluralism and Empires, 1500–1850*, eds. Lauren Benton and Richard Ross (New York: New York University Press, 2013), 21–48.
21. Assumed to be the forerunners of the Merchant Adventurers and the Eastland Company: William Scott, *Constitutions of English Companies* (Cambridge: Cambridge University Press, 1912), 1:9–10; Carr, *Select Charters*, xxii; also compare the charter to the Prussia merchants, 1391, Rymer, *Foedera*, VII, 693.
22. Eli Heckscher, *Mercantilism* (London: Allen Unwin, 1962); Philip J. Stern and Carl Wennerlind, eds., *Mercantilism Reimagined: Political Economy in Early Modern Britain and Its Empire* (Oxford: Oxford University Press, 2014); Lars Magnusson, *Mercantilism: The Shaping of an Economic Language* (London: Routledge, 2015); Steve Pincus, "Rethinking Mercantilism: Political Economy, the British Empire, and the Atlantic World in the Seventeenth and Eighteenth Centuries", *William and Mary Quarterly* 69, no. 1 (2012): 3–34.
23. Thomas Nachbar, "Monopoly, Mercantilism, and the Politics of Regulation", *Virginia Law Review* 91, no. 6 (2005): 1313–79; David Harris Sacks, "The Greed of Judas: Avarice, Monopoly, and the Moral Economy in England, ca.1350–ca.1600", *Journal of Medieval and Early Modern Studies* 28, no. 2 (1998): 263–307.
24. *The East India Company v. Sandys* (1683), in William Cobbett, ed., *State Trials and Proceedings for High Treason and other Crimes and Misdemeanors*, vol. 10 (London, 1811), col. 426; *Nightingale v. Brydges* (1689), 1 Show., 135, 89, *English Reports*, 496–502; and discussed in Pettigrew, *Freedom's Debt*, 89–91.
25. Pettigrew, *Freedom's Debt*, Chap. 3.
26. Richard Dale, *The First Crash: Lessons from the South Sea Bubble* (Princeton: Princeton University Press, 2016).
27. Harris, *Industrializing English Law*, 61–81.
28. C. Hunt, "The Joint-Stock Company in England, 1830–1844", *Journal of Political Economy* 43, no. 3 (1935): 331–64 (331).

29. Harris, *Industrializing English Law*, 58–61. Attempts were made to suggest the influence of the unincorporated company, DuBois, *The English Business Company after the Bubble Act*.
30. James Taylor, *Creating Capitalism: Joint-Stock Enterprise in British Politics and Culture, 1800–1870* (Woodbridge, UK: Boydell & Brewer, 2014).
31. Adam Smith, *An Inquiry into the Nature and Causes of the Wealth of Nations*, eds. R. H. Campbell and A. S. Skinner (Indianapolis, IN: Liberty Fund, 1981), 2: 741.
32. Boyd Hilton, *The Age of Atonement: The Influence of Evangelicalism on Social and Economic Thought, 1795–1865* (Oxford: Oxford University Press, 1988).
33. *The Monthly Review* 3 (1826), 26–27.
34. Henry N. Butler, "Nineteenth-Century Jurisdictional Competition in the Granting of Corporate Privileges", *Journal of Legal Studies* 14:1 (1985); The literature on the British statutes is growing: Rob McQueen, *A Social History of Company Law : Great Britain and the Australian Colonies 1854–1920* (Farnham: Ashgate, 2009); Donna Loftus, "Capital and Community : Limited Liability and Attempts to Democratize the Market in Mid-Nineteenth-Century England", *Victorian Studies* 45, no. 1 (2002): 93–120; Taylor, *Creating Capitalism*; Marie-Laure Djelic, "When Limited Liability Was (Still) an Issue: Mobilization and Politics of Signification in 19th-Century England", *Organization Studies* 34, no. 5–6 (2013): 595–621; Josephine Maltby, "UK Joint Stock Companies Legislation 1844–1900: Accounting Publicity And 'mercantile Caution", *Accounting History* 3, no. 1 (1998): 9–32; R. A. Bryer, "The Mercantile Laws Commission of 1854 and the Political Economy of Limited Liability", *Economic History Review* 50, no. 1 (1997): 37–56; Henry N. Butler, "General Incorporation in Nineteenth Century England: Interaction of Common Law and Legislative Processes", *International Review of Law and Economics* 6, no. 2 (1986): 169–88.
35. McQueen, *Social History of Company Law*, 85.
36. McQueen, *Social History of Company Law*, 57–76; Torben Christensen, *Origin and History of Christian Socialism, 1848–1854* (Leiden: Brill, 1962); on cooperation, see G. D. H. Cole, *A Century of Co-operation* (Manchester: Allen & Unwin, 1944); John Wilson, Anthony Webster, and Rachael Vorberg-Rugh, *Building Co-operation: A Business History of*

the Co-operative Group, 1863–2013 (Oxford: Oxford University Press, 2013).

37. See Jocelyn Paul Betts, "John Stuart Mill, Victorian Liberalism, and the Failure of Co-operative Production", *Historical Journal* 59, no. 1 (2016): 153–74.
38. Surveyed in Porter, *Rise of Big Business*; Leslie Hannah, *The Rise of the Corporate Economy* (London: Routledge, 1976).
39. David Millon, "Theories of the Corporation", *Duke Law Journal* 39, no. 2 (1990): 201–62 (213); on fiction theory see Arthur W. Machen, "Corporate Personality", *Harvard Law Review* 24, no. 4 (1911): 253–67.
40. Holdsworth, "English Corporation Law", 406; and Maitland, *State, Trust, and Corporation*, 63.
41. *Citizens United v. Federal Election Commission* 558 US 310 (2010); and related commentary about the evolution of the corporate form, Reuvan S. Avi-Yonah, "*Citizens United* and the Corporate Form", *Wisconsin Law Review* (2010), no. 4, 999–1047.
42. Adolf Berle, "Corporate Powers as Powers in Trust", *Harvard Law Review* 44, no. 7 (1931): 1049; These ideas were more famously worked out in Adolf Berle and Gardiner Means, *The Modern Corporation and Private Property* (New York: Macmillan, 1936).
43. *Dodge v. Ford Motor Company*, 170 NW 668 (Michigan, 1919); though the actual value of the case as precedent has been questioned by Lynn Stout in "Why We Should Stop Teaching Dodge v. Ford", *Virginia Law and Business Review* 3, no. 1 (2008), 164–90, and *The Shareholder Value Myth: How Putting Shareholders First Harms Investors, Corporations, and the Public* (San Francisco: Berrett-Koehler Publishers, 2012).
44. Ronald Coase, "The Nature of the Firm", *Economica* 4, no. 16 (1937), 386–405; Michael Jensen and William Meckling, "Theory of the Firm: Managerial Behavior, Agency Costs and Ownership Structure", *Journal of Financial Economics* 3, no. 4 (1976), 305–60; though compare Jensen's later work on the uses of stakeholder theory, "Value Maximization, Stakeholder Theory, and the Corporate Objective Function", *Journal of Applied Corporate Finance* 22, no. 1 (2010): 32–42.
45. Milton Friedman, "The Social Responsibility of Business is to Increase Its Profits", *New York Times Magazine*, September 13, 1970, 32.
46. E. Merrick Dodd, "For Whom Are Corporate Managers Trustees?" *Harvard Law Review* 45, no. 7 (1932): 1157.

47. Ibid., 1161; Millon, "Theories of the Corporation", 216–18.
48. Howard Bowen, *Social Responsibilities of the Businessman* (Iowa City: University of Iowa Press, repr. 2013), 6.
49. Ibid., 75, 77.
50. Ibid., 72.
51. Ibid., 75; Bowen also adopts Dodd's argument that managers become focused on the "welfare of the corporation", which leads them to think about the "impact of the corporation upon the various groups affected by it" (ibid., 88).
52. Keith Davis, "Can Business Afford to Ignore Social Responsibilities?" *California Management Review* 2, no. 3 (1960): 71, 63.
53. Keith Davis, "The Case For and Against Business Assumption of Social Responsibilities", *Academy of Management Journal* 16, no. 2 (1973): 313; and Clarence Walton, *Corporate Social Responsibilities* (Belmont, CA: Wadsworth Publishing, 1967), 18.
54. Lizabeth Cohen, *A Consumers' Republic: The Politics of Mass Consumption in Postwar America* (Princeton: Princeton University Press, 2003), 119–29.
55. Peter Drucker, "The New Meaning of Corporate Social Responsibility", *California Management Review* 26, no. 2 (1984): 53–63; Archie B. Carroll and Kareem M. Shabana, "The Business Case for Corporate Social Responsibility: A Review of Concepts, Research and Practice", *International Journal of Management Reviews* 12, no. 1 (2010): 85–105.
56. Michael E. Porter and Mark R. Kramer, "Strategy and Society: The Link Between Competitive Advantage and Corporate Social Responsibility", *Harvard Business Review* 84, no. 12 (2006): 78–92; and for attempts to model how these ideas are operationalized within the current business context, see Stefan Heck, Matt Rogers, and Paul Carroll, *Resource Revolution: How to Capture the Biggest Business Opportunity in a Century* (New York: New Harvest, 2014).
57. J. J. Asongu, "Innovation as an Argument for Corporate Social Responsibility", *Journal of Business and Public Policy* 1, no. 3 (2007): 1–21; Ülle Übius and Ruth Alas, "Connections between Corporate Social Responsibility and Innovation Climate", *EBS Review*, no. 26 (2009): 58–71; Yunhee Kim, "Corporate Social Responsibility Driven Innovation", *Innovation* 27, no. 2 (2014): 175–96.
58. Kenneth E. Aupperle, Archie B. Carroll, and John D. Hatfield, "An Empirical Examination of the Relationship between Corporate Social

Responsibility and Profitability", *Academy of Management Journal* 28, no. 2 (1985): 446–63; Philip L. Cochran and Robert A. Wood, "Corporate Social Responsibility and Financial Performance", *Academy of Management Journal* 27, no. 1 (1984): 42–56; Markus Kitzmueller and Jay Shimshack, "Economic Perspectives on Corporate Social Responsibility", *Journal of Economic Literature* 50, no. 1 (2012): 51–84.

59. S. P. Sethi, "Dimensions of Corporate Social Performance: An Analytical Framework", *California Management Review* 17, no. 3 (1975): 58–64; and the recent reinterpretation emphasizing the many levels, including institutional, of CSP, Donna J. Wood, "Corporate Social Performance Revisited", *Academy of Management Review* 16, no. 4 (1991): 691–718.
60. Sethi, "Dimensions of Corporate Social Performance", 60.
61. Ibid., 62.
62. Ibid., 59.
63. Archie B. Carroll, "A Three-Dimensional Conceptual Model of Corporate Performance", *Academy of Management Review* 4, no. 4 (1979): 497–505 (500).
64. R. Edward Freeman, *Strategic Management: A Stakeholder Approach* (Cambridge: Cambridge University Press, repr. 2010); R. Edward Freeman et al., *Stakeholder Theory: The State of the Art* (Cambridge: Cambridge University Press, 2010). Also, see the recent criticism of CSR models as overly static, Dima Jamali, "A Stakeholder Approach to Corporate Social Responsibility: A Fresh Perspective into Theory and Practice", *Journal of Business Ethics* 82, no. 1 (2007): 213–31.
65. J. E. Parkinson, *Corporate Power and Responsibility: Issues in the Theory of Company Law* (Oxford: Clarendon Press, 1995), 43.
66. McBarnet et al., eds., *The New Corporate Accountability: Corporate Social Responsibility and the Law* (Cambridge: Cambridge University Press, 2009); David Detomasi, "The Political Roots of Corporate Social Responsibility", *Journal of Business Ethics* 82, no. 4 (2008): 807–19; Laura Albareda et al., "The Government's Role in Promoting Corporate Responsibility: A Comparative Analysis of Italy and UK from the Relational State Perspective", *Corporate Governance* 6, no. 4 (2006): 386–400.
67. Carroll, "Corporate Social Responsibility", 268; Asli Yüksel Mermod and Samuel O. Idowu, *Corporate Social Responsibility in the Global Business World* (Springer Science & Business Media, 2013); Dirk

Matten and Jeremy Moon, "'Implicit' and 'Explicit' Csr: A Conceptual Framework for a Comparative Understanding of Corporate Social Responsibility", *Academy of Management Review* 33:2 (2008): 404–24.

68. Geoffrey G. Jones, "Debating the Responsibility of Capitalism in Historical and Global Perspective", Working Paper 14-004 (Cambridge MA: Harvard Business School, 2013); Bryan Husted, "Corporate Social Responsibility Practice from 1800–1914: Past Initiatives and Current Debates", *Business Ethics Quarterly*, 25:1 (2015): 126.
69. Patrick Fridenson and Kikkawa Takeo, eds., *Ethical Capitalism: Shibusawa Eiichi and Business Leadership in Global Perspective* (Toronto: University of Toronto Press, 2017); and the special issue "Japanese Approaches to CSR", *Journal of Corporate Citizenship*, no. 56 (2014); Holtschneider Uwe, *Adoption of Corporate Social Responsibility by Japanese Companies* (Munich: IUDICIUM Verlag, 2015).
70. Morrell Heald, *The Social Responsibilities of Business, Company, and Community, 1900–1960* (Cleveland: Press of Case Western Reserve University, 1970), 7–10.
71. Randy Evans et al., "History of Management Thought About Social Responsibility", *Journal of Management History* 19, no. 1 (2013), 8–32, at 9.
72. Archie B. Carroll, "A History of Corporate Social Responsibility: Concepts and Practices", in *The Oxford Handbook of Corporate Social Responsibility*, eds. Andrew Crane et al., (Oxford: Oxford University Press, 2008), 19–46 at 20–22; and Daniel Wren, *The History of Management Thought* (Hoboken, NJ: Wiley, 2005); Evans et al., "History of Management Thought", 9–10.
73. Nicholas N. Eberstadt, "What History Tells Us About Corporate Responsibility", *Business & Society Review/Innovation* 7 (1973): 76–81 (77).
74. Eberstadt, "What History Tells Us About Corporate Responsibility", 77.
75. Husted, "Corporate Social Responsibility", 126.
76. Ibid., 136.
77. Archie B. Carroll et al., *Corporate Responsibility: The American Experience* (Cambridge: Cambridge University Press, 2012); Archie B. Carroll, "A History of Corporate Social Responsibility: Concepts and Practices"; W. Randy Evans et al., "History of Management Thought About Social Responsibility"; C. A. Wells, "Cycles of Corporate Social Responsibility: An Historical Retrospective for the Twenty-First Century", *Kansas Law Review* 51 (2002), 77–140; History of Corporate Responsibility Project, *Corporate Social Responsibility: The*

Shape of a History, 1945–2004 (Center for Ethical Business Cultures, 2010); Rosamaria C. Moura-Leite and Robert C. Padgett, "Historical Background of Corporate Social Responsibility", *Social Responsibility Journal* 7, no. 4 (2011): 528–39.

78. Carroll, "History of Corporate Social Responsibility", 109.
79. Andreas Georg Scherer and Guido Palazzo, "Toward a Political Conception of Corporate Responsibility: Business and Society Seen from a Habermasian Perspective", *Academy of Management Review* 32, no. 4 (2007): 1096–1120.

2

Leadership and the Social Agendas of the Seventeenth-Century English Trading Corporation

William A. Pettigrew and Aske Laursen Brock

The study of business leaders and commercial leadership has been a far greater preoccupation for management scholars than for historians of business.[1] Few historians who have been interested in leadership have noted it as a field in business history prior to the twentieth century.[2] Historians of seventeenth-century corporations have concentrated less on the leadership of those bodies and more on their civic, participatory cultures.[3] Philip Stern has recently warned convincingly against reading the modern business corporation into its early modern progenitor.[4] One connection between the early modern and modern period nonetheless suggests itself—the social dimension of business. The recent expectation that twenty-first-century multinationals ought to operate in socially responsible ways offers the most concrete way to connect and compare the modern multinational with its distant ancestor. While modern corporations seek to market themselves with reference to their awareness of the non-financial needs of the societies within which they operate,

W.A. Pettigrew (✉) · A.L. Brock
University of Kent, Canterbury, England
e-mail: W.Pettigrew@kent.ac.uk

W.A. Pettigrew and D.C. Smith (eds.), *A History of Socially Responsible Business, c.1600–1950*, Palgrave Studies in the History of Finance,
DOI 10.1007/978-3-319-60146-5_2

the early modern corporation was an instinctively and inherently social entity.[5] This chapter examines how the leadership cultures, practices and personnel of the early modern trading corporations were designed to ensure that their financial goals remained embedded within a socially responsible framework.

The chapter analyses the significance of the trading corporations' social obligations (at home and abroad) to the seventeenth-century English understanding of what constituted good corporate leadership. It explores the theories and practice of socially determined leadership styles as well as the prosopography of corporate leaders in this period. It discusses leadership at the individual level and the conciliar level. The chapter stresses that leadership in early modern trading corporations was principally about forging positive relationships with constituencies typically characterised as external to the corporation: the labour force, the state, suppliers, the needy and the public. Leaders spent much of their time forming relationships outside the membership of the company and were chosen because of their experience as leaders within their broader communities and within society at large. Leadership was societal and therefore helped to ensure that trading corporations upheld their social obligations. Social and commercial concerns operated symbiotically, however. Satisfying social obligations often helped to cement commercial relationships. Through engagement in corporate projects such as "the Stock for putting Poor French protestants to work", directors of multinational companies were instrumental in improving society while aiding sociability that facilitated strategic network-building. Understanding corporate leadership offers a distinctive and important lens on the social imperatives of the early modern company. Who, how and why people led trading corporations over the seventeenth century reveals the cultural alignment and (at times) tensions at the heart of early modern corporate activity between individual or oligarchic financial gain and social utility.

Leadership, for seventeenth-century trading companies, combined Ralph Stogdill's modern definition of "the process of influencing the activities of an organised group in its efforts toward goal setting and goal achievement" with the early modern expectation that leaders had a responsibility to live up to societal expectations associated with high office.[6]

In seventeenth-century England, the goal and the expectation were fused into the broad and elastic notion of the "national interest". The national interest was the inversion of the individual interest—a concept emerging in the seventeenth century and seen as likely, if left unregulated, to dissolve the bonds of society. The national interest was therefore a route to social and political stability.[7] Corporations were to ensure that the economy served national, public, social interests rather than exclusively the individual, mercantile or oligarchic interests contained within their membership. Corporations often mentioned the national interest when justifying their monopoly (and other) privileges. Corporate monopolies were understood to serve social agendas. They upheld the interest of the people by keeping prices on consumer goods low and wages high, and by maximising employment. They prevented the ravaging of natural resources by developing state apparatus such as the naval marine without depleting the nation's resources of forests.[8] Trading corporations supported community infrastructure by continuing the philanthropic work of their guild predecessors. Corporate leadership was therefore bound to the deep-seated cultural expectation that commerce ought to serve the public good. In the seventeenth century, almost every aspect of social welfare was managed by corporate bodies: parish vestries, charitable trusts, civic corporations and companies of merchants.[9] The overlapping networks constituted by these bodies created and disseminated a collective corporate culture, by which the leaders of companies were obliged and influenced. During the seventeenth century, merchants (alongside other professionals) set up their own organisations to combat competition and business failure. Leadership of corporations was as much a matter of promoting the broader social good as it was a matter of generating returns for investors.[10]

A key additional characteristic of successful leaders in seventeenth-century English trading corporations (as in modern corporates) was the ability to adapt to internal and external changes.[11] The seventeenth century was a period of profound commercial and constitutional change. Spearheaded by trading corporations, England made an impressive push to expand its international trading networks in the Atlantic and in South Asia. The seventeenth century also saw protracted and bloody disagreement about the workings of the English constitution, which culminated in the Civil Wars and then the constitutional settlement known as the Glorious Revolution. These two changes created huge opportunities for business, but also introduced uncertainty as regulatory frameworks altered. Corporate leaders had to uphold the long-established culture of public service at the same time as negotiating a rapidly and constantly changing business environment. New leadership styles emerged during this period, but these faced challenges from state regulation as the cultural expectation for commerce to serve the public good became diluted by conspicuous commercial gain and new theories that suggested how individual interests ought to be liberated to further the national good.[12]

Executive leadership within a corporation was paradoxical. Corporations existed to uphold a pervasive civic culture that denied the notion of the individual leader.[13] Through a legal process, corporations gave individual legal personality to groups of individuals. This incorporation process was meant, however, to sustain the collective into a convenient legal person, rather than celebrating individual action over the collective good. Indeed, the state instituted corporations in the sixteenth and seventeenth centuries to prevent social corruption through greed in a rapidly commercialising society.[14] The process of incorporation conferred governmental functions upon commercial ambitions that could be, if left unmanaged, socially enervating. The governmental functions within corporations—most importantly the leadership roles themselves—were designed to ensure that corporations operated to uphold this civic and socially responsible culture.

Although this culture was mostly national in focus, trading corporations also helped to develop the view that their operations ought not to undermine the societies they interacted with overseas. Trading corporations were meant to uphold the national interest. But as transnational entities they had to negotiate a double standard. Initially conceptualised as bodies that could ensure trade would be conducted solely in the interest of the English nation, over the course of the seventeenth century, as experience of non-European trading environments increased and theories of international trade became more sophisticated, corporations began to disabuse earlier mercantilist precepts that suggested a natural tension between one nation's commercial gain and another's loss. Corporations increasingly understood that international commercial success was often a function of facilitating mutual commercial gains across national and cultural lines. This insight socialised and internationalised the national interest in the short term as English corporations began to celebrate the ways in which their operations would outlive their European competitors because English trade benefited non-Europeans as well as the English national interest.[15]

The social purpose of the seventeenth-century English trading corporation was typically spelt out in its charter. The first charter of the East India Company (1600) outlined the company's purpose as being "for the Honour of this our Realm of England, as for the Increase of our Navigation, and Advancement of Trade of Merchandize...for the Benefit of our Common Wealth".[16] Trading companies were expected to take on social responsibilities, and the language of improvement can be found, for instance, in the pamphlets written for the Virginia Company, founded in 1606. Robert Johnson, a prominent member of the Company, argued in 1609 that the Company would be "for the singular good and benefite that wil vndoubtedly arise to this whole Nation".[17] Similar language can be found in seventeenth-century pamphlets defending the East India Company's monopoly.[18]

For many writers of the early seventeenth century, it was the job of sound governance to prevent trade from undermining the commonwealth. State regulation, often in the form of corporate organisation, was understood to provide this governance. In 1622, the Jacobean pamphleteer and merchant Gerald Malynes explained:

> Some Merchants doe deale all for Commodities, others for Monyes, and other some altogether for Exchanges or all three, or that which yeeldeth them most gaine: and commonly without consideration had of the good of the Commonwealth, which is the cause that Princes and Gouernours are to sit at the sterne of the course of Trade and Commerce.[19]

Prevailing interpretations of the best characteristics for corporate leaders derived from depictions of merchants themselves and the public role they ought to play. The mixture of commercial and governmental ambitions that corporations embodied began to offer a recipe for the socially responsible merchant. In 1641, the East India Company director Lewes Roberts argued that the English public would be effectively supported if "States-Merchants" had a large role to play in the management of the economy as well as the prosecution of war and the negotiation of peace.[20] Again, trade was not to be left to operate without governance (or properly functioning leadership).

Throughout the seventeenth century, corporate governance reflected broader constitutional debates about the best way to combine executive and conciliar mechanisms. These intensified in the corporate setting, because corporate governance emphasised the need for deliberation and collective decision-making. In all cases, the collective will of the corporation's court remained supreme. It is highly instructive that the notion of the individual company director was resisted in the English setting throughout much of the seventeenth century and was associated with the more unilateral style of corporate governance that the English saw in the Dutch companies.[21] Corporate constitutions nonetheless always included an executive figure—usually a governor, though in some cases in the second half of the century, including the Royal African Company, the governor was a figurehead and the deputy governor assumed executive power.

At the beginning of the seventeenth century, the governor was understood to be a servant of the board of directors. An East India Company minute of 1607 records that the board (or Court of Committees) was to have the "direction of the voyages", while the executive branch (the governor and deputy governor) were to oversee the board's relationship with the shareholders (the General Court) and the making and implementation of the society's laws.[22] The governor also had the important responsibility of informing shareholders about the annual dividend and paying suppliers.[23] Company minutes are also full of gubernatorial initiatives to "relieve poverty" in the hope that good works would cultivate "prayers for the good and prosperity of the Company's voyages".[24] Final authority to perform such works, however, rested with the board.

In the 1621 printed edition of the East India Company's by-laws, the specifics of the governor's role were clearly outlined. The governor was supposed to summon and host Court of Committee meetings, supervise the corporate oath and ensure good order in all meetings. He (and it was always a he) was to be the implementer of the will of the Court of Committees, rather than the originator of commercial strategy.

The governor, however, was to have an important influence in developing the corporation's public profile and ensuring that it enjoyed good relations with outside bodies. He was entrusted with the strategic task of digesting intelligence from overseas agents of the company and to lead the board in scrutinising all information. The most important role for the governor was "attending his Majesty". The governor was a crucial point of contact between the company and the state privileges that defined it. Such privileges could be sustained and enlarged with the help of a diplomatically savvy governor.[25] The governor's responsibilities therefore ranged across the development and enforcement of internal regulations, the performance of critical financial roles to do with suppliers and shareholders, and—most important—the "interposition" between corporate and state interests.[26] Any reader of the early modern corporation's minute books can't help but be impressed by the dedication corporate leaders clearly felt to the task in hand. In May 1641, the governor of the East India Company and the Court of Committees travelled across London to their dockyard facility at Blackwall to collectively "inspect the defective sluice there". Such inspections would also have served the purpose of helping the company leadership maintain their social profile in a community that supplied much of the company's workforce.[27]

Which people became governors and why? The governor almost always had previous experience of service on the Court of Committees.[28] The East India Company appears to have appointed Nathaniel Herne as governor in 1674 because of his exemplary attendance as a director.[29] An additional key factor that appears to have influenced which board members became governors was the extent of policy experience outside the corporation. Of the sixty-six governors of the East India, Levant, Virginia, Hudson's Bay and Massachusetts Bay companies (or deputy governors of the Royal African Company) and of the Bank of England across the seventeenth century, 45% had served as a member of Parliament, 41% had enjoyed civic office—most often within the City of London Corporation—and 15% boasted experience of commercial contexts overseas. For the much larger community of directors, just 19% had been members of Parliament, 9% had served in civic office, and 10% had lived overseas. Clearly, the extent of service within the broader community and—to a lesser extent—their understanding of international commercial contexts influenced their ability to serve in an executive capacity.[30] Executive leadership was expected from those who had the social contacts beyond the company—especially within the City of London and Parliament—and with experience and contacts in international settings.[31]

Wealth and success as directors may very likely also have influenced who became governors. Governors were expected to be rich. This expectation was based not on any importance attached to the commercial skill of a merchant, but on the belief that wealthier officials would be less likely to compromise the public good. Governors received modest annual gratuities. At times, they could be substantial but were often rejected. The founding governor of the East India Company, Thomas Smith, was offered a gratuity of £500 for "procuring the first and second patents [charters]", but he refused to take his oath of office until the sum had been reduced to £250.[32] Office was not meant to provide wealth. Leadership, therefore, was best offered by those who were already wealthy. As John Smith, promoter of the Virginia Company, explained in 1624:

> There are some merchants and others, I am confidently perswaded, doe take more care and paines, nay, and at their continuall great charge, than they could be hired for the love of money, so honestly regarding the general good of this great worke, they would hold it worse than sacrilege to wrong it by a shilling, or extort upon the common souldier a penny.[33]

Smith's words came after a lengthy debate within the Virginia Company. The two factions fighting over power, one led by the aforementioned Thomas Smith and the other by the gentleman Edwin Sandys, disagreed over directors' salaries among other things. Sandys and his supporters wanted large salaries to take care of a central part of the tobacco trade, which a number of the stockholders found unacceptable.[34] John Smith's comment should be seen in that light. In 1635, the draper William Scott made the point about the need for governors to be rich and therefore more watchful of the public benefit more explicitly:

> [Governors] ought to be rich for these reasons. Wealth is a pledge of their care of the Commonwealth: it is likely, he that hath done well for himself, will know how to do well for the public good...[it] being gotten, their minds may with more diligence intend the public affairs' ... In Ruling, there must be power and command, which a poor man cannot have, all the world despises him...to have a poor governor is a great plague.[35]

However, as the historian Richard Grassby summarised, the purchasing of company stock and service on corporate boards provided significant opportunities to exercise patronage and power, and offered substantial returns on investments.[36]

The best way to analyse the changing significance of social priorities for seventeenth-century corporate leaders is through the careers of a sample of East India Company governors over the course of the century. Each of the following case studies demonstrates the development of different leadership priorities.

Sir Thomas Smith, the founder governor of the East India Company, was at the same time governor of the Muscovy, Levant and Virginia companies. His career offers a striking early example of corporate interlock and of the ways in which experience of different corporate settings transferred across the different companies.[37] Smith developed specialist skills as a corporate governor and was often invited to serve or to continue to serve at the insistence of the King.[38] He proved a particularly effective interlocutor with the monarch and used bribery and persuasion to expand the provisions of the company's charter.[39] He clearly defined his role as an external-facing official and styled himself as a servant of the Court of Committees, rejecting compensation from the company on several occasions. He was the quintessential Jacobean corporate magnate who led companies to satisfy the national interest and used a good profile with the state to develop each company's trade.

Gubernatorial service posed some challenges for Smith, however. As governor, he literally housed the company, using his own home at Philpot Lane in the City of London to host the Court of Committees meetings in ways that underscored the early modern corporation's elision of public/private distinctions. The social obligations to which the East India Company was subject meant that his house was often besieged by outside stakeholders who wished to influence company practice or have grievances redressed. In July 1615, a group of mariners' wives arrived in Philpot Lane clamouring for payment of their husbands' wages. The minute books of the Court of Committees noted that Smith was "so troubled with their clamours and petitions as that he cannot have that freedom in his house which is needful for preservation of his health".[40] In July 1621, fatigued by his own efforts and success as governor, Smith pleaded ill health in an attempt to dodge the habitual reappointment each year and "begged the Company would spare him, that they should see he could as well obey as command".[41]

While Smith may have resented the ways in which his corporate office placed him at the mercy of the society around him, he was conscientious about understanding and cultivating the far-flung societies that the East India Company relied upon for its trade. Smith took his international intelligence very seriously, and others understood the extent of his international expertise. His tomb records how "he got intelligence" from "all the famous rivers, lands, and seas betwixt this place and our Antipodes".[42] He was acutely conscious of the need for corporate servants to behave responsibly overseas and create a good impression on the non-European societies within which they operated. Smith worked hard to develop a corporate culture for the early East India Company and especially to instil the corporatist, socially minded culture of the City of London in those travelling overseas on the company's behalf. In February 1614, he called the soon-to-depart officials into his parlour at Philpot Lane to brief them on the corporate values they should uphold overseas, exhorting

> them to discharge their trusts conscientiously, to avoid private trade, and acquaints them with the Company's care to furnish them with things needful for their spiritual comfort and the health of their bodies…also books of divinity for the soul, and history to instruct the mind…tells them of the offensive behaviour of some of the Company's factors in the East Indies, and admonishes them 'to be the more respective and shun all sin and evil behaviour, that the heathen may take no advantage to blaspheme our religion by the abuses and ungodly behaviour of our men'… 'they are also advised to be careful to dispatch their bonds, are informed

> that many have counterfeit ballast rubies, which will disgrace the nation and bring the Company into discredit'...'by making the people hate us and destest us before we be settled amongst them'[43]

Smith clearly worried about the social, moral profile of the company's employees overseas and saw this profile as something that could better facilitate durable trading relationships.

In the late 1630s and early 1640s, the assured dividends and intimate relations with the Crown that Smith had sustained as governor were a distant memory. The governorship of Sir Christopher Clitheroe demonstrates an alternative style of leadership during a period of profound financial crisis. Facing near bankruptcy and the onset of political turmoil, the investors not serving as directors began to flex their muscles through the General Court (the seventeenth-century equivalent of the annual general meeting) and to decentre the company's decision-making. The power of the governor was questioned. A proposal to limit the term of the governor, who was portrayed as a potentially "perpetuall dictator", gathered speed.[44] But this proposal (which had also been made earlier in the 1630s) was understood to have discouraged investment.[45]

The 1670s and 1680s were, by contrast, decades of success for the company, when its import trade accounted for about 14% of the nation's total.[46] In this context, the governor was able to use personal experience to craft corporate strategy directly (rather than in response to external threats). These conditions of commercial buoyancy helped to strengthen the power of individual leadership. Sir John Banks became governor in the 1670s and then again in the 1680s. Banks used his experience as a money lender to the Crown to reorient the corporate strategy of the East India Company. Banks had pioneered the financial technique of advancing loans to the King as a way of settling customs obligations and then used the company's capital in a similar fashion as a go-between with the treasury.[47] These loans became a significant new source of funds for the company and helped sustain intimate relations with the King. Over time they would come to reorient the role of chartered companies within public life as state financiers, a process that culminated with the foundation of the Bank of England.

The financial successes of the East India Company helped the company to argue that its main contribution to the public was state finance. This enlarged public role as national financier appears to have been the personal vision of Governor Sir John Banks.

The corporation's overall strategy and social profile, however, were determined more by the board as a whole and were the collective preserve of the directors rather than the executive responsibility of the governor. Networks of directors as well as individual directors were as important to corporate strategy as governors; their collective involvement in social projects is impressive. The directors of trading corporations, like other social leaders, wished to contribute to social improvement. Improvement for the directors meant more than improving corporate forms, overseas plantations or maximising profits. The term "improvement" covers bettering English infrastructure and social amelioration through the development of new personal styles and manners. By linking the world together and integrating their business into it, merchants were of the opinion that they improved the world: "They applied what they learned in the economic sphere to the conduct of life in the social sphere, and vice versa".[48] The directors were in a similar situation; they used their knowledge of civic governance to conduct trade and allowed their economic sense to affect their involvement in civic governance. For the directors—although they did not use the expression themselves—improvement referred to improving the commonwealth and being active agents in the "national incorporation".[49] This activity was ritualised. In the Muscovy and Levant companies, it was common that new freemen donated to the poor box before they could become members of the company.[50] But socially responsible initiatives also provided ways to expand and fortify social networks and legitimise participation in economic enterprises.[51]

Merchants were at the forefront of philanthropy in the City of London throughout the sixteenth and seventeenth centuries. The company directors were with little variation drawn from the top tiers of merchant society in London and were among the major contributors to the different charities in London. The long-time Levant and East India director Sir George Smith donated £50 to the governors of Christ Church to take care of poor children in his 1667 will. However, his trading partner and

Table 2.1 Social structure of charitable benefactions in London (amended), 1480–1660[a]

Number of donors	Social status	Per cent of all donations	Per cent of all donors	Amount in £
9	Crown	6.29	0.12	118,766
607	Nobility & Gentry	6.21	8.22	117,149
168	Yeomen & Husbandmen	2.15	2.27	5198
180	Clergy	7.35	2.44	138,224
438	Great merchants	48.04	5.93	907,623
2239	Lesser merchants	8.49	30.29	160,260
788	Burghers	2.64	10.66	49,809
518	Artisans	0.16	7.01	3030
490	Professional	6.59	6.63	124,524
867	Unknown	8.81	11.73	166,409

[a]W. K. Jordan, *The Charities of London, 1480–1660: The Aspirations and the Achievements of the Urban Society* (London: George Allen & Unwin, 1960), 48.

fellow East India director William Ryder was even more generous. He donated £50 to the poor of Wembury in Devon, £20 to the poor of the Trinity Corporation, £80 to the poor of Stepney Parish in London, £20 to the poor of St Andrew Undershaft and finally £50 to the "Free Schoole of Poplar erected by the Hon:ble East India Companie".[52] In total, he gave £220 to different charitable corporations. The directors were often generous donators.

As Table 2.1 shows, merchant elites (consisting of merchants who became the masters of their livery companies, served as lord mayor or sheriffs of London or left a fortune of £4000 or more in their will) were particularly active. During the period in question, their donations to charitable institutions and schools for the poor constituted 48.04% of the total amount gifted.[53] Forty per cent of the amount gifted by merchants went to poor relief and most frequently in the form of endowments.[54] The charitable donations above were from the wills of individuals and not from the companies themselves. However, a number of the wills specified that money should be donated either to the livery companies or to the trading companies, which in turn should put it to use for various charities such as schools and poor relief. Merchants were actively engaged in improving the human capital of society. W. K. Jordan, who examined the charitable nature of England expressed in donations in wills, found that merchants of London supported educational schemes across the country in 27.55% of the instances they donated, in particular grammar schools, which received £178,132 (or 19.63%) of the total amount donated by merchants.[55] Company directors were prominent within this group of elite merchants. For instance, Thomas Kerridge, a former factor in India and East India Company director, donated £100 to the company to "be by them employed for and towards the relief of the poor of their almshouses at Popler Blackwall".[56] Similarly, the Levant and East India director William Vincent donated generously to the housekeepers in the Northampton parish where he was born, to the poor in St Martin Outwich in London, to the children at Christ's Hospital, to the sick at St Bartholomew's and to the Grocers to pay for a young man's entry into the company.[57] Through their own investments and the charitable donations of former employees, the early modern companies frequently provided support for the poor when and where the state could not. The creation of new companies with the specific purpose of improving society was an alternative to the companies' and their directors' charitable giving and active engagement in corporate sociability. Such companies brought the commercial and civic elite together, forming networks that came to shape the future English state and political economy.

Just as directors participated in charitable acts, so the idea of the corporation as a vehicle for philanthropic and socially minded acts was realised through directorial agency. Formed in early 1681 by sixty-eight individuals, the adventurers in the Stock raised for setting the Poor French Protestants to work at Ipswich in the linen manufacture was one such company.[58] The purpose of the company, as its name stated, was to provide work for the Protestants who fled France following religious persecution. The adventurers (led by an unknown number of trustees/directors) purchased flax, hemp and looms for the workers, and rented a house in which the poor French could work.[59] In August the same year, the Royal African Company decided to donate £10 to the French Protestants.[60] The Stock for Poor French Protestants was not a hugely profitable company, but in all likelihood that was never the purpose. When the treasurer, Thomas Papillon, stepped down in 1684, he transferred £173 3s in cash to the new treasurer as well as an unspecified amount of cloth, which the company was supposed to sell.[61] Even the meagre amount of £173 was an increase of 686% on the result from the previous year. The year before, in 1683, however, the treasurer still held eighty-six pieces of half Holland cloth and ninety-five pieces of coarse linen, which undoubtedly made the stock more valuable.[62]

Trading company directors were prevalent as investors in this initiative to provide work for the French Protestants. During the five years in which the stock was functional, twenty-four (38.7%) of the investors were active as directors or governors of the overseas trading companies. Another seven of the investors either had been or would become directors. These individuals were on the fringes of the director community in the period, but were still an integral part of the larger commercial community. Some of the directors who invested had a direct interest in the scheme, being descendants of French Protestants, but that was not the case for all of them. The stock had the backing of an impressive selection of the most important London merchants. Besides the twenty-four company directors, the adventurers counted the governor of the East India Company and a former governor, the governor of the Levant Company, a former treasurer of the Levant Company, six 1681 MPs, the Lord Mayor of London and seven previous Lord Mayors, nine aldermen, four members of the Royal Society, the Bishop of London, the Dean of Canterbury (who was also the future Archbishop) and the Dean of St Paul's.[63] The stock was a veritable who's who of influential people who, through the means of a trading corporation, worked to improve society.

The stock functioned as a social company and created connections between influential individuals who were only tangentially connected. It brought a number of directors together with other important members of the upper echelons of society. Besides forming ties among the elites of English society, the stock also—to some extent—cemented a commercial community that was fracturing over its organisation and market

Table 2.2 Distribution of investors in the Stock for Poor French Protestants in trading companies

	East India company	Levant company	Royal African company	Muscovy company
1681	13	2	3	2
1682	13	1	2	1
1683	10	2	1	1
Total	36	5	6	4

shares.[64] The Levant Company and the East India Company, which previously enjoyed a large overlapping directorate, publically disagreed about the nature of the East India trade. The Levant Company felt it was being squeezed out of the silk trade due to cheaper silk from India, and as a result, Levant merchants lobbied to break down the East India monopoly. The East India Company defended its monopoly by claiming that a joint stock, rather than a regulated company, would be better for the English nation.[65] The Stock for Poor French Protestants, formed at the height of the conflict, poured oil on troubled waters by bringing adversaries together in a charitable company. Though the majority of the director-participants were from the East India Company, the stock had members from all the other companies. The strategic goal of investing in the stock, beyond the improvement of society, may also have been to tie the community closer together and stem the destructive debate between the companies (Table 2.2).

The Stock for Poor French Protestants therefore served three different purposes. First, it was successful in addressing the issue it set out to alleviate, namely providing work for the French Protestants. It helped improve the society of which it was a part. Second, the company created a platform for the creation and strengthening of new ties between important people in London. Through participation in the stock, the elites of London came to invest together and share an interest. The participation in this charitable corporate joint venture provided an opportunity to create ties with directors who held knowledge of markets and mechanisms the parent company did not have at the time.[66] Third, at a time when the director community and the commercial corporate sphere were fracturing over different commercial approaches, the stock provided a temporary space for networking across commercial differences. The same can be said for political difference in society: the stock brought together political adversaries for the good of society.

The example of the Stock for Poor French Protestants underlines the importance of corporate sociability to seventeenth-century English notions of collective corporate leadership. The directors held an individual social responsibility, as illustrated by their charitable donations, investments in charities and involvement in intellectual societies—but the responsibility frequently manifested itself within the collective, corporate form. They donated to corporations, they formed corporations, and they governed corporations for both private and public good. Improvement was a strategic decision serving the public good and the private interest of the companies and their adventurers, as well as the individual ends of the directors. In a fashion that would be formative of later companies, socially minded enterprise provided a means to help build local relationships of trust and consolidate the local merchant community, at the same time as doing good for those beyond that community. Corporations formed for dual charitable and commercial ends became commonplace in the eighteenth century.[67]

By the 1670s and 1680s, directors of corporations began to promote strong and concentrated (rather than deliberative) leadership. They did so not by seeking executive office as governors, but by consolidating huge shareholdings to engross power within the boardroom. Apologists for an increasingly powerful and less deliberative East India Company management whose stock was increasingly engrossed by a small cabal of directors, led by Sir Josiah Child, suggested that strong corporate leadership had been implied by the company's founders. They declared that there had always been a strong man in both the English and the Dutch East India Company. In the opinion of the company, a strong man was necessary to run business. Using Machiavelli, the company argued that "The state of Florence when it was a Commonwealth never prospered, but when some one Citizen arrived at Reputation enough to moderate the Councils of the Commonwealth".[68] Overall, the guild-like fellowship model of corporate sociability appears to have been substituted during the 1680s for a more hierarchical model that allowed particular investors to engross power within the seventeenth-century company boardroom.[69] Such centralisation of corporate power did not, of course, necessarily produce less socially responsible outlooks. Child himself had, in a similar period, written a pamphlet called "Proposals for the Relief and Employment of the Poor" and had argued that corporations were best placed to solve social problems because they were "the best Administrators of what is left to Charitable Uses".[70] A corporation such as the one proposed by Child would channel funds into different social projects, alleviate an actual problem in society and create a platform where experienced leaders could create common ties. Child's scheme did not become a reality in his time, but a part of the proposal—erecting petty banks and providing so-called Lombard credit for the poor—was at the heart of the Charitable Corporation for the Relief of the Industrious Poor chartered in 1707.[71] Though corporations and corporate sociability were changing rapidly, the charitable companies and directors made it into the eighteenth century.

The assaults on traditional modes of corporate leadership were depicted during public and state scrutiny as antithetical to public interest at home and abroad and were censured. Such self-serving engrossment of capital and power within the East India Company's Court of Committees was blamed for some disastrous corporate decision-making as well as some nefarious practices (including insider trading and the bribery of parliamentary officials) and led, ultimately, to the state's decision to reform the corporate governance of the East India Company (and others) during what amounted to a compliance revolution in the 1690s.[72] Under the leadership of Child and then the large-scale bullion merchant Sir Thomas Cooke, directors (including governors) concentrated their stock holdings and therefore their control over company strategy. In 1689, the company declared war on the Mughal Emperor and suffered a major defeat, thereby bringing into question the future of its trading relationships in its most promising markets. Cooke and others profited hugely from selling their own bullion to the company and authorised huge bribes to parliamentary officials (most notoriously the Speaker of the House of Commons, who received £50,000) in exchange for agreeing to favour the company's hopes of receiving a new charter. Parliament duly stepped in and restored Jacobean governance motifs to prevent the re-emergence of corporate titans like Child by preventing individual directors from acquiring huge shareholdings.[73] Overmighty corporate leadership was blamed for socially irresponsible activity at home and abroad, and the English state—through Parliament—altered governance arrangements.[74] Even though directors like Child were careful to indicate how their more centralised form of leadership made corporations more dynamic in upholding their traditional social roles, regulators levelled the charge of social irresponsibility against these aberrant and pernicious leadership structures.

This chapter's examination of social responsibility as a determinant for successful corporate leadership shows that the founding century of corporate leadership in overseas trading companies is a rise and fall narrative in which state regulation to uphold the public utility of corporations would substitute for long-established cultures that expected corporations to behave in socially responsible ways. At the beginning of the seventeenth century, deeply entrenched cultures required mercantile prioritisation of public and social concerns to alleviate the compunction felt about individual gain. The corporation and its governance arrangements—and therefore leadership styles—upheld this culture. By the end of the century, more centralised corporate governance regimes had been reformed with the help of state intervention on the understanding that overmighty leadership posed an inherent challenge to the public good. Corporate autonomy could be relied upon to express society's suspicion of individual interest until a more ambitious state at the end of the century substituted for that culture. Throughout the period, and beyond, the social functions of the corporations remained and expanded as non-profit corporates (such as the Stock for Poor French Protestants) were formed for charitable and social as well as commercial ends and also helped to structure cross-corporate mercantile communities who used social and philanthropic activity to augment their oligarchic status.

Notes

1. For works that have proved especially formative for the approach adopted here, see the *Handbook of Leadership Theory and Practice*, ed. Nitin Nohria and Rakesh Knurana (Boston, MA: Harvard Business

Press, 2010). See also Daan van Knippenberg and Michael A. Hogg, *Leadership and Power: Identity Processes in Groups and Organizations* (London: Sage, 2003); Edgar Schein, *Organisational Culture and Leadership* (San Francisco, CA: Jonssey-Bass, 2004).

2. Walter A. Friedman, "Leadership and History", in *Handbook of Leadership Theory and Practice*, 291–301.
3. Phil Withington, *The Politics of Commonwealth: Citizens and Freemen in Early Modern England* (Cambridge: Cambridge University Press, 2005); Paul Halliday, *Dismembering the Body Politic: Partisan Politics in England's Towns, 1650–1730* (Cambridge: Cambridge University Press, 1998).
4. Philip J. Stern, "The English East India Company and the Modern Corporation: Legacies, Lessons, and Limitations", *Seattle University Law Review* 39, no. 2 (2016).
5. For the contemporary debate on corporate social responsibility, see David P. Baron, "Private Politics, Corporate Social Responsibility, and Integrated Strategy", *Journal of Economics & Management Strategy* 10 (2001): 41–42; N. Craig Smith, "Business as Usual Is Not the Answer to Society's Problems", in *Mainstreaming Corporate Responsibility*, ed. N. Craig Smith and Gilbert Lenssen (Chichester: Wiley, 2009), 8–9; Andrew M. Pettigrew, "Corporate Responsibility in Strategy", in *Mainstreaming Corporate Responsibility*, ed. N. Craig Smith and Gilbert Lenssen (Chichester: Wiley, 2009), 12–20.
6. Ralph Stogdill, "Leadership, membership and organization", *Psychological Bulletin* 47, 3.
7. Albert Hirschman, *The Passions and the Interests: Political Arguments for Capitalism before Its Triumph* (Princeton, 2013).
8. This summary of the meaning of the national interest amounts to a summary of what historians have agreed to call the "mercantilism" mentality. These ideas are largely repeated across the seventeenth century. For a useful recent commentary on mercantilism, see the chapters assembled in Philip J. Stern and Carl Wennerlind's *Mercantilism Reimagined: Political Economy in Early Modern Britain and its Empire* (New York, 2013).
9. Paul Slack, *The Invention of Improvement: Information and Material Progress in Seventeenth-Century England* (Oxford: Oxford University Press, 2015), 65.
10. Peter Clark, *The Cambridge Urban History of Britain. Vol. 2, 1540–1840* (Cambridge: Cambridge University Press, 2000), 11–12.

11. Michael Porter, "What is leadership: The CEO's Role in Large, Complex Organizations", in *Handbook of Leadership Theory and Practice,* 427–438.
12. The emergence of these theories is canonically an eighteenth-century story, but opposition to corporate monopolies generated early incarnations of such ideas in the seventeenth century. See Hirschman, *Passions and Interests* and William A. Pettigrew, *Freedom's Debt: The Royal African Company and the Politics of the Atlantic Slave Trade, 1672–1752* (Chapel Hill, 2013), Chap. 3.
13. Phil Withington, "Public Discourse, Corporate Citizenship, and State Formation in Early Modern England", *American Historical Review* 112 (2007): 1036.
14. Keith Wrightson, *Earthly Necessities: Economic Lives in Early Modern Britain* (New Haven, 2000), 154.
15. English merchants in Surat justified the use of bullion as their principal trading good because "whereby much good may be done, for that divers of the country people are constrained to sell to engrossers at very low prices for want of money to supply the needful" see *Letters Received by the East India Company from its servants in the East* 6 vols. (London, 1896—1902), ed. F. C. Danvers and W Foster, Vol. 1, 1602—1613, 153. Needless to say other European companies argued this is well. See Blair B. King and M. N. Pearson, *The Age of Partnership: Europeans in Asia before Dominion* (Honolulu, Hawai UP, 1979).
16. For the first charter of the East India Company, see *Charters Granted to the East-India Company, from 1601; Also the Treaties and Grants, Made with, or obtained from, the Princes and Powers in India, from the years 1756 to 1772* [London, 1774?], 5–22.
17. Robert Johnson, "Nova Britannia Offering Most Excellent Fruites by Planting in Virginia" (London: Printed for Samuel Macham, 1609), 5.
18. See, for instance, Thomas Papillon, "The East-India-Trade a Most Profitable Trade to the Kingdom and Best Secured and Improved in a Company and a Joint-Stock: Represented in a Letter Written Upon the Occasion to Two Letters Lately Published Insinuating the Contrary" (London, 1677), 2. "It's Foreign Trade that renders us Rich, Honourable and Great, that gives us a name and esteem in the World, that makes us Masters of the Treasures of other Countries, and begets and maintains our Ships and Seamen".
19. Gerald Malynes, *The Maintenance of Free Trade according to the Three essentiall parts of traffique; namely, commodities, moneys and exchange*

of moneys (London, 1622), 3–4. This depiction of corporations remained the same throughout the seventeenth century. See *Certain Considerations Relating to the African Company of England* (1680).
20. Lewes Roberts, *Treasure of Traffick* (London, 1641), 52.
21. Robert Boyle, "A Letter of the Honorable Robert Boyle Concerning the Vegetable Nature of Amber Greece, According to an Extract Taken out of a Dutch East Indian Journal", *Philosophical Transactions*, 8 (1673), 6113.
22. *Calendar of State Papers: East Indies, China and Japan, 1513–1615*, ed. W Noel Sainsbury (London, 1862) (hereafter *CSP*).
23. *CSP*, no. 374, July 29 1607, 157 (dividend); *CSP*, no. 447, June 20 1609, 187 (suppliers).
24. *CSP*, no. 772, Oct 10 1614, 326.
25. [East India Company], *Lawes and Standing Orders* (London, 1621).
26. *A SPEECH Made by the RIGHT HONOURABLE GEORGE EARL of BERKELEY, TO THE LEVANT Company at their Annual Election, February ix. 1680* (London, 1680).
27. *A Calendar of the Court Minutes of the East India Company, 1640–1643* ed. Ethel Bruce Sainsbury, William Foster (London, 1909 hereafter *Minutes of EIC*), 165/166.
28. Exceptions include the following governors: the Duke of York, Prince Rupert, Lord Marlborough or George Berkeley in the Levant Company (though he had experience from other companies).
29. D. C. Coleman (rev. Anita McConnell), "Herne, Sir Nathaniel (d. 1679)", in *Oxford Dictionary of National Biography* (Oxford, 2004).
30. See Multinationals Database compiled by Aske Laursen Brock. The database contains data on the individuals elected director of the overseas trading companies between 1600 and 1708. The 1600 charter of the Levant Company and the 1672 charter of the Royal African Company are from Cecil T. Carr, *Select Charters of Trading Companies, A.D. 1530–1707* (London: Bernard Quaritch, 1913), 30–42, 186–192. EIC charters can all be found in East India Company, *Charters Granted to the East-India Company, from 1601; Also the Treaties and Grants, Made with, or Obtained from, the Princes and Powers in India, from the Year 1756 to 1772* (London: East India Company, 1774). The minute books, which constitute the core of the database: BoE: Minutes of the Court of Directors 1694–1725 (available on www.bankofengland.co.uk/archive); EIC: BL IOR/B/1–50, BL IOR/H/764; NEIC:

BL IOR/B/47 & 50; HBC: TNA BH 1–2; LeC: TNA SP105/147–156; MBC: Nathaniel Bradstreet Shurtleff, *Records of the Governor and Company of the Massachusetts Bay in New England* (Boston, Mass.: The Massachusetts Historical Society, 1853–1854); MuC: LMA CLC/B/195/MS11741/001–003; RAC: T70/100–102; VaC: Susan M. Kingsbury, *The Records of the Virginia Company of London: The Court Book, from the Manuscript in Library of Congress* (Washington: Government Printing Office, 1906). Information on relationship between directors, their family and their surrounding environment has been found in probates, The National Archives, Kew (hereafter TNA), Prob/11: the wills and probates of 303 directors have been successfully identified. Further information on 236 of the directors can be found in the Oxford Dictionary of National Biography; 232 of the directors can be found on the History of Parliament Online; 127 directors who were active in the civic government in London can be found in Alfred P. Beaven, *The Aldermen of London Temp Henry Iii—1912* (London: Guildhall Library, 1908); John Noorthouck, *A New History of London Including Westminster and Southwark* (London: R. Baldwin, 1773), p. appendix. Information on the directors relationship within and to the livery companies has been found on "The Records of London's livery companies Online" (ROLLCO) (www.londonroll.org). This online database contains membership information on a number of the Livery Companies in London for the seventeenth century: clothworkers', drapers', goldsmiths', mercers', bowyers', girdlers', salters', musicians' and tallow chandlers' company.

31. Key strategic breakthroughs, however, were often initiated by governors who came to the board as outsiders or newcomers. The best example of this is the governorship of the East India Company in the 1650s of Maurice Thomson, the former Atlantic interloper who sought to rebuild the East India Company as a plenipotentiary body—thus underpinning its huge expansion in the 1670s and 1680s.
32. *CSP*, no. 448, July 4, 1609, 187.
33. John Smith, *Generall Historie [of Virginia]* (London, 1624), 120.
34. Kingsbury, *The Court Book*, 175–197.
35. William Scott, An essay of drapery: or, the compleate citizen trading justly. Pleasingly. Profitably (London, 1635), 117.
36. Richard Grassby, *The Business Community of Seventeenth-Century England* (Cambridge, 1995), 218.

37. A. M. Pettigrew, "On Studying Managerial Elites", *Strategic Management Journal* 13, no. S2 (1992): 163–182.
38. *CSP*, no. 873, July 8, 1620, 379.
39. *CSP*, no. 77, Nov 18, 1619, 323.
40. *CSP*, no. 1003, July 11, 1615, 418.
41. CSP, no. 1039, July 4, 1621, 435.
42. Stanley Spurling, *Sir Thomas Smythe, knt* (New York, 1955), 19.
43. *CSP*, no. 691, Feb. 8, 1614, 275.
44. *Minutes of EIC*, on "perpetuall dictator" see "A Quarterly General Court", 28 May 1641.
45. *Minutes of EIC*, "General Court", 17 April 1640.
46. D. C. Coleman, *The Economy of England* (New York: Oxford University Press, 1977), 141.
47. D. C. Coleman, *Sir John Banks: Baronet and Businessman* (Oxford, 1963), 70.
48. David Hancock, *Citizens of the World: London Merchants and the Integration of the British Atlantic Community, 1735–1785* (Cambridge: Cambridge University Press, 1995), 17.
49. Phil Withington, *Society in Early Modern England: The Vernacular Origins of Some Powerful Ideas* (Cambridge: Polity, 2010), 217–218.
50. See, for instance, Muscovy Company: LMA CLC.B.195. MS11741.001; Levant Company: TNA SP105/151.
51. Koji Yamamoto, "Piety, Profit and Public Service in the Financial Revolution," *EHR*, CXXVI (2011), 833–834.
52. TNA PROB 11/324/368; TNA PROB 11/331/110.
53. Ibid., 64.
54. Ibid., 66.
55. Ibid., 66–67. The lesser merchants were considerably less interested in education. Like the greater merchants, they gave the majority of their donations to the poor, but the second largest group was social rehabilitation: people in jail. In all probability, it was the fear of debtors' jail that made lesser merchants remember their unfortunate colleagues.
56. TNA PROB 11/272/491.
57. TNA PROB 11/305/443.
58. KHLC U1015/Q21/1–5.
59. KHLC U1015/Q21/2. The total cost of the adventure at the time was £2195, which was—unsurprisingly——exactly the same as the subscription.

60. TNA T70/78, f. 164.
61. KHLC U1015/Q21/4.
62. KHLC U1015/Q21/1. The increase in percent from £22 in 1683 to £173 in 1684: 173–22 = (151/22)*100.
63. There are some overlaps, but the list is still impressive. EIC governors: Joseph Herne, Josiah Child. Deputy governor: Thomas Papillon. Levant Company governor: George Berkeley. Levant Company treasurer: Charles Thorold. The MPs: Robert Clayton, John Lawrence, John Moore, Jacob Lucy, Thomas Papillon, John Pollexfen. The Lord Mayors: John Moore, Robert Clayton, John Frederick, Robert Viner, James Edwards, Patience Ward, William Turner, William Pritchard. Aldermen: Robert Clayton, John Lawrence, Jacob Lucy, John Moore, William Pritchard, William Turner, Robert Viner, Henry Cornish, Patience Ward. Royal Society: John Lawrence, Edward Stillingfleet, Patience Ward, John Tillotson. Bishop of London: Henry Compton. Dean of St Paul: Edward Stillingfleet. Dean of Canterbury: John Tillotson.
64. The relationships described here are decided by who the directors worked with in the company boardrooms, in the civic corporation of London, Parliament in 1681 and the Stock for putting Poor French Protestants to work. EIC BL B/35–36 Levant Company: TNA SP105/154; RAC: TNA T70/78; Muscovy Company: LMA CLC.B.195.MS11741.001. Aldermen of London: Alfred P. Beaven, "Chronological list of aldermen: 1651–1700", in *The Aldermen of the City of London Temp. Henry III—1912* (London, 1908), 75–119.; Parliament of 1681: Adventurers of the Stock for putting Poor French Protestants to work: KHLC U1015/Q21/2.
65. For this debate, see, Anon, *Two Letters Concerning the East-India Company* (London, 1676); Papillon, *The East-India-Trade a Most Profitable Trade*; Anon, *The Allegations of the Turky Company and Others against the East-India-Company* (London, 1681); Josiah Child, *A Treatise* (London, 1681).
66. For the importance of the commercial knowledge economy, see Natasha Glaisyer, *The Culture of Commerce in England, 1660–1720* (Woodbridge: Boydell, 2006). For a recent example of the importance of knowledge economy and networks, see Edmond J. Smith, "Networks of the East India Company, c.1600–1625," (Magdalene College, University of Cambridge, 2016).

67. See the Charitable Corporation, Foundling Hospital and the proposed reinvention of the Royal African Company as a charity to regulate the pawnbroking trade in London in the 1740s. See Pettigrew, *Freedom's Debt*, 201.
68. East India Company, *Answer to All the Material Objections against the Present East-India-Company* (London, 1689), 2.
69. For more on this broad thesis, see David Veevers, "The Early Modern Colonial State in Asia: Private Agency and Family Networks in the English East India Company" (University of Kent, 2015), Chap. 1 and David Veevers, "'Inhabitants of the Universe': Global Families, Kinship Networks, and the Formation of the Early Modern Colonial State in Asia *", *Journal of Global History* 10 (2015).
70. Josiah Child, *Sir Josiah Child's Proposals for the Relief and Employment of the Poor* (1670?), 6. The British Library has dated the pamphlet as 1670, but Josiah Child was not knighted until 1678, so it is undoubtedly published later than the proposed date.
71. Josiah Child, "Sir Josiah Child's Proposals for the Relief and Employment of the Poor" (1670?), 5; Peter Brealey, "The Charitable Corporation for the Relief of Industrious Poor: Philanthropy, Profit and Sleaze in London, 1707–1733", *History*, 98 (2013), 709–711; Carr, *Select Charters*, 257–258.
72. *Some Remarks on the Present State of the East-India Company's Affairs* (1690), 6; *Reasons humbly offered against establishing, by Act of Parliament, the East-India-trade, in a company, with a joint-stock, exclusive of others, the subjects of England* (1693), 3; Daniel Defoe, *An Essay on Projects* (1697), 29; *An Essay towards a Scheme or Model for Erecting a National* East-India *Joynt Stock or Company* (1691), 2.
73. *Some Remarks on the Present State of the East India Company's affairs* (1690), 8. In 1693, the Crown added provisions to the Company's new charter that expanded its stock and altered its governance to prevent the engrossing of shares and power into single "overmighty" directors like Josiah Child by limiting each member to a maximum of ten votes. See W. R. Scott, *The Constitution and Finance of English, Scottish, and Irish Joint Stock Companies to 1720* (2 vols, 1912), i. 340; ii. 155.
74. For further details of this "compliance revolution", see William A. Pettigrew and Tristan Stein, "The Public Rivalry between Regulated and Joint Stock Corporations and the Development of Seventeenth Century Corporate Constitutions", *Historical Research*, December 2016.

References

Archives

British Library, India Office Records (BL IOR): B/1–50.
Kent History and Library Centre (KHLC): U1015/Q21.
London Metropolitan Archives (LMA): CLC.B.195.MS11741.001.
The National Archives, Kew Gardens (TNA): BH 1–2.
TNA: PROB 11.
TNA: SP105/151.
TNA: T70/100–102.

Primary Published Material and Calendars

Anon, *Two Letters Concerning the East-India Company* (London, 1676).

Anon, *Certain considerations relating to the Royal African Company of England. In which, the original, growth, and national advantages of the Guiney trade, are demonstrated: as also that the same trade cannot be carried on, but by a company and joint-stock* (London, 1680).

Anon, *The Allegations of the Turky Company and Others against the East-India-Company* (London, 1681).

Anon, *Some Remarks on the Present State of the East-India Company's Affairs* (1690).

Anon, *An Essay towards a Scheme or Model for Erecting a National East-India Joynt Stock or Compan*' (1691).

Anon, *Reasons humbly offered against establishing, by Act of Parliament, the East-India-trade, in a company, with a joint-stock, exclusive of others, the subjects of England* (1693).

Beaven, Alfred P., *The Aldermen of London Temp Henry III—1912* (London: Guildhall Library, 1908).

Berkeley, George, *A speech made by the Right Honourable George Earl of Berkeley to the Levant company at their annual election, February ix* (Printed for Roy Royston, London: 1680).

Boyle, Robert, 'A Letter of the Honorable Robert Boyle Concerning the Vegetable Nature of Amber Greece, According to an Extract Taken out of a Dutch East Indian Journal', *Philosophical Transactions*, 8 (1673).

Carr, Cecil T., *Select Charters of Trading Companies, A.D. 1530–1707* (London: Bernard Quaritch, 1913).
Child, Josiah, 'Sir Josiah Child's Proposals for the Relief and Employment of the Poor' (1670?).
Child, Josiah, 'A Treatise' (London: printed by J.R. for the Honourable the East-India Company, 1681).
East India Company, 'Answer to All the Material Objections against the Present East-India-Company' (London, 1689).
East India Company, 'Charters Granted to the East-India Company, from 1601; Also the Treaties and Grants, Made with, or obtained from, the Princes and Powers in India, from the years 1756 to 1772' (London, 1774?).
Johnson, Robert, 'Nova Britannia Offering Most Excellent Fruites by Planting in Virginia' (London: Printed for Samuel Macham, 1609).
Kingsbury, Susan M., *The Records of the Virginia Company of London: The Court Book, from the Manuscript in Library of Congress* (Washington: Government Printing Office, 1906).
Malynes, Gerald, 'The Maintenance of Free Trade according to the Three essentiall parts of traffique; namely, commodities, moneys and exchange of moneys' (London, 1622).
Noorthouck, John, *A New History of London Including Westminster and Southwark* (London: R. Baldwin, 1773).
Papillon, Thomas, 'The East-India-Trade a Most Profitable Trade to the Kingdom and Best Secured and Improved in a Company and a Joint-Stock: Represented in a Letter Written Upon the Occasion to Two Letters Lately Published Insinuating the Contrary' (London, 1677).
Roberts, Lewes, 'The treasure of traffike, or, A discourse of forraigne trade wherein is shewed the benefit and commoditie arising to a commonwealth or kingdome, by the skilfull merchant' (London, 1641).
Sainsbury, Noel W. (ed.), *Calendar of State Papers: East Indies, China and Japan, 1513–1615* (London, 1862).
Sainsbury, Ethel Bruce (ed.), *A Calendar of the Court Minutes of the East India Company, 1640–1643* (London, 1909).
Scott, William, An essay of drapery: or, The compleate citizen Trading iustly. Pleasingly. Profitably (London, 1635).
Shurtleff, Nathaniel Bradstreet, *Records of the Governor and Company of the Massachusetts Bay in New England* (Boston, MA: Massachusetts Historical Society, 1853–54).

Smith, John, 'The generall historie of Virginia, New-England, and the Summer Isles with the names of the adventurers, planters, and governours from their first beginning. ano: 1584. to this present 1624' (London, 1624).

Secondary Literature

Baron, David P., "Private Politics, Corporate Social Responsibility, and Integrated Strategy," *Journal of Economics & Management Strategy* 10 (2001), 7–45.
Brealey, Peter, 'The Charitable Corporation for the Relief of Industrious Poor: Philanthropy, Profit and Sleaze in London, 1707–1733', *History* 98 (2013), 708–729.
Clark, Peter, *The Cambridge Urban History of Britain. Vol. 2, 1540–1840* (Cambridge: Cambridge University Press, 2000).
Coleman, D. C., *Sir John Banks: Baronet and Businessman* (Oxford: Clarendon Press, 1963).
Coleman, D. C., *The Economy of England* (New York, Oxford University Press, 1977).
Glaisyer, Natasha, *The Culture of Commerce in England, 1660–1720* (Woodbridge: Boydell, 2006).
Grassby, Richard, *The Business Community of Seventeenth-Century England* (Cambridge: Cambridge University Press, 1995).
Friedman, Walter A., 'Leadership and History' in *Handbook of Leadership Theory and Practice*, Nitin Nohria and Rakesh Knurana (eds.) (Boston, MA: Harvard Business Press, 2010), 291–304.
Halliday, Paul, *Dismembering the Body Politic: Partisan Politics in England's Towns, 1650–1730* (Cambridge: Cambridge University Press, 1998).
Hancock, David, *Citizens of the World: London Merchants and the Integration of the British Atlantic Community, 1735–1785* (Cambridge: Cambridge University Press, 1995).
Hirschman, Albert, *The Passions and the Interests: Political Arguments for Capitalism before Its Triumph* (Princeton: Princeton University Press, 2013).
Jordan,W. K., *The Charities of London, 1480–1660: The Aspirations and the Achievements of the Urban Society* (London: George Allen & Unwin Ltd., 1960).
King, Blair B. and M. N. Pearson, *The Age of Partnership: Europeans in Asia before Dominion* (Honolulu, Hawai University Press, 1979).
Nohria, Nitin and Rakesh Knurana (eds.) *Handbook of Leadership Theory and Practice* (Boston, MA, 2010).

Pettigrew, Andrew M., 'On studying Managerial Elites', *Strategic Management Journal*, Volume 13, Issue S2, Winter (1992), 163–182.

Pettigrew, Andrew M., 'Corporate Responsibility in Strategy', in *Mainstreaming Corporate Responsibility*, ed. by N. Craig Smith and Gilbert Lenssen (Chichester: Wiley, 2009), 12–20.

Pettigrew, William A., *Freedom's Debt: The Royal African Company and the Politics of the Atlantic Slave Trade, 1672–1752* (Chapel Hill: University of North Carolina Press 2013).

Pettigrew, William A. and Tristan Stein, 'The Public Rivalry between Regulated and Joint Stock Corporations and the Development of Seventeenth Century Corporate Constitutions', *Historical Research* (Dec. 2016).

Porter, Michael, 'What is leadership: The CEO's Role in Large, Complex Organizations' in the *Handbook of Leadership Theory and Practice*, Nitin Nohria and Rakesh Knurana (eds.) (Boston, MA, 2010), 427–438.

Schein, Edgar, *Organisational Culture and Leadership* (San Francisco: Jonssey-Bass, 2004).

Scott,W. R., *The Constitution and Finance of English, Scottish, and Irish Joint Stock Companies to 1720*, vol. I (Cambridge: Cambridge University Press, 1912).

Scott,W. R., *The Constitution and Finance of English, Scottish, and Irish Joint Stock Companies to 1720*, vol. II (Cambridge: Cambridge University Press, 1910).

Slack, Paul, *The Invention of Improvement: Information and Material Progress in Seventeenth-Century England* (Oxford: Oxford University Press, 2015).

Smith, N. Craig, 'Business as Usual Is Not the Answer to Society's Problems', in *Mainstreaming Corporate Responsibility*, ed. by N. Craig Smith and Gilbert Lenssen (Chichester: Wiley, 2009), 8–11.

Smith, Edmond J., 'Networks of the East India Company, C. 1600–1625' (Magdalene College, University of Cambridge, 2016).

Spurling, Stanley, *Sir Thomas Smythe, knt* (New York: the Newcomen Society in North America 1955).

Stern, Philip J. and Carl Wennerlind (eds.), *Mercantilism Reimagined: Political Economy in Early Modern Britain and tis Empire* (New York: Oxford University Press, 2013).

Stern, Philip J., 'The English East India Company and the Modern Corporation: Legacies, Lessons, and Limitations,' Seattle University Law Review, 39 (2: 2016).

Stogdill, Ralph, 'Leadership, membership and organization, *Psychological bulletin*, 47 (1950), 1–14.

Van Knippenberg, Daan and Michael A. Hogg, *Leadership and Power: Identity Processes in Groups and Organizations* (London, Sage, 2003).

Veevers, David, "Inhabitants of the Universe': Global Families, Kinship Networks, and the Formation of the Early Modern Colonial State in Asia', *Journal of Global History*, 10 (2015), 99–121.

Withington, Phil, *The Politics of Commonwealth: Citizens and Freemen in Early Modern England* (Cambridge: Cambridge University Press 2005).

———, 'Public Discourse, Corporate Citizenship, and State Formation in Early Modern England', *The American Historical Review*, 112 (2007), 1016–1038.

———, *Society in Early Modern England: The Vernacular Origins of Some Powerful Ideas* (Cambridge: Polity, 2010).

Wrightson, Keith, *Earthly Necessities: Economic Lives in Early Modern Britain* (New Haven, 2000).

Yamamoto, Koji, 'Piety, Profit and Public Service in the Financial Revolution', *EHR*, CXXVI (2011), 806–834.

3

Socially Responsible and Responsive Business in Seventeenth-Century England

Edmond J. Smith

Seventeenth-century chartered corporations, such as the East India Company (EIC), were designed and operated with specific social responsibilities in mind. They were expected to contribute to the commonwealth of the kingdom, in terms of both increasing the wealth of society and responding to the welfare needs of their particular constituents.[1] Supporting these constituents—that is, a company's members and employees, and people living close to their operations—was vitally important for early modern companies; it justified their privileges and allowed them to stave off attacks from interlopers and proponents of free trade.[2] Undertaking socially responsible activities was not just good for public relations; it was part of a corporation's very reason to exist. At the heart of early modern business, there was a social contract between corporation and society intended to ensure positive gains for both.[3]

E.J. Smith (✉)
University of Kent, Canterbury, England, UK
e-mail: e.j.smith@kent.ac.uk

W.A. Pettigrew and D.C. Smith (eds.), *A History of Socially Responsible Business, c.1600–1950*, Palgrave Studies in the History of Finance,
DOI 10.1007/978-3-319-60146-5_3

To achieve this aim, corporations participated in initiatives ranging from building schools and hospitals to giving pensions to the elderly and developing medical provisions for their workers. While such initiatives were usually ordered by company directors, they were developed through collaboration with various constituents from across society.[4] In particular, constituents had a voice within early modern businesses through regular meetings where petitions could be presented to company boards directly. These meetings were an important way in which companies developed their socially responsible agendas and ensured their activities responded to the needs of the people they were trying to help and influence. Social responsibility in a seventeenth-century business was far more responsive than initiatives in many companies today.[5]

This chapter focuses on a key mechanism that allowed broader constituents of corporations to hold directors to account and ensure they upheld their social obligations—the petition. Through analysing the detailed accounts of EIC board meetings, this chapter examines how petitions were received, considered and responded to by early modern businesses. This will demonstrate the importance of social responsibility for early modern companies, how different constituents could approach the companies, and what sorts of petition received positive responses. To do so, the chapter will assess the petitioning culture of the 1620s in detail before briefly examining the later 1670s and 1680s. By examining petitions across a fifty-year period, the chapter will show how social responsibility became an ingrained part of the governance of corporations, with sophisticated mechanisms in place to ensure businesses kept the end of the social bargain that made their existence possible. The chapter suggests that the EIC worked hard to satisfy a series of social obligations to a broad array of petitions. In most cases, the individuals concerned had some connection with the EIC but were not members of the corporation in the strictest sense. They were, however, members of a broader corporate constituency whose breadth confirms that, despite their exclusivity, corporations depicted themselves as inseparable from the social basis that supplied their labour force, customer base and social environment.

This important relationship between companies, the public and the state was sustained in part by the contractual arrangements in corporate charters, but it was also built on the cultural values that underpinned early modern commerce, in particular trust and creditability.[6] Trust between merchants, corporations, customers, employees and regulators was a vital foundation for commercial interaction, with actors relying on the reputation of potential partners to assess the viability of commercial projects.[7] From helping to attract investment to efficiently underwriting transactions, the reputation of corporate bodies was a key determinant of their success.

Social legitimacy was an important area in which corporate bodies could demonstrate their creditability. Institutional reputations underpinned the social legitimacy of corporations in the early modern world. Corporations in early modern Europe were built on networks of overlapping interests, relationships and businesses. These networks enabled the development of new types of corporate bodies—most famously the joint-stock model best represented by the East India Company—that relied heavily on support from the broader communities within which they operated. This included attracting investment, employees and political support, all of which depended on the willingness of a wide variety of people to participate in a company's agenda. Within this environment, corporations depended on the socially responsible activities of their leaders and members to retain support and ensure their continued viability in the public sphere.

The EIC was founded in a period where merchants and civic corporations spent considerable time and effort on socially responsible activities and the new company developed its own strategies in this area in response to these. During the early modern period, people in London, principally merchants, "were to provide an almost incomprehensibly large total of charitable wealth" as they sought to assuage the social challenges of the growing metropolis. Indeed, between 1480 and 1660 almost two million pounds of charitable donations were made by just over seven thousand donors. The average donation was £255 12s 2d—a considerable sum of money that far exceeded the national average rate of giving. These funds were used in a range of different ways as London's merchants sought to undertake "a great variety of experimental efforts for the social rehabilitation of the poor". Just over a third of donations were made to specific individuals but the vast majority were used to establish institutions that provided essential social facilities, such as hospitals, almshouses or schools.[8] Even when charitable institutions were not the direct recipients of this funding, they were often managed by institutional bodies, particularly London's livery companies.[9]

Livery companies in London had a long-standing charitable role in society, both in terms of managing bequests from their members and through directly undertaking charitable works as an organisation. Their social activities foreground the social responsiveness of the trading companies. These would often relate to the specific interests of the company—such as protecting their members and their legacies—but were also intended to benefit society more broadly. For example, the Mercers' livery company, whose hall in Ironmonger Lane placed them at the very centre of London's political and economic landscape, undertook numerous socially responsible activities. In 1608, after receiving news "touching certain decay in the company's chapel" the wardens of the company decided to "give order for the repairing the ruins thereof".[10] Ten years later, following a report about the "decayed" window of the parish church of St Lawrence Jewry, which "was first founded and made by Sir William Eastfield knight, a famous man of this society in his age and a great benefactor to the company and in general to the whole City", it was agreed that "the same shall be repaired at the cost and charges of this company".[11] In each case, support for religious institutions stemmed from their connection to the company—supporting them demonstrated the company's historical and current support for society.

Yet, while there was support for projects of this sort, much more time and money was spent within livery companies in connection with more immediate charitable activities. Considerable attention was given to respond to the changing needs of younger company members, and attempts were made to ensure children and apprentices connected to the company could enter the working world in the best possible position. For instance, each year the wardens of the Grocers' Company used funds provided by deceased members to pay "for the benefit and advancement of young men" of the company and to loan to people outside the company. Each loan followed the same pattern, with a principal recipient supported by at least one other person offering surety.[12] These loans were an important means for younger members to access funds required for establishing their own business or family and amounted to tens of thousands of pounds in the early seventeenth century. Similarly, livery companies also supported access to formal education, offering support for students and scholars at Oxford and Cambridge as well as educational activities in London.[13] In London, salaries and funds to support schools were a long-term investment for companies, with payments for schoolmasters, tutors and buildings a constant charge in the account books of these corporations.[14] Contributing to society through these activities not only provided an essential means of responding to social needs, but also helped cultivate a large community of individuals who could later be relied upon to support the company and who had the essential skills and values for participating in corporate activities in England and overseas.

In addition to these long-term charitable activities, livery companies would also respond to specific charitable needs. Providing some sort of safety net for the poor in London was expected, and support for corporations could depend in part on their effective contribution to the social demands of the city. When they failed to do so, it would be quickly noted, both by merchants in London but also powerful political figures on whose support the companies depended. When the Mercers' received a letter from the Lord Mayor suggesting that the company should refrain from conspicuous and expensive public dinners and give the money to charity instead, the company was quick to agree.[15] Such complaints were rare, though, and the companies didn't usually require a push to undertake charitable works. Regular collections were held to raise funds, and these were supplemented by the distribution of clothes and other essentials to the poor.[16] In addition to direct donations, companies also supported long-term pensions, such as the Clothworkers' agreement to award fourteen "aged and impotent persons" with payments each quarter.[17] Charitable activities were not made without thought, as petitioners seeking aid could face inquiries seeking to understand "by what means he came into decay" before receiving funds.[18] Much like the EIC, whose socially responsible activities are discussed in detail below, livery companies sought to support a wide range of activities to improve the lives of their members and those of people living in the communities within which they operated.

As new ventures took on corporate forms for trade and empire, they were built on a long-standing tradition of social responsibility that sat at the heart of company culture in early modern London.

As London's fortunes waxed and waned, so too could charitable giving, and it was the early decades of the seventeenth century that witnessed the greatest upsurge in charitable activity. Between 1601 and 1640, a vast sum of money was donated by London's benefactors.[19] During this period, London continued to attract considerable numbers of migrants from elsewhere in England and the city grew at a prodigious rate. At the same time, its wealth grew as London's merchants took advantage of trading and colonial activities across the globe. As bumper profits coincided with a rising population and challenges to the social fabric of the city, there was a growing demand for resources to battle poverty and tackle unemployment and to ensure that future generations had the necessary skills to meet the demands of a rapidly changing economy.

During the Stuart period, "the frontal assault on poverty" included several forms of poor relief that amounted to almost £10,000 a year across four decades, in addition to the endowment and construction of almshouses.[20] Some of these provisions were made for the general benefit of the poor in London, but many were made to support social groups connected to particular benefactors—members of a livery company would often specify in their wills that their charity should be used primarily for needy constituents of the same institution. Corporations had long played an important role in responding to the challenges facing English society, and the incorporation of livery companies from the fourteenth century onwards had been taken, in part, as a response to social forces. Through incorporation livery companies obtained rights and privileges that were essential for their continuing relevance—particularly, the right to own land—but in doing so they took on a greater role in society. They sought to regulate the activities of members, sometimes by forcing individuals to curtail activities deemed unsuitable, but also by providing an important safety net and social structure.[21]

In addition to poor relief, "the aspirations of the London burghers and their incredible generosity are perhaps best exemplified in the steady and massive support which they lent to education".[22]

This included founding and supporting grammar schools (that often included spaces for poorer students), the establishment of scholarships and support for universities.[23] This focus on the future, and attempts to improve the livelihoods of individuals, can also be traced to the role of corporations in society. First, corporations were built on a well-developed system of apprenticeships that sought to guarantee certain levels of education and social support for members. Second, livery companies and certain trading companies took care to support schools. Companies depended on both of these methods to provide education for their constituents and train potential future employees, and coupled with support for almshouses and hospitals, these represent some of the ways they sought to act responsibly in society.

Although these strategies allowed companies to undertake long-term charitable activities, they were not the main recourse for social responsibility in early modern corporations. Day to day, corporations' social responsibility was much more responsive. In the EIC, the Court of Committees—essentially the board of directors—received thousands of petitions across the seventeenth century. These came from shareholders, employees, their families and sometimes from people with no previous connection to the company at all.

Between July 1624 and July 1625, the EIC received 166 petitions.[24] These can be divided between five main subjects: wages and payments; requests for charity; applications for employment; the repatriation of goods; and crime. The most common requests came from employees or their families regarding wages—sometimes when these had not been paid by the company, but more often when families requested a portion of the wages of husbands or children who were working for the EIC overseas. Eighty-six petitions related to this area, twice as many as any other area. A further forty-three petitions came from people seeking employment in the company, nineteen from people seeking poverty relief, twelve relating to crime and five regarding the return of goods.

These divisions are not perfect, and many petitions were couched in terms of the particular circumstances of petitioners—often their poverty, health or service to the company. For example, when Giles Shepherd, "an old servant of the company", petitioned the EIC for employment at its ironworks in Blackwall, he was already receiving aid, living in the almshouse in Deptford. Unfortunately for Shepherd, the company did not require further workers in this position, but in respect to his previous service and current circumstances, it took his petition seriously and promised to think of him again if a position became available.[25] In the case of Shepherd, his petition for employment was linked closely with his poverty and long-term relationship with the EIC.

For many petitioners, this existing relationship was the main cause for their appearance before the Court of Committees, and dozens of employees sought redress through this facility. Many simply sought the payment of wages from their time overseas. Mr Worden, "lately returned out of the Indies … made suit at the Court that the company would be pleased to let him have some part of the monies owed unto him for wages".[26] Nicholas Woodcock "petitioned the Court for wages due to him in the *Whale*, the *Blessing*, the *Reformed* and the *Dolphin*".[27] Each man was told "that he shall have what appears due into him".[28] As these two examples suggest, some petitions were fairly straightforward, and where a petitioner had cause and evidence and had not acted against the company's rules and regulations, it was usually a fairly standard process.

In other cases, the company could be less responsive, particularly when petitioners sought to improve their position within the company. When William Walker sought an increase of salary, "the Court gave no care unto it" and the matter was not discussed further.[29] Even when the company was more supportive, such as when James Remmant sought employment, it would seek to match the company's requirements with support for the applicant. In this case, where Remmant reported how his "father lost his life casually in the company's service", the company assessed his particular skills and "because he had been formerly at sea" decided "he can serve as a mariner" if a position became available.[30] The company wanted to deliver a responsive agenda, but it would not sacrifice its financial and operational interests without good cause.

The difficulties in petitioning the court for cases that were less clear-cut could be more problematic for relatives of employees than for employees themselves. When Elizabeth Courtney, the "late wife of Robert Courtney … petition[ed] for her said husband's estate", the court could not immediately respond in her favour. She was instead referred to a further committee, responsible for mariners, whose report into Robert would assess whether Elizabeth could receive his wages.[31] Information relating to family members was often held by different parts of the company, and even if a petition was not referred to a different committee, such as Mary Sherwood's request for part of her husband's wages, it was commonly referred to the company secretary who would assess the matter.[32] Another wife of a company employee, Katherine Searle, submitted a similar petition, asking for part of her husband's wages "to relieve her and her poor child"; again, the court was unable to respond immediately and could only promise "that if it might appear that her husband desire it for her relief she shall have it".[33] This need to provide additional information was an endemic problem for petitioners requesting payment relating to family overseas.

The challenges of obtaining a quick response from the company could be overcome on occasion when petitioners' circumstances—usually poverty—demanded an immediate response. When Mary Johnson, the widower of Ottwall Johnson, a boatswain on one of the company's ships, "petitioned the Court for their charitable relief to her and her poor sick orphan", she was granted the immediate succour of 10s from the poor box.[34] Similarly, when Elizabeth Healing, "that lost her husband in the company's service petitioned the Court for some relief", she was given 5s.[35] When faced with the poverty of petitioners, particularly if caused in part by the death of family members in the company's service, the company could respond with speed and seems to have been willing to adopt a less strict attitude towards evidence before offering charitable relief.

The company took a similar approach to employees who had suffered serious injury in its service, and providing support for them was an important means for the company to demonstrate its socially responsible credentials.[36] When Joane Atkinson reported how her husband Richard Atkinson, "being amongst others at Blackwall at the lathing of a mast in the company's yards", had suffered a shock accident when "the tackle broke [and] it broke his leg into many pieces to the extreme peril of his life", the court ordered that she should receive "20s out of the poor box" and also paid for the company's surgeon to oversee his recovery.[37] The next month, when Joane returned to the company for further aid "towards the relief of her husband and 5 small children", the court, "considering the poor man's misery … was content to bestow upon him 40s more out of the poor box".[38]

This level of support for an injured employee was not a one-off occurrence. In the same year, the company granted charitable aid to a number of other injured petitioners. Thomas Smyth, "one of the labourers in the company's service at Blackwall, having broke his leg casually in doing his labours", approached the company with support from two witnesses and was given 20s.[39] Edward Hart "humbly prayed that they would bestow upon him some charitable relief" after he broke his collar bone working on the *Dolphin* and received 20s.[40] John Allen, a ship's carpenter who "had caught a sore hurt which made him unable to labour", was allowed to receive pay from his two servants employed overseas.[41] Another man, John Purre, was granted 10s after being hurt by a falling bale of silk on condition that he brought a certificate proving his assertion.[42] So long as the injured could support their petitions with witnesses or other evidence, the company was very likely to give support.

The provision of evidence was easier when petitioners had been injured working for the company in London, but injuries suffered overseas could still lead to charitable aid. When Samuel Pritchett, a mariner from Limehouse, entered a petition after he "received a hurt in his shoulder in doing them service in the Indies, by means whereof he is become lame of his said shoulder and arm", the company was provisionally supportive. He also claimed "that by the fall of the topmast aboard the *London* he had broke his thumb".[43] Even though the injuries had been suffered overseas, the company was willing to grant aid if Pritchett could provide evidence. Direct charitable contributions to injured or poverty-stricken petitioners were a fairly easy means by which the company could remonstrate its positive social contribution.

Yet direct monetary aid was not the only means by which the company sought to support its constituents when they suffered injury. Like Pritchett, Thomas Joyce came before the court following injury in the company's service overseas. He informed the company how his "right hand was cut off by an Arabian at the siege of Ormuz, and having learned to write well with his left hand, petitioned for a benevolence and employment". The company referred the issue "until he brought testimony to approve the truth of his petition", which Joyce was able to do ten days later when Mr Bangham and Mr Willis wrote in support.[44] With proof in hand, the company granted Joyce an immediate payment of 20 nobles—the equivalent of 80s—and promised to consider his employment on the next ships sailing for the East Indies.[45] This remarkable story, of the injured soldier retraining to perform a new role for the company, suggests how the company provided support for employees that far exceeded the norm during this period. Through its willingness to offer continued employment to people like Joyce, and medical provisions for employees who suffered injury, the EIC provided an essential social role for their constituents and made a considerable contribution to the localities in which it belonged. Like livery companies, the EIC understood the benefits of supporting individuals through times of struggle as a means of securing ongoing support from the wider community and for securing the loyalty of people with the skills, education and experience necessary for undertaking trade in Asia.

However, while the company did have a fairly open-door policy regarding petitions and was willing to receive them from all manner of people, it was not an organisation that would hand over money without thorough examination of each request. Petitions were made in person to the Court of Committees, and petitioners were expected to provide evidence in support of their request. In many cases, petitioners were well aware of this expectation and attended the company with a range of evidence. When Mrs Read, the widower of William Read who had died in the Indies, approached the company, she "produced letters of administration granted unto her for the goods of her deceased husband, whereunto was also annexed a will made by the same".[46] The wife of Andrew Workes, "now serving the Indies at Amboyna", was similarly well prepared when seeking £10 of her husband's wages and "provided a letter from her said husband authorising her to receive so much". The company checked its own records and agreed to pay her £5.[47] When letters of administration from family members were held by petitioners, the EIC usually responded positively to their petitions.

In situations when this was not possible other evidence was provided. When Constance Manley sought £10 from her husband's wages, she was not able to provide a letter from him personally. Instead, she provided a letter of recommendations from Sir William Bushell to support her claim. Coupled with her husband's good reputation and long service within the company, this letter of recommendation was enough to persuade the company to accept her suit.[48] The importance of a good reputation was vital for petitioners who lacked the necessary evidence, and this could be particularly challenging for people who, unlike Manley, did not live in London or have support from reputable, well-known merchants. For example, when Sara Vincent made a similar request for part of her husband's wages, "alleging her extreme poverty, and brought a certificate thereof from the inhabitants of the town of Newington in the county of Surrey", the EIC was willing to accept this evidence only of her need, rather than evidence of her husband's support for the payment, and ordered that she should receive two months' pay.[49] Distance could also make the company more sceptical of evidence provided. When Constance Dale sought her husband's wages, "she alleged that she dwells far off", and the company clearly found it difficult to trust her claim. It recorded how she "brought a letter of attorney of her husband's hands (as she said) for the same, together with other provable attestations from the town where she dwells", but was still unwilling to give her money without further investigation by the directors.[50] Evidence was only as good as the trust the company placed in it.

In addition to the challenges of presenting trustworthy evidence, the company often refused petitions because it possessed information that could challenge a claim. The EIC regularly referred petitions to the company accountant to check details of previous payments or specific wages, and the company secretary could draw on the organisation's extensive records for further evidence. This was an important mechanism for the company to ensure its socially responsible activities were undertaken accurately and in good faith, and highlights the careful consideration given to successful petitions as much as unsuccessful ones.

When petitions sought redress for activities that occurred outside London, either at sea or in Asia, the company took care to collect the necessary information before making decisions. When Elizabeth Johnson, the daughter of John Johnson, a gunner on the *Exchange*, petitioned the company for a package of cloves worth £44 that her father had sent from Asia, the court sent letters to the ship's purser "to certify the truth of this business".[51] While seeking additional information, the company might still find in favour of the petitioner, but this was not always the case. John Wood, who had served as mate on the *Pansgrove*, "upon some information from the company's President at Jacatra was denied his wages". Wood had waited for the President to return, but now that he had died sought to persuade the company to finally provide his pay. However, "the Court made answer that albeit that President be dead, yet his letters are alive, and they do and must give credit to their President as well in this as they do in matters of far greater moment".[52] With the internal evidence against him, Wood had no recourse.

Beyond evidence obtained by petitioners and information held by the company, other sources of information and other legal mechanisms for seeking redress further influenced and complicated the ways in which the EIC responded to petitioners. Robert Munden petitioned the EIC regarding 150 ryalls-of-eight that were owed him by Mr Newbeggen. Munden had already sought to obtain the silver through the Admiralty court, and he presented the company with two depositions from witnesses sworn in this court. While the EIC had no authority to seize the money from Newbeggen, Munden hoped they would stop the money passing into Newbeggen's hands while the proceedings continued. Newbeggen was owed wages from the *Swan* and the *Defence*, and the EIC ordered that the books of each ship should be searched before making a decision.[53] In the overlapping jurisdictions of London's commercial community, the EIC saw a clear hierarchy of evidence, where their own records surpassed other material. For petitioners, service to the company or other means of obtaining its trust could be more important for obtaining support than other forms of evidence. The EIC sought to uphold its social obligations but kept tight controls on how this process worked.

In some circumstances, information held by the company could run counter to the assertions made by petitioners. When Joyes Davies sought to obtain the estate of her husband's brother, Henry Davies, whose will she believed could not be executed because both of the executors were deceased, she was surprised to find out that the EIC held a copy of Henry's will "and neither she nor her husband are named therein".[54] While in this case, the petitioner seems to have been caught out by inaccurate or missing information on her part, the EIC was not always trusting of the people who came before the court.

Taking care to verify the information was essential, and fear of fraudulent activity was pervasive in the Court of Committees. In a period when information could only be transmitted through word of mouth or in writing, the company (and indeed the wider commercial community) viewed information sceptically. A series of possible frauds were attempted by petitioners, and they all depended on false papers and the challenges of proving identity.[55] The first such case, which seems to have provoked a more suspicious response to requests for charity afterwards, was revealed when Oliver Havers returned from Asia to discover that £14 of his wages had been paid to his wife each year. His shock and assertion that fraud had taken place rested on one issue—he was not married. "It was said that the first payment had been allowed and that he had acknowledged that woman that received it, to be his wife", but Havers insisted the evidence presented must have been false.[56] Two months later, Havers was still trying to obtain redress and had now identified a certain Mr Atkinson who had claimed the money "for the use of his wife whereas in truth he had no wife". The court "took knowledge that £7 10s had been paid by virtue of a letter of attorney was showed in Court under the hand of Havers" and sought to call Atkinson's executors to court. The executor refused to appear, "but returned answer that he would pay nothing without suit", and the company was forced to pay £10 10s to Havers out of its own account.[57] The fraudulent letter of attorney shown to the court had cost the company a significant sum of money.

In the following months, the company took a stricter approach to evidence presented in similar circumstances. Elizabeth Davies found her petition to receive part of her husband's wages, while he was overseas in the *Lyon*, rejected because the court, "resting unsatisfied that her husband had authorised her so to do", denied her request.[58] She returned the following month, "pretending a letter from her husband for his wages ... but the Court was informed that there is suspicion of fraud and therefore would grant her nothing".[59] A similar petition from Joan Selby, the wife of the bricklayer John Selby, was refused until "she bring good certificate that she is his wife".[60] Yet, when she provided "a letter from her husband in that behalf", the court "sent the letter into Mr Hunts office to be compared with the hand of the said Selby, found it suspicious that the hand was counterfeit, and therefore would do nothing in it".[61] In each case, the presentation of letters considered fraudulent led the company to reject the women's petitions. Yet, as the case of Selby suggests, proving or discovering fraud could be highly problematic when comparing simple signatures was often the extent of verifying material. The provision of evidence was in most circumstances essential in gaining a positive response from the company, and the administration of numerous requests could be an arduous process that depended on the continuing interest of senior figures in the EIC.

While the company depended on evidence and was suspicious of fraudulent activity, it was also highly responsive to the needs of its constituents and would often take the particular circumstances of petitioners into account before making decisions about accepting or rejecting aid. For example, when Gibbert Lodge sought part of his servants' wages who were employed by the company "for the relief of himself and his wife", his petition rested on evidence that "he being aged above 100 years and in great distress" was "ready to be turned out of doors".[62] Lodge understood that the success of his petition depended on the company taking pity on his circumstances. Other petitioners were successful in using similarly emotive techniques to persuade the company to support them. Aaron Ellis "exhibited a petition to the court entreating that in respect of his poverty" they might aid him financially, and "the court was contented in regards of the poverty of the man" to forgive his debts and give him 20s.[63] Elizabeth Elgar "alleged great poverty, sickness and a charge of children", and the company agreed "in such case of extremity" they would "help the distressed and therefore granted her desire".[64] Later, "Thomas Bell a very old man petitioned the Court for their charity and had 10s out of the poor box".[65] Mrs Alexander, who was "near fourscore years of age (as she said) and is poor", was similarly granted aid by "the Court in respect of her age and remote dwelling".[66] Ellen Geronimo, "being very poor", told the company that her husband was "one of those that went to the Manilias" and was given 10s from the poor box.[67] Extreme age, poverty and childcare were all issues that motivated the company to lend support.

Other circumstances similarly motivated the EIC to offer support to its petitioners, particularly when connected to extraordinary service to the company. When Pricilla Rickman petitioned the company, she was careful to highlight how "her husband had served in the company's ship the *Expedition* seven or eight years past, where (at such) time as the ship was taken by the Flemings he lost all that he had, that afterwards returning in the *Charles* he died by the way, and left her a poor widow with three small children". The eldest child was twelve or thirteen years old, and "she humbly prayed that the Company would take into their service, and to send him into the Indies in their ship the *London* now outward bound". The court agreed to employ the child, but only on condition that "the mother shall leave him wholly to the Company's care, and for so long as her son shall be living shall not require any part of his wages from the Company".[68] Rickman's desperate situation, and her husband's previous service, provided the circumstance for a successful petition to the company. Another petitioner, Thomas Ladbrooke, claimed to have also suffered at the hands of the Dutch. He informed them that in Cambella he "was put in irons by the Dutch" and had suffered the ignominious loss of a parrot and 30 ryalls. Yet, while the company sympathised with Ladbrooke, it declined to offer compensation as his losses were part of the conflict around the "massacre of Amboyna" for which the company was seeking redress from the Dutch.[69] The company did not always satisfy petitioners who had suffered in service to the company, but such service was certainly an important factor in encouraging their support.

Dutch aggression was a popular complaint during this period, but the petition of Ralph Moore far exceeded Rickman's in terms of demonstrating his extraordinary suffering in service to the company. Moore approached the company with a petition describing how he had served in the company's ship the *Bull* and "being by night commanded to him to lie in the ships boat to free her from water, being then foul weather, the hawser that fastened the boat by violence of a storm by night broke". Castaway in the ship's small boat, Moore had "saved his life by cutting his clothes to make a sail thereof" and had used such propulsion to reach "a strange coast, where he was taken and kept a slave" for thirty months. Eventually, he had been ransomed, for 100 marks, but his "whole wages are swallowed up in that ransom" and he had been left penniless. He "humbly therefore prayed the benevolence of the company towards this great loss".[70] The court called a witness, Mr Munden, the master of the *Exchange*, to assess the issue. Munden's additional detail only made the harrowing events more dramatic, and he accounted how Moore "had no means to keep himself alive but by drinking his own water" and had "endured a heavy slavery". Munden understood that Moore had been made "utterly destitute of all means to help himself".[71] With Munden's testimony confirming Moore's incredible story, "the company took pity of the man", cleared his debts "and rewarded him with £10 more, which he thankfully accepted".[72] Moore approached the company as a debtor—still owing part of the 100 marks ransom that had been paid—but left with a conclusion in his favour. The unique circumstances of his situation and the damage to the company's reputation that might have been sustained if they did not support him gave Moore a powerful platform. In a period when accounts of travel calamity were still popular, the company had considerable incentive to support employees who suffered during service.

Whereas Rickman and Moore obtained favourable outcomes as a result of their exceptional service, the company would also take into account disloyal or inadequate service. Thomas Wolley had travelled to Asia "in the company's service in the *London* and came home in the *Dolphin*" and approached the company for wages relating to this service. While examining his petition, the court "took knowledge that he had run away from the company and had served the Portuguese". Wolley confessed to this betrayal, but sought to bargain with the company, offering his unique knowledge regarding ports and commodities controlled by the Portuguese in Asia. Information regarding these areas was desperately sought after and the court promised to consider his petition if he handed over his journal.[73] Wolley provided the journal, which, "being too tedious to be read in court", was given to a director to read.[74] Yet, in spite of the journal, the company was "unsatisfied of his fitness" and denied his request.[75] A few weeks later, Wolley was offered a position as steward's mate in the *Palsgrave* if he "put in good security for his honest dealing", but this was later rescinded when the court, "remembering he had been formerly rejected", refused to read his petition.[76] In spite of his considerable experience working in Asia, and willingness to share his journal, Wolley was unable to obtain a positive response from the EIC. He was rejected not because his petition lacked merit or evidence, but because his previous actions had damaged his creditability, and the company was no longer willing to work with him.

A breakdown in trust between the EIC and its petitioners was one reason why requests for support were rejected. For the EIC, controlling the activities of its employees in Asia could be particularly problematic and it relied on them following the customs and laws of the company when overseas. This issue came to the fore when Ann Lane sought payment of her servants' wages who had come home without leave from the company. After reviewing the petition, the court was informed that "diverse carpenters and others are come home in the same manner" and was "likewise given to understand that by the order of the sea in such cases, where men return without leave, they are to have no wages for the time they were upon their voyage homewards".[77] Lane's case was joined first by that of John Rose, who petitioned the court complaining that his wages "homeward bound are detained for him"; the court "considered that he came home without order, and therefore would pay him no wages homeward".[78] Over the following month, "diverse persons petitioned for their wages who conveyed themselves into the Company's ships homeward bound, and came home without leave". These individuals had failed to follow the instructions of the company, and while not an outright betrayal this meant they lacked the moral authority that other petitioners could call upon. The company "ordered that there shall be no haste made in paying them at all". Its focus shifted towards ensuring the future control of employees and approached the Admiralty "to endeavour to procure some punishment upon them".[79]

This hard-minded disregard of their employees' complaints demonstrates the sometimes transactional nature of EIC social responsibility. The company did provide wide-ranging support, but it expected to receive the loyalty and support of its constituents in return. When William Mountford petitioned the company for charity, his long-term employment, poverty and "infirmity of body occasioned by sundry bruises in his journeying for the company's services" were not enough to obtain aid. While these circumstances would often have been enough to elicit a sympathetic response, Mountford was not so lucky. The court "remembered that he had been a low performer of his duty, always negligent", and that he owed the company £60—"the court therefore gave no care to the petition".[80] Mountford's case exposes the balance of interests that informed corporate decision-making regarding social responsibility.

Half a century later, the EIC was still undertaking similar activities to support the livelihoods of its constituents.[81] By now, the activities had become ingrained in the structure of the company, and it operated well-established almshouses, hospitals and churches – in England as well as overseas. The EIC's almshouse in Poplar had been expanded and developed over the course of the seventeenth century, and a debate about the facility from 1679 reveals how the company understood its relationship with poorer communities in London and its suburbs. The almshouse continued to be administered by the company and continued to receive funds from the organisation, but much of its endowment had been received through individual donations from members of the company.[82] Similarly, a stock had been raised for a hospital through funds from the company directors, who had agreed that a proportion of their gratuities would be contributed to the same. This agreement had been made in 1625 and was still the main source of income for the company's welfare facilities. By March 31, 1626, a £71 stock had been raised but these funds had been depleted during the 1640s and 1650s and a new stock worth £2350 was contributed to the almshouse as part of the restructuring of the company in 1658.[83]

During a debate in 1679, the directors charged with assessing the facilities were well aware of their heritage. They recounted how the hospital in Poplar provided charity that was "first given to wounded and maimed mariners and such as otherwise were fallen to decay" but noted how "there was little in the way of regulation to enforce this expenditure". The Committee for Shipping believed that "this Court may if they see cause give of the charity to such of their factors, or servants, as have deserved".[84] For over fifty years the company had continued to offer support to a range of people who sought their aid, primarily those who had served the company and particularly those who had suffered injury in its service, but also people from communities in London with little direct connection to the company. The EIC also paid £20 per annum to the "poor widows of Stepney".[85]

In addition to the provision of care for people who had "fallen into decay", the EIC's activities included the operation of a school in Poplar designed to enable "twenty-five youths [between the ages of seven and fourteen] to be taught in the school". These places were open to all, but preference was given to those "whose father have been in the company's service and are poor".[86] Students at the school were expected to "every day read some part of the Holy Scripture and pray in the school room" and to "be taught to read and write English, and be instructed in the knowledge of arithmetic". The minister and schoolmaster were also expected to attend the alms people in Poplar to instruct them "in the principles of the Christian religion".[87] The suggestion is that the company's educational priorities were focused as much on providing a moral education for people who depended on the company and on ensuring children of company employees might develop the necessary skills to contribute to society at large as they were on training a labour force for the company itself.

Many of the company's social activities were directed through these institutions, but it was still willing to receive petitions directly to the Court of Committees. Over the two-year period between April 1678 and April 1680, the company received seventy-five petitions.[88] Of these, fourteen were requests for assistance against poverty, five regarded wages, five employment, three the return of goods and a single petition regarded crime. In addition to these, which were recorded in considerable detail as with those from 1624 to 1625, the court minutes of the company include forty-seven petitions where no specific topic was defined. For these, the court simply referred the petitioner to one of the standing committees that now existed to administer a particular aspect of the company's business. In the preceding decades, the company had undergone considerable administrative change and social responsibility was no longer a priority for the principal Court of Committees. That is not to say the company relied on social responsibility any less, but because it was now administered outside the court, there are fewer records of their changing approach.

When the petitions were heard and discussed in detail in the Court of Committees, we can see similar priorities as those found in the earlier period. The same consideration was given to the trustworthiness and circumstances of petitioners, which continued to motivate the company. For example, when Joan Rouse, the daughter of Hewise Rouse, the late warehouse keeper at Leadenhall, petitioned the company, it was "pleased in consideration of his long, diligent and faithful service" and of her "poor and mean condition" as well as four children to "bestow the sum of £20 upon them for her relief".[89] Isabella Pywel received a similarly positive response when she informed them how her husband had died in the South Seas in the company's service. Her plight encouraged the company not only to consider her own poverty but to discuss the possibility of expanding the almshouse at Poplar to maintain six more women.[90] In each case, the family of loyal servants to the company was supported through its welfare activities.

In addition to positive responses to petitions from family members of employees, EIC directors in the 1670s were still willing to offer support to people injured in the company's service. When William Allison, a seaman who had "for many years served the company", petitioned the EIC following "the loss of the use of his limbs" and great poverty, he requested a place in the company's almshouse in Poplar and, with the support of Captain Prowd who "certified the matter of fact to be true", he was admitted to the facility.[91] Another injured man, William Fisher, who had fallen "between decks into the bottom of the hold by which he is very much bruised in his body and at present in a very mean and distressed condition", was given a stipend of 5d a week and the help of a surgeon until he fully recovered.[92] As these examples suggest, the company of the later seventeenth century retained its interest in protecting its employees and their families in times of poverty and injury.

While these responses to the company's London constituents suggest a level of continued support, the EIC was facing increasing challenges in terms of its transnational and colonial activities.[93] Although the details are slight, the company did receive numerous petitions relating to these areas. For instance, the company received a petition from a Portuguese seaman who had travelled from India in an EIC ship and sought transportation back to India.[94] Other petitions, including those from Mary Rawlins and two other maids who sought passage to Bombay, from Mary Sanderson who hoped to join her husband in Fort St George and from the astronomer Edmond Halley who desired the repayment of his transportation fee from St Helena, all suggest the growing, global web of responsibilities that the company was attempting to manage.[95] The company was going through a rapid process of development in response to growing overseas demands, but its Court of Committees retained a deep interest in supporting its local constituents in London.

During the 1670s and 1680s, when the EIC was discussing the most appropriate ways of helping its constituents in London, the prominent EIC director Josiah Child wrote a treatise outlining how he believed charitable activity was declining because people were unsure as to the best strategies for successfully using funds.[96] One of his more radical proposals was to create a company dedicated to oversee the welfare of the poor.[97] His proposed company, the "Fathers of the Poor", would be managed by members of livery and trading companies because "the several corporations in London are the best administrators of what is left to charitable uses".[98]

This assertion that the companies of London were best suited to taking on further charitable responsibilities demonstrates just how important they were in providing welfare in early modern London. Merchants, and their companies, provided vast sums over the course of this period to provide for the poor and establish schools, almshouses, hospitals and other essential facilities. This expenditure was part of the expected activities of corporate bodies. Social responsibility was one of the reasons they were given unique privileges by the government. It was also one of the reasons they could depend on a deep well of support from their local constituents and employees. This was of course good for business as well, because the EIC, like other companies, often recruited locally.

Early modern business was built in part on a social contract between corporation and society that was believed to ensure positive gains for both. In addition to providing funds for welfare and poor relief, companies were expected to respond effectively to the particular needs of their constituents. They did this through allowing constituents a voice during regular meetings in which petitions from employees, their families and local people could be heard by the company directors. By adopting an open-door policy in this regard, early modern corporations were able to develop socially responsible agendas that directly responded to the needs of the people they were intended to help. In the seventeenth century, social responsibility was not an afterthought, a public relations exercise or something that only thought about in the good times—social responsiveness was an essential part of corporate activity.

Notes

1. For a detailed examination of the relationship between corporate bodies and the idea and practice of Commonwealth, see Phil Withington, *The Politics of Commonwealth: Citizens and Freemen in Early Modern England* (Cambridge: Cambridge University Press, 2005).
2. Public service could also help legitimise corporations in the eyes of the state, nobility and gentry. See Koji Yamamoto, "Piety, Profit and Public Service in the Financial Revolution", *English Historical Review* 126, no. 521 (2011): 833–34.
3. This relationship between corporation and state has lost its appeal as shareholder value has become the predominant focus for publicly listed companies. See Milton Friedman, "The Social Responsibility of Business is to Increase its Profits", *New York Times Magazine*, September 13, 1970.
4. Phil Withington, "Public Discourse, Corporate Citizenship and State Formation in Early Modern England", *American Historical Review* 112, no. 4 (2007): 1036.
5. Even where social responsibility is integrated into corporate strategy, it is often disconnected from wider concerns. See David P. Baron, "Private Politics, Corporate Social Responsibility, and Integrated Strategy", *Journal of Economics and Management Strategy* 10, no. 1 (2001): 41–42; Andrew M. Pettigrew, "Corporate Responsibility in Strategy", in *Mainstreaming Corporate Responsibility*, ed. N. Craig Smith and Gilbert Lenssen (Chichester: John Wiley, 2009), 12–20.

6. Anne Goldgar and Robert L. Frost, eds., *Institutional Culture in Early Modern Society* (Leiden: Brill, 2004); Steve Rappaport, *Worlds Within Worlds: Structures of Life in Sixteenth-Century London* (Cambridge: Cambridge University Press, 1989).
7. Craig Muldrew, *The Economy of Obligation: The Culture of Credit and Social Relations in Early Modern England* (Basingstoke: Palgrave, 1998); Nuala Zahedieh, "Credit, Risk and Reputation in Late Seventeenth-Century Colonial Trade", *Research in Maritime History* 15 (1998): 53–74.
8. W. K. Jordan, *The Charities of London, 1480–1660: The Aspirations and Achievements of the Urban Society* (Abingdon, Routledge: 2006 [1960]), 1–3. This data is considered in more detail in William Pettigrew and Aske Brock's chapter in this volume.
9. For the important role of institutions in the management of social welfare, see Paul Slack, *The Invention of Improvement: Information and Material Progress in Seventeenth-Century England* (Oxford: Oxford University Press, 2015), 65.
10. Mercers' Company Hall, Acts of Court 1595–1629, f. 86.
11. Ibid., f. 174.
12. Guildhall Library, Ms 11732.
13. Mercers' Company Hall, Acts of Court 1595–1629, f. 194.
14. Mercers' Company Hall, Renter Wardens Accounts 1619–1629, discharges 1629.
15. Mercers' Company Hall, Acts of Court 1595–1629, f. 289–90.
16. Drapers' Company Hall, MB 13, May 2, 1604.
17. Clothworkers' Company Hall, CL/B/1/4, Orders of Court, f. 85.
18. Mercers' Company Hall, Acts of Court 1595–1629, f. 229.
19. Jordan, *Charities of London*, 24–25.
20. Ibid., 88, 135.
21. George Unwin, *The Gilds and Companies* (London, Allen and Unwin: 1938 [1908]), 155–75.
22. Jordan, *Charities of London*, 206, 215, 251–67.
23. Ibid.
24. BL IOR/B/9. This differs greatly in scale from the activities of other trading companies, such as the Levant Company, which recorded only 16 petitions during the same period: TNA SP 105/109; TNA SP 105/148.
25. BL IOR/B/9, March 9, 1625.

26. BL IOR/B/9, July 7, 1624.
27. BL IOR/B/9, November 3, 1624.
28. Ibid.
29. BL IOR/B/9, December 22, 1624.
30. BL IOR/B/9, December 8, 1624.
31. BL IOR/B/9, July 7, 1624.
32. BL IOR/B/9, January 5, 1625.
33. BL IOR/B/9, July 26, 1624.
34. BL IOR/B/9, November 6, 1624.
35. BL IOR/B/9, February 21, 1625.
36. This became a particularly important issue after the EIC opened a dockyard in Blackwall in 1609. This facility had its own surgeon, and the company took great care to listen to, and work with, people from the surrounding areas in Wapping and Shadwell.
37. BL IOR/B/9, August 13, 1624.
38. BL IOR/B/9, September 18, 1624.
39. BL IOR/B/9, November 24, 1624.
40. BL IOR/B/9, February 28, 1625.
41. BL IOR/B/9, December 17, 1624.
42. BL IOR/B/9, September 20, 1624.
43. BL IOR/B/9, January 5, 1625.
44. BL IOR/B/9, September 8, 1624; September 18, 1624.
45. BL IOR/B/9, September 18, 1624.
46. BL IOR/B/9, July 9, 1624.
47. BL IOR/B/9, July 26, 1624.
48. BL IOR/B/9, September 3, 1624.
49. BL IOR/B/9, November 19, 1624.
50. BL IOR/B/9, March 7, 1625.
51. BL IOR/B/9, September 20, 1624.
52. Ibid.
53. BL IOR/B/9, November 6, 1624.
54. BL IOR/B/9, July 26, 1624.
55. The challenges of assessing identity in the early modern world are most elegantly explored in Natalie Zemon Davis, *The Return of Martin Guerre* (Boston, MA: Harvard University Press, 1984).
56. BL IOR/B/9, July 26, 1624.
57. BL IOR/B/9, September 8, 1624.
58. BL IOR/B/9, September 20, 1624.

59. BL IOR/B/9, October 20, 1624.
60. BL IOR/B/9, October 15, 1624.
61. BL IOR/B/9, January 12, 1625.
62. BL IOR/B/9, November 6, 1624.
63. BL IOR/B/9, September 25, 1624.
64. BL IOR/B/9, October 20, 1624.
65. BL IOR/B/9, December 1, 1624.
66. BL IOR/B/9, August 13, 1624.
67. BL IOR/B/9, August 18, 1624.
68. BL IOR/B/9, November 12, 1624.
69. BL IOR/B/9, October 29, 1624.
70. BL IOR/B/9, August 4, 1624.
71. BL IOR/B/9, August 13, 1624.
72. BL IOR/B/9, August 18, 1624.
73. BL IOR/B/9, December 20, 1624.
74. BL IOR/B/9, December 31, 1624.
75. BL IOR/B/9, January 7, 1625.
76. BL IOR/B/9, January 24, 1625; February 14, 1625.
77. BL IOR/B/9, July 7, 1624.
78. BL IOR/B/9, July 26, 1624.
79. BL IOR/B/9, August 13, 1624.
80. BL IOR/B/9, August 20, 1624.
81. Although there is no equivalent study of Jordan's *Charities of London* for this period, insight into the social activities of merchants can be found in Perry Gauci, *The Politics of Trade: The Overseas Merchant in State and Society, 1660–1720* (Oxford: Oxford University Press, 2001).
82. BL IOR/B/35, April 10, 1679.
83. BL IOR/B/35, January 24, 1679.
84. Ibid.
85. Ibid.
86. Ibid.
87. Ibid.
88. BL IOR/B/35.
89. BL IOR/B/35, May 1, 1678.
90. BL IOR/B/35, March 19, 1680.
91. BL IOR/B/35, February 18, 1680.
92. BL IOR/B/35, August 30, 1678.

93. The challenges faced by the EIC when developing forms of governance and social organisation overseas is explored in detail in Philip J. Stern, *The Company-State: Corporate Sovereignty and the Early Modern Foundations of the British Empire in India* (Oxford: Oxford University Press, 2011). Or, to compare to the Hudson's Bay Company, see Edward Cavanagh, "A Company with Sovereignty and Subjects of its Own? The Case of the Hudson's Bay Company, 1670–1763", *Canadian Journal of Law and Society* 26, no. 1 (2011): 25–50.
94. BL IOR/B/35, September 18, 1678; February 5, 1679; December 24, 1678.
95. BL/IOR/B/35, February 5, 1679.
96. Josiah Child, *Sir Josiah Child's Proposals for the Relief and Employment of the Poor* (London: 167[?]). Often dated to 1670, this pamphlet is almost certainly from a later date as Child was not knighted until 1679.
97. The development of private companies for charitable ends was not a proposal unique to Child. See Aske Brock and William Pettigrew's chapter in this volume for a further examination of this approach to social responsibility.
98. Child, *Relief and Employment of the Poor*, 4–6.

References

Primary Material

BL IOR/B/9.
BL IOR/B/35.
Child, Josiah. *Sir Josiah Child's Proposals for the Relief and Employment of the Poor*. London, 167[?].
Clothworkers' Company Hall, CL/B/1/4.
Drapers' Company Hall, MB 13.
Guildhall Library, Ms 11732.
Mercers' Company Hall, Acts of Court 1595–1629.
Mercers' Company Hall, Renter Wardens Accounts 1619–1629.
TNA SP 105/109.
TNA SP 105/148.

Secondary Material

Baron, David P. "Private Politics, Corporate Social Responsibility, and Integrated Strategy." *Journal of Economics and Management Strategy* 10, no. 1 (2001), 41–42.

Cavanagh, Edward. "A Company with Sovereignty and Subjects of its Own? The Case of the Hudson's Bay Company, 1670–1763." *Canadian Journal of Law and Society* 26, no. 1 (2011): 25–50.

Davis, Natalie Zemon. *The Return of Martin Guerre.* Boston, MA: Harvard University Press, 1984.

Friedman, Milton. "The Social Responsibility of Business is to Increase its Profits." *New York Times Magazine*, September 13, 1970.

Gauci, Perry. *The Politics of Trade: The Overseas Merchant in State and Society, 1660–1720.* Oxford: Oxford University Press, 2001.

Goldgar, Anne and Robert L. Frost, eds. *Institutional Culture in Early Modern Society.* Leiden: Brill, 2004.

Jordan, W. K. *The Charities of London, 1480–1660: The Aspirations and Achievements of the Urban Society.* Abingdon: Routledge, 2006 [1960].

Muldrew, Craig. *The Economy of Obligation: The Culture of Credit and Social Relations in Early Modern England.* Basingstoke: Palgrave, 1998.

Pettigrew, Andrew M. "Corporate Responsibility in Strategy." In *Mainstreaming Corporate Responsibility*, edited by N. Craig Smith and Gilbert Lenssen, 12–20. Chichester: John Wiley, 2009.

Rappaport, Steve. *Worlds Within Worlds: Structures of Life in Sixteenth-Century London.* Cambridge: Cambridge University Press, 1989.

Slack, Paul. *The Invention of Improvement: Information and Material Progress in Seventeenth-Century England.* Oxford: Oxford University Press, 2015.

Stern, Philip J. *The Company-State: Corporate Sovereignty and the Early Modern foundations of the British Empire in India.* Oxford: Oxford University Press, 2011.

Unwin, George. *The Gilds and Companies.* London: Allen and Unwin, 1938 [1908].

Withington, Phil. *The Politics of Commonwealth: Citizens and Freemen in Early Modern England.* Cambridge: Cambridge University Press, 2005.

———. "Public Discourse, Corporate Citizenship and State Formation in Early Modern England." *American Historical Review* 112, no. 4 (2007): 1016–38.

Yamamoto, Koji. "Piety, Profit and Public Service in the Financial Revolution." *English Historical Review* 126, no. 521 (2011): 833–34.
Zahedieh, Nuala. "Credit, Risk and Reputation in Late Seventeenth-Century Colonial Trade." *Research in Maritime History* 15 (1998): 53–74.

4

Profit and Surety: The British Chartered Trading Companies and the State

Michael Wagner

In 1580, when a charter for a company to trade with the Ottoman Empire was under consideration, Francis Walsingham, Queen Elizabeth I's secretary, wrote to the Queen explaining: "In all trades two things principally are to be considered, profit and surety; for if they not be joined together they are in no wise to be attempted".[1] What did Walsingham mean by profit and surety? By profit, Walsingham referred to benefits to the Crown, not the ability of merchants to earn money in the trade. Walsingham defined these benefits to the Crown by listing a series of broader military and social advantages. The first consideration he mentioned was the employment of a great number of ships "in work whereby your navy shall be maintained". Maritime trade, including that of the chartered trading companies, was viewed as providing a "nursery for seamen" which could be called upon by the navy in time of war. Walsingham also mentioned the opportunity to export and import

M. Wagner (✉)
University of Oxford, Oxford, UK
e-mail: mikewagner.oudce@gmail.com

W.A. Pettigrew and D.C. Smith (eds.), *A History of Socially Responsible Business, c.1600–1950*, Palgrave Studies in the History of Finance,
DOI 10.1007/978-3-319-60146-5_4

goods, for consumption in England and elsewhere in Europe. This was potentially profitable to the Crown, as both exports and imports could be taxed. By surety, Walsingham referred to the ability to secure benefits for the Crown. Walsingham foresaw potential attacks on English ships from the Venetians, French, Spanish and Barbary pirates. Furthermore, Walsingham anticipated that French and Venetian diplomats in Constantinople would seek to discredit the English. To counter these threats, Walsingham recommended that heavily manned and armed ships be employed in the trade, but he saw these ships being provided and operated by the company rather than the Royal Navy. Walsingham also thought it would be necessary to use diplomacy to obtain safe conduct from the Turks, but the model employed in the Levant required the Levant Company rather than the state to pay the substantial costs of the ambassador and other diplomatic staff in the Ottoman Empire.[2] Both surety and profit were to be supplied by the trading corporation rather than the state.

What does Walsingham's comment reveal about how state support for trade in the early modern period interacted with the social obligations of trading corporations? Walsingham viewed a chartered company as a means of providing benefits to the state, but he believed that the state should incur minimal expense and should provide minimal assistance to a company. Profits, for the Elizabethan official mind, were state profits, and these were often defined with reference to broader social benefits. Yet, for Walsingham, such social profits could not appear without state sanction for trading companies that would assume the state's prerogatives of military protection and diplomacy. Trading corporations would receive the support of the Elizabethan state if they could protect and support trade using pseudo-state powers to produce profits that benefited the nation as a whole. What has been called the mercantilist mindset highlighted social benefits—such as employment and charity—as advantages that corporations would supply to the public (or national) interest in return for the privileges that the state conferred on them, especially monopoly rights. The social obligations of the corporation cannot therefore be understood without a broader account of the relationships formed between the trading corporations and the state. This chapter examines the changed relationship between the communities of merchants that formed the core memberships of early modern trading corporations and the state authorities that chartered and conferred privileges upon them. It concentrates on the public funds used to support the companies' operations and on a fundamental social obligation for the corporations and other legal persons—tax contributions that the companies made to the state that supported them. Trading corporations were not only obliged to contribute to the public purse but also enjoyed access to it to support their trades. From the beginning of their existence, trading companies celebrated the social role as the providers of employment and as syphons for legitimate (as opposed to smuggled) trade that could be taxed. Similarly, the state protected the companies with tariffs that also helped finance the naval convoys that offered protection in a different form. These transactions were the focus of the trading corporations' relationship with the state and represent an essential insight into the public and social consequences of corporate activity. The chapter examines the sureties provided by the state, such as convoys, and the tariff system that simultaneously protected the company's domestic manufactures and helped finance the overseas military protection. It also outlines the social profits, or taxes, supplied by the companies to the Crown and the alliances and lobbies formed between the state and corporate interests that allowed this collaboration to function until global commercial predominance allowed private corporations to concentrate on profit as trading companies entered a long slow decline through the nineteenth century.

The mid- to late-nineteenth-century relationships between corporations and the British state seem inconsistent with Walsingham's vision. Free trade became an attractive proposition as the Industrial Revolution gave Britain an unassailable advantage in manufacturing, and imperial expansion created a vast network of protected markets. Corporations became vehicles for investing the country's rapidly accumulating wealth, and the drive for profit maximization became the overwhelmingly dominant corporate objective. The state provided little direct assistance to companies but took on greater responsibility for a series of social issues resulting from Britain's rapid population growth, urbanization and industrialization. The state provided the surety of military protection, while the corporations provided profits. Social obligations of the early modern corporation had been largely surrendered to the state. This is a familiar story, but what is perhaps less well understood is the period of closer relations between the British state and corporations in the eighteenth century. This chapter considers the ways in which the later seventeenth- and eighteenth-century contexts for English trading corporations altered Walsingham's provisos. Following the Glorious Revolution of 1688, the state became much more directly involved in ensuring that the chartered companies provided profit and surety. This chapter examines why the state became more interventionist and describes how the relationships between companies and the government worked in the first half of the eighteenth century, when there were five significant chartered trading companies: the East India Company (EIC), the Levant Company, the Russia Company, the Hudson's Bay Company (HBC) and the Royal African Company (RAC).[3]

The chartered companies are sometimes viewed by historians as becoming less relevant after a number of their monopolies were challenged in Parliament in the late seventeenth century, but the five companies that survived into the eighteenth century were responsible for British trade to a very large proportion of the world.[4] The EIC was responsible for trade to both India and China. The Levant Company had a monopoly on British trade to the Ottoman Empire, which at the time encompassed most of the Near East, the Middle East and south-eastern Europe. The Russia Company had a monopoly on imports from the vast Russian Empire. The HBC had a trade monopoly in Rupert's Land, the drainage basin of Hudson's Bay, which covered an area roughly equivalent to a third of modern-day Canada. The RAC traded with West Africa and supplied African slaves to the hugely profitable sugar colonies in the West Indies.

"The chartered company was a device whereby a European government, by granting a monopoly of a particular trade to a particular group among its subjects, could delegate to that group the duties of administration, jurisdiction and defence", observed J. H. Parry, echoing Walsingham.[5] Indeed, the charters of the five companies reflect the intention of the state to use the companies as nurseries for seamen and for the companies to be largely responsible for their own defence. An act of 1566 required the Russia Company to use only English ships, to be sailed "for the most part" by English seamen.[6] The Levant Company charter of 1592 gave the company the right to employ four ships adequately equipped with ordnance, munitions and crew subject to being commandeered by the navy during the time of war.[7] The original charter of the EIC in 1600 gave it similar rights to employ armed ships, and its charter of 1661 went further by giving it the power to build forts in India, export munitions from England and wage war with non-Christian princes.[8] The charters of the HBC in 1670 and the RAC in 1672 contain similar provisions to the EIC charter of 1661 (all three charters being issued during the reign of Charles II), enabling them to send ships of war, build and man forts, send ammunition and declare war on non-Christians.[9] The companies used these delegated military powers in the seventeenth century, including the power to wage war.[10] However, these powers were insufficient to provide surety of trade in the eighteenth century.

During the first half of the eighteenth century, the government was forced to deploy the Royal Navy more often to provide protection for the companies. In addition, the government became increasingly involved in managing the profit aspect of the profit-surety equation. This was not regulation in the modern sense of how governments regulate utilities. In the eighteenth century, the British government was not in the business of consumer protection, but rather sought to help companies succeed against their foreign rivals through diplomacy and protective legislation governing imports.

International rivalry was a fundamental influence that affected the business of the companies, the development of the state and relations between companies and the state. From the Glorious Revolution of 1688, England was engaged in a fierce rivalry with France. William III's accession triggered the Nine Years' War (1688–97), followed by the War of the Spanish Succession (1702–13) and the War of the Austrian Succession (1744–48).[11] In addition to military rivalry, there was an intense commercial rivalry between Britain and France. The Dutch had been England's great commercial rival in the seventeenth century, but the intensity of this rivalry diminished in the eighteenth century.[12] Instead, the focus of Britain's commercial rivalry turned towards France. The period 1735–55, when France's trade growth outstripped Britain's, has been termed *l'âge d'or* of French commerce.[13] The sheer size of the French population (roughly three times that of England) also meant that France's total manufacturing output was much larger than Britain's during this period.[14] War and commerce were very much interrelated, and all of the British chartered trading companies suffered either directly or indirectly from hostilities with the French. War fused profit and surety into a single concern when the English state considered the trading corporations.

War between England and France triggered privateering activity from St Malo, Dunkirk and other ports along the French coast, which reached a peak between 1694 and 1713 and proved to be the principal threat to British trade in the eighteenth century.[15] In addition to privateers, or corsairs as they were known in France, English commercial shipping was subject to attack by the French navy. At the beginning of the Nine Years' War, English naval resources were insufficient to provide convoys for all commercial shipping. For the Levant Company, whose ships sailed south along the French coast and through the straits of Gibraltar, this proved to be disastrous. French naval activity in the Channel virtually suspended Levant trade between 1690 and 1692. When a joint Anglo-Dutch fleet set out for Smyrna in 1693, it was destroyed by the French. The loss of the Smyrna fleet was a national disaster.[16] The Admiralty was severely criticized for the loss and, thereafter, implemented a more regular system of convoys.[17] As Nicholas Rodger has described, the distinctive feature of British defence expenditure in the eighteenth century was that almost half was spent on the navy.[18] Naval protection for the companies relied upon the expansion of the navy, and, more broadly, increased government expenditure on capital projects involving dockyards and shipbuilding also benefited commercial shipping. Such expenditure from the public purse offers the most dramatic insight into the social costs of trading corporations in this period.

However, the prolongation and scope of warfare with the French meant that the British naval resources needed to protect commercial shipping continued to be stretched. In 1697, a French naval victory in Hudson's Bay resulted in the HBC losing all but one of its posts on the bay, and those posts were not restored to the company at the end of the war. The RAC was particularly vulnerable to the loss of ships going from Africa to England, laden with precious cargo, such as gold and ivory, which tended not to receive the same level of convoy protection as shipping to and from the West Indies.[19] In September 1704, the RAC stated that 26 of its 37 ships that year had been taken by the French.[20] In India, the French under Governor General Dupleix presented a real military threat to the EIC's army as well as its shipping. Dupleix developed a network of alliances with local powers, and despite the dispatch of a small Royal Navy squadron to Indian waters, the French captured Madras in 1746.[21] Such setbacks jeopardised the existence of the trading companies.

The Russia Company was only indirectly affected by French privateers and the French navy, but it too required the support of the Royal Navy. During the Great Northern War (1700–21) between Sweden and Russia, Swedish privateers preyed upon Baltic shipping.[22] To obtain convoy support, the Russia Company had to compete with other British commercial interests subject to attack by the French. Diplomatic support proved to be of greater long-term significance for the Russia Company than naval support from the British government. British merchants in Russia had a series of complaints about doing business in Russia, including the Russian tendency to commandeer British seamen for their own ships and falsely package goods such as hemp destined for export to Britain. To put Anglo-Russian commerce on a more predictable basis, a commerce treaty between the two countries was discussed at the Board of Trade as early as 1716.[23] However, diplomatic relations between Britain and Russia were strained following the accession of George I, who was suspicious of Russian designs in the Baltic, and the commerce treaty was not concluded until 1734. That treaty made Britain Russia's preferred western trading partner and blocked the development of Franco-Russian trade.[24] This provided the springboard for the explosive growth in Anglo-Russian trade that made Russia the most important source of European imports to Britain in the second half of the eighteenth century.[25]

Protective tariffs were another important means by which the state supported the trading companies. The series of wars with France led to a massive increase in British government expenditure, and as Ralph

Davis indicated, the increase in customs duties was motivated by the fiscal needs of the state rather than any theories of political economy.[26] Nevertheless, customs duties provided protection both for British manufacturers and for British chartered trading companies. Before 1688, the general level of customs duties was 5%. This was progressively increased until it reached 25% in 1759.[27] The prohibitive duties that were placed specifically on French imports during the Nine Years' War remained in place during the first half of the eighteenth century. The Levant Company particularly benefited from tariff protection. The effective block on French imports protected the English silk industry, which the Levant Company supplied, from being overwhelmed by the export of silk to England from the much larger French silk industry.[28] The Levant Company was also protected by a 20% surcharge on the EIC's imports of Bengal and Chinese silk, introduced in 1690. Tariffs neatly suggest how the state's relationship with the trading companies was based principally on a fiscal need that nevertheless protected the commerce of the trading companies at home and financed the military protection of the companies overseas.

Having seen how the government acted to provide greater surety of trade, how did the five surviving chartered companies provide profit to the state in the first half of the eighteenth century? The EIC was an important source of government finance. The state periodically extracted money from the company in the context of its charter renewals. In 1698, the New East India Company was chartered when it loaned the government £2 million at 8% interest, and a further £1.2 million was loaned interest-free in 1708 when the United East India Company was formed. In 1730, the EIC obtained a charter renewal when it paid the government £200,000 and agreed to reduce the overall interest rate on its outstanding loan of £3.2 million from 5% to 4%. In 1744, the company loaned the government a further £1 million at 3% and, in exchange, had its charter termination date extended from 1766 to 1780.

The huge imports of the companies also provided a significant annual contribution to the state in the form of customs duties. The Levant trade was reasonably balanced between exports and imports, but the Russian/Baltic and East Indies trades were heavily weighted towards imports. There was not only a great volume but also a great variety of imports from the East. Naval stores and iron from Russia and the Baltic, silk from the Levant, as well as spices, calicoes and tea from the East Indies and China, provided raw materials for key British manufacturing industries (such as shipbuilding) and introduced a range of exotic new products to British consumers. The exports of the two newest chartered companies, the HBC and the RAC, were insubstantial. The main purpose of both companies was to provide imports into Britain. In total, the value of the goods these five companies imported into Britain was more than twice as great as the value of the trade goods that they exported.[29] By the middle of the eighteenth century, the value of their imports was well over £1 million. Customs duties on those imports were at least £400,000 annually by mid-century, and duties paid by the companies roughly trebled between mid-century and the eve of the war with revolutionary France.[30] In total, the companies generated about a third of British customs duties. This represented the honouring of a considerable social obligation, and companies often made the case for their social role with reference to their contributions to the public purse.[31]

A consequence of escalating customs duties was that it gave rise to wide-scale smuggling into Britain. This made trade through chartered companies relatively more attractive to the government and was a crucial part of their public utility. Importing goods through chartered companies increased the likelihood that customs duties would be paid as the ultimate sanction for a chartered company, if it was caught smuggling, was to have its charter revoked. Furthermore, other countries in Western Europe also put protective tariffs in place, leading to a stagnation of European trade and making the trade of the five remaining chartered companies, outside of Western Europe, even more important to the British economy.

In addition to these direct financial contributions to the state, the companies were responsible for significant employment both in the London port trades and among the suppliers and customers who were their economic stakeholders. This was an important benefit for the state in a period when the cost of poor relief was escalating, and over half the prison population was incarcerated because of their inability to pay their debts. In the case of the Levant Company, it was estimated that, in 1684, it employed four or five thousand sailors and that it found work for about three thousand others in the port of London.[32] At the beginning of the eighteenth century, the company was also the chief supplier of raw silk to the large silk-weaving industry based in Spitalfields. Peter Earle estimated that 40,000–50,000 people were employed in London silk manufacturing and allied trades in the early eighteenth century.[33] In addition, there were thousands of people in the woollen cloth-making industry who were economically dependent on the Levant Company. Some of these were in London, where the cloth exported by the company was dyed, but many more were in Worcestershire and Gloucestershire, the main sources of cloth exported to the Levant. The companies understood their role in producing these social benefits and often celebrated it in public. Indeed, the provision of employment was high on the list of obligations that the company's charters imposed on them from the beginning.

The Levant Company was not the only chartered company to generate significant employment and benefits that were not confined to London. Scots enthusiastically took up opportunities provided by the companies, and they were disproportionately prominent in the HBC and the EIC. The EIC directly employed thousands of British seamen and several hundred British soldiers in the first half of the eighteenth century.[34] Like the Levant Company, the EIC generated a vast amount of activity in the port of London. The EIC also exported a significant amount of woollen cloth from the West Country, and its imports fuelled an explosion in retail activity. The naval stores imported by the Russia Company were used in the Royal Navy's dockyards in southern England, and the iron imported by the company was sold to customers located in the Midlands and north-eastern England. The HBC was the major supplier of beaver fur to the thriving hat-making industry based in Southwark on the south bank of the Thames. The key function of the RAC was to supply slaves to sugar plantations in the West Indies whose output was to become the most valuable British import of all in the eighteenth century. This supported employment in London, Bristol and Liverpool.

Having considered how the government provided surety and the companies provided profit, it is now worth considering how the state and the companies worked together. To a large extent, the way in which the government and the companies interacted was shaped by the personal relationships between political and business leaders. The dominant political figure in Britain during the first half of the eighteenth century was Sir Robert Walpole, first minister from 1721 to 1742. Walpole had very mixed relationships with merchants. J. H. Plumb observed that Walpole "disliked merchants as a class".[35] There was a perception that he was "hated by the city of London, because he never did anything for the trading part of it, nor aimed at any interest of theirs, but a corrupt influence over the directors and governors of the great monied companies".[36] Unlike his dealings with smaller merchants in unregulated trades, more structured trading organizations, such as the chartered companies, offered Walpole greater ability to direct their behaviour through his preferred approach—personal management.[37] Walpole's favourable disposition towards the chartered companies in general is reflected in his record of support for them in Parliament. In 1730, over the opposition of many smaller merchants in London, the EIC obtained the renewal of its charter, and the RAC was granted an annual subsidy in parliament. The relationship between Walpole and Samuel Holden, the governor of the Russia Company, helped to ensure government support for the Anglo-Russian commerce treaty of 1734.[38] Although less cosy, government relations with the Levant Company were also mediated successfully through individuals. The first Earl De La Warr, who became governor of the Levant Company in 1736, was a loyal supporter of Walpole who took an active role in attacking the government's opponents.[39] Even though Desmond Clarke, the biographer of the HBC's chief critic, Arthur Dobbs, described Walpole as a "good friend and influential patron" of Dobbs, Walpole was not enthusiastic about the idea of launching a voyage of discovery for a north-west passage.[40] It was only in 1741, when Walpole's position had become precarious, that Dobbs was able to send an expedition using ships provided by the Admiralty.[41] The personal management of Walpole appears, on balance, to have assisted the trading companies' prospects after the great public onslaughts against them in Parliament in the 1690s.

Walpole was a master of political management, but he could not personally deal with all economic controversy. A development whose significance has been underestimated was the establishment of the Board of

Trade in 1696. The main remit of the Board concerned colonies or trade affecting the colonies, but less well appreciated, is the role the Board played in a number of other commercial policy debates in the first half of the eighteenth century, including those involving chartered companies. An indication of the importance of the Board to Walpole is the fact that the office of Surveyor and Auditor General of Plantations, which was held by Horatio Walpole throughout his brother's administration, was added as an *ex officio* member of the Council of Trade and Plantations in 1721.[42] Of the five chartered companies, it was the RAC that attracted most attention from the Board because of the interest of the West Indian and American colonies in acquiring a reliable supply of slaves. Major activity by the Board concerning the company preceded significant changes in the regulation of the company. At the beginning of the eighteenth century, the Board was concerned with the dispute between the RAC and private traders regarding the need for private traders to provide a subsidy to the company.[43] In 1712, private traders were relieved of the requirement to pay a 10% duty towards the upkeep of the company's forts. Under the direction of the Duke of Chandos, the company initiated an ambitious plan in 1720 to diversify its activities away from the slave trade and, instead, develop a bilateral trade with Africa featuring African botanical and mineral resources.[44] Despite receiving a £30,000 loan from the Bank of England, it became apparent by the end of 1724 that the diversification plan was not working.[45] In 1726, there was a major inquiry by the Board into the company's forts.[46] The company argued that it could not support the forts on its own, and the private traders argued that the forts were no better than sheds or warehouses. In 1730, the government began to provide a £10,000 annual subsidy to the company. In 1744, the Duke of Newcastle initiated a fresh examination of the financial requirements of the RAC's forts by the Board.[47] The governmental subsidy was temporarily increased to £20,000 that year but withheld entirely after 1746.[48] In 1748, the Duke of Newcastle, in William Pettigrew's words, finally "hammered the nails into the RAC's coffin" in a report to the Board.[49] The company was dissolved in 1752.

The HBC also attracted considerable attention from the Board early in the century. Understandably, the company's focus was to recover the forts it had lost to the French during the Nine Years' War. During the

War of the Spanish Succession, officials were sent to Utrecht to argue the company's case in 1709 during preliminary peace negotiations. In February 1712, the company sent the Board a memorial outlining what it wanted from the final treaty, and the Treaty of Utrecht of 1713 restored the company's forts. The Board then turned to an evaluation of the credibility of the company's claims for compensation from the French.[50] The company mounted a major effort in 1719, presenting the Board with a large amount of documentation, and the company's governor, Sir Bibye Lake, urged the Board to seek full reparations.[51] Although they were ultimately unsuccessful, Colonel Bladen of the Board joined Lake in Paris that year to argue the company's case.

Even for companies that had very little dealing with colonies, there were some important interventions by the Board. In addition to acting as a forum for discussion of the commerce treaty with Russia, the Board was instrumental in granting the Russia Company the right to trade with Persia in 1740–41.[52] In the cases of the Levant Company and the EIC, the main role of the Board was to collect data that would inform the making of trade policies and provide input to the series of parliamentary debates that involved the companies.[53] In these cases, the Board provided the House with copies of materials it had collected as part of its role in monitoring trade, particularly British exports.[54] Overall, the trading corporations proved more effective lobbyists with ministers than with the Board of Trade. As privileged entities, the companies perhaps preferred personal channels than the glare of statistical inquiry that the Board seemed to impose on them.

The expansion of the empire and the growth of the British state that gathered pace during and after the second half of the eighteenth century transformed the roles of two of the companies—the EIC and the HBC. Philip Stern has indicated that the EIC was acting as a hybrid "company-state" as early as the seventeenth century.[55] The populations that the company governed in India in the seventeenth century were not insignificant in English terms. For example, Madras, the most important English trading centre in India in the late seventeenth century, had a population of some 40,000 in the 1670s.[56] This was roughly equivalent to the combined population of Bristol and Norwich, the second and third most populous English cities.[57] Nevertheless, this was a small fraction of the territory and population that would come under the company's control a century later. There was a massive expansion in the scope of the EIC's jurisdiction following the 1765 grant of the *diwani* (right to collect taxes) from some twenty million people in Bengal, Bihar and Orissa. The company's army grew to be significantly larger than the peacetime British army.[58] The scale of the administrative challenge in India made the case for state intervention increasingly compelling, and the India Act of 1784 formalized the assumption of governmental control by the British state. As the role of the British state expanded, the monopoly privileges of the company were withdrawn in the nineteenth century.[59]

In North America, the HBC, while confining its trade to posts on Hudson's Bay during the first century of its existence, began to take on enhanced governmental responsibilities as it expanded into the interior of the continent, spurred on by competition with the Northwest Company.[60] Unlike the situation in India, much of western Canada remained unexplored by Europeans, and the British government was willing to delegate additional responsibility to the company even into the nineteenth century. When the HBC and the Northwest Company merged in 1821, the British government granted the merged company exclusive trading rights in British North America from Rupert's Land Land west.[61] It was only in 1870 that the HBC sold Rupert's Land to the Canadian government.[62]

The other two surviving chartered trading companies, the Russia Company and the Levant Company, reached commercial peaks in the late eighteenth and early nineteenth centuries but faded away thereafter. During this period, in both the Russia and the Ottoman Empires, there was an increasing separation between British diplomatic staff and overseas representatives of the companies. Diplomats clearly became representatives of the state and lost some of their quasi-commercial functions. The Russia Company benefited from the insatiable demand for naval stores during the Napoleonic wars and burgeoning demand for industrial raw materials such as iron, but the company became less significant later in the nineteenth century as alternative sources of naval stores, such as Canadian timber, were developed, and Germany emerged as Russia's key trading partner in Western Europe. The Levant Company enjoyed a renaissance as an importer of raw cotton to feed

British factories in the early stages of the Industrial Revolution but relinquished its charter voluntarily in 1825 as the American south became the primary source of raw cotton for British factories.

The new British companies formed in the nineteenth century were unlike the chartered trading companies. Mercantile enterprise came to be dominated by commission agents, financial services became more specialized and, most significantly, new capital-intensive manufacturing companies were formed as Britain industrialized. These new companies operated in an environment where Britain was the largest imperial and industrial power in the world. The umbrella of protective customs duties was dismantled by the government in the second quarter of the nineteenth century. Unlike the first half of the eighteenth century, when Britain's place in the world was less secure and trading companies required state intervention to provide profit and surety, Britain's economic dominance in the nineteenth century meant that British companies required less assistance from the state and were free to focus on their commercial operations. Seventeenth- and eighteenth-century English trading corporations formed intimate and mutually supporting relationships with the state (just as Walsingham advised). By the nineteenth century, however, the international commercial predominance that Walsingham's surety-profit equation had helped secure was reformulated to allow a new breed of private corporation to return profits for their investors, while the state continued its role as provider of surety and extended its social obligations into territory once occupied by the trading corporations.

Notes

1. *A consideration of the trade into Turkey, 1580, by Mr. Secretary Walsingham*, State Papers Domestic, Elizabeth, vol. 44, no. 70. The great naval battle of Lepanto in 1571, where the Ottoman navy was defeated by a Christian coalition, led by Spain, created new possibilities for English trade to the eastern Mediterranean. A charter was granted to the Turkey Company in 1581. In 1592, the Turkey Company merged with the Venice Company (charter granted in 1583) to form the Levant Company.

2. It was only in 1767 that the British government began to make a contribution towards diplomatic costs in the Ottoman Empire.
3. In 1700, there were, in fact, two English East India Companies. A second company was chartered in 1698, but the old company quickly purchased some of its shares, and a united company was formed in 1709. The RAC had already lost its monopoly by 1700. Separate traders had by far the largest share of the English slave trade, and their operation was sanctioned by Parliament in 1698, subject to their payment of contributions to the RAC for the upkeep of forts in Africa. By 1712, separate traders were no longer required to pay a subsidy for the RAC's forts. The South Sea Company, established in 1711, was essentially a financial organization. Its operations as a trading company were minor.
4. The Eastland Company lost its monopoly on trade to Scandinavia in 1673, and most leading Eastland merchants joined the Russia Company in 1699 when a tobacco trade to Russia was opened, and the Russia Company was forced to lower its admission fee. The Merchant Adventurers continued to operate in the eighteenth century but no longer enjoyed a monopoly on woollen cloth exports to Germany.
5. J. H. Parry, *Trade and Dominion: The European Oversea Empires in the Eighteenth Century* (London: Phoenix, 1974 [1971]), 86.
6. See T. S. Willan, *The Early History of the Russia Company, 1553–1603* (Manchester: Manchester University Press, 1956), 76.
7. A. Wood, *A History of the Levant Company* (London: Frank Cass, 1935), 21.
8. See J. E. Thomson, *Mercenaries, Pirates and Sovereigns* (Princeton: Princeton University Press, 1996), 35–6.
9. For the HBC charter, see *Charters, Statutes, Orders in Council etc. Relating to the Hudson's Bay Company* (London, 1949). For the RAC charter, see C. Thomas Carr, *Select Charters of Trading Companies, 1530–1707* (London: Bernard Quaritch, 1913), 186–92.
10. The EIC fought a losing war against the Mughal Empire in the late 1680s.
11. These first three major wars were followed by three more: the Seven Years War (1756–63), the American Revolutionary War (1775–82) and the French Revolutionary and Napoleonic Wars (1792–1815).
12. There were a number of reasons for the decline in the Anglo-Dutch rivalry, including the Navigation Acts and Anglo-Dutch wars of the seventeenth century which cut the Dutch out of much trans-Atlantic trade, the accession of a Dutch king to the English throne in 1688

who was a bitter enemy of France, and the development of a financial market in England which provided attractive opportunities for Dutch investors.

13. F. Crouzet, "Angleterre et France au XVIIIe siècle: Essai d'analyse comparée de deux croissances économiques", *Annales: Economies, Societes, Civilisations* 21 (1966): 264.
14. Total French manufacturing output was estimated to be twice that of Britain in 1750, B. R. Tomlinson, "Economics: The Periphery", in A. Porter, ed., *The Oxford History of the British Empire: The Nineteenth Century* (Oxford: Oxford University Press, 1999), table 3.8, 69.
15. P. Crowhurst, *The Defence of British Trade, 1689–1815* (Folkestone: Dawson, 1977), 15.
16. Wood, *Levant Company*, 111. The estimated losses were some £600,000.
17. Crowhurst, *Defence of British Trade*, 47. Convoy acts of 1798 and 1803 mandated the use of convoys for commercial shipping during the wars with revolutionary France.
18. N. A. M. Rodger, "War as an Economic Activity in the Long Eighteenth Century", *International Journal of Maritime History* 22, no. 2 (2010): 13.
19. Crowhurst, *Defence of British Trade*, 56. With the outbreak of the War of Jenkins' Ear in 1739, the Spanish became a significant additional threat to British shipping in the West Indies.
20. Board of Trade Minutes, Journal Book 1, 20 September 1704.
21. Parry, *Trade and Dominion*, 214. Madras was restored to Britain by treaty in 1748.
22. See M. Wagner, "Misunderstood and Unappreciated: The Russia Company in the Eighteenth Century, *Russian History* 41, no. 3 (2014): 409. The Russia Company estimated its losses to Swedish privateers at over £100,000.
23. Board of Trade Minutes, Journal 3, 20 March 1716.
24. The Board of Trade played an important role in finalizing the terms of the 1734 treaty. Drafts of the treaty were discussed at several stages.
25. H. Kaplan, *Russian Overseas Commerce with Great Britain during the Reign of Catherine II* (Philadelphia, PA: American Philosophical Society, 1995), 9.
26. R. Davis, "The Rise of Protection in England, 1689–1786", *Economic History Review*, new series, vol. 19, no. 2 (1966), 306.

27. There was also a 5% tax on exports, which was eliminated in 1722.
28. The proposed French Commerce Bill of 1713 would have removed these prohibitive tariffs but was defeated in Parliament. The Levant Company lobbied forcefully against the bill.
29. Roughly 80% of exports of the EIC in the first half of the eighteenth century consisted of treasure (as opposed to trade goods), see K. N. Chaudhuri, *The Trading World of Asia and the English East India Company, 1660–1760* (Cambridge: Cambridge University Press, 1978), appendix 5, table C.4. Actual commodity exports of the EIC were about £200,000 annually in the 1740s, Chaudhuri, table C.3. This was roughly equal to the level of commodity exports by the Levant Company, where exports and imports were balanced, R. Davis, *Aleppo and Devonshire Square* (London: Macmillan, 1967), 31. The Russian trade was similarly skewed to the EIC trade, and imports were about four times the level of exports, Wagner, *Misunderstood and Unappreciated*, 412. Annual commodity exports of the Russia Company were under £100,000 by the middle of the century. Even adding in the small commodity exports of the HBC and the RAC, total commodity exports by the companies were likely about £500,000. Annual imports of the EIC from Asia averaged over £700,000 in the 1740s, Chaudhuri, table C.2. Imports from the other companies might have doubled this amount by the middle of the century.
30. This is a conservative estimate. K. N. Chaudhuri estimated customs paid by the EIC alone averaged just under £400,000 in the 1740s, table A.24. The duties paid by the Levant Company were relatively low, Davis, *Aleppo*, 232. However, the Russia Company paid high duties on its imports, in excess of 30% on some commodities, Wagner, 416–17. The rapid growth of the Russian trade and the growth of the EIC's tea trade in the second half of the eighteenth century significantly increased customs paid by the companies. By 1786/7, the EIC alone was paying the government over £1 million in customs and tea duties, H. V. Bowen, *The Business of Empire* (Cambridge: Cambridge University Press, 2006), 39. Imports from Russia already exceeded £800,000 in the 1760s, Wagner, 407. Thus, customs duties paid by the Russia Company would likely have exceeded £200,000 annually by the 1780s, and duties paid by the EIC and Russia Company would likely have exceeded £1.2 million.
31. Patrick O'Brien estimated customs duties levied on retained imports of £1.4 million in 1750 and £3.3 million in 1785, "The Political

Economy of British Taxation, 1660–1815", *Economic History Review*, 2nd series, XLI, 1988, table 4, 9.

32. E. Chamberlayne, *The Present State of England*, fifteenth edition, second volume (1684), 32.
33. Peter Earle, *The Making of the English Middle Class: Business, Society and Family Life in London, 1660–1730* (London: Methuen, 1989), 20.
34. Huw Bowen estimated that there were 8000–10,000 men in the company's maritime service in the 1760s and that perhaps two-thirds of them originated from the British Isles, *The Business of Empire* (Cambridge: Cambridge University Press, 2006), 269.
35. J. H. Plumb, *Sir Robert Walpole, the King's Minister* (London: Cresset Press, 1960), 241.
36. *Some Materials towards Memoirs of the Reign of King George II by John Lord Hervey*, ed. R. Sedgwick (1931), I:138.
37. Patronage was at the heart of Walpole's approach to personal management, E. Cruickshanks, "The Political Management of Sir Robert Walpole, 1720–42", in *Britain in the Age of Walpole*, ed. J. Black (Basingstoke: Macmillan, 1984), 25.
38. Wagner, 400–1.
39. M. E. Clayton, "West, John, first Earl De La Warr (1693–1766)", *ODNB*, Oxford University Press, 2004; online edn., May 2005 [http://ezproxy.ouls.ox.ac.uk:2117/view/article/29087, accessed 14 March 2012].
40. D. Clarke, *Arthur Dobbs Esquire, 1689–1765* (London: Bodley Head, 1958), 51.
41. Ibid., 48–49. In 1745, Parliament offered a £20,000 reward for discovery of the passage.
42. J. C. Sainty, "Council of Trade and Plantations 1696–1782", *Office Holders in Modern Britain: Volume 3: Boards of Trade 1660–1870* (1974), 28–37.
43. Parliament instructed the Board of Trade to inquire into the African trade in 1708, and the Board's report helped to legitimize the cause of the private traders, William A. Pettigrew, "Regulatory Inertia and National Economic Growth", in *Regulating the British Economy, 1660–1850*, ed. Perry Gauci (Farnham: Ashgate, 2011), 34.
44. For a discussion of this period, see Matthew D. Mitchell, "Legitimate Commerce in the Eighteenth Century: The Royal African Company of England under the Duke of Chandos, 1720–1726", *Enterprise and Society* 14, no. 3 (2013): 544–78.

45. Ibid., 571–72.
46. Board of Trade Minutes, Journal 5, March–June 1726.
47. Board of Trade Minutes, Journal 8, May–July, 1744.
48. K. G. Davies, *The Royal African Company* (New York: Atheneum, 1970), 345.
49. W. Pettigrew, *Freedom's Debt* (Chapel Hill: University of North Carolina Press, 2013), 176.
50. For example, see National Archives, Colonial Office Records, CO134/3, letter from the HBC to the Earl of Dartmouth dated 19 February. 1711, fo. 77. The figure agreed was £108,000.
51. Board of Trade Minutes, Journal 4, 13 August 1719.
52. See M. Wagner, "The Levant Company under Attack in Parliament, 1720–53", *Parliamentary History* 34, no. 3 (2015): 301–2.
53. Ibid., 295–313.
54. This data collection tended to precede a parliamentary debate on the issue by a few years. For the Levant Company, the collection of data on Italian trade in 1715–16 preceded the parliamentary debate of 1720. The collection of data in 1727 preceded a 1729 dispute between the Levant Company and the clothiers of Worcester. In the case of the EIC, the major issue in 1719–20 concerned the impact of calico imports.
55. Philip J. Stern, *The Company-State* (New York: Oxford University Press, 2011).
56. The population of Madras was estimated by Thomas Bowrey, a sailing master, to be about 40,000 in the 1670s. See *A Geographical Account of the Countries Round the Bay of Bengal, 1669 to 1679*, ed. R. C. Temple (Cambridge: Hakluyt Society, 1905).
57. R. Sweet, *The English Town, 1680–1840* (Harlow: Longman, 1999), table 1, 3.
58. It was only following the mass mobilization during the Napoleonic wars that the size of the British army was comparable to the Indian army.
59. The monopolies of trade with India and China were lost in 1813 and 1833, respectively.
60. The Northwest Company was founded in 1779 and largely took over the old French fur-trading network.
61. J. S. Galbraith, *The Hudson's Bay Company as an Imperial Factor, 1821–1869* (Cambridge: Octagon Books, 1957), 8.
62. The price was £300,000 but the HBC retained ownership of its prime trading posts and some land for exploration.

References

Archives

The National Archives (TNA): Colonial Office Records, CO134.

Primary Published Material and Calendars

Board of Trade Minutes, Journal 3, March 20, 1716.
Board of Trade Minutes, Journal 5, March–June 1726.
Board of Trade Minutes, Journal 8, May–July 1744.
Carr, Cecil Thomas. *Select Charters of Trading Companies, 1530–1707*. London, 1913.
Chamberlayne, E. *The Present State of England*. Fifteenth edition, vol. 2. London, 1684.
Hudson's Bay Company. *Charters*, Statutes, Orders in Council etc. Relating to the *Hudson's Bay Company*. London, 1949.
Sainty, J. C. "Council of Trade and Plantations 1696–1782," In *Office Holders in Modern Britain: Volume 3: Boards of Trade 1660–1870* (1974).
Temple, R. C., ed., *A Geographical Account of the Countries Round the Bay of Bengal*, 1669 to 1679. Cambridge: Hakluyt Society, 1905.

Secondary Literature

Bowen, H. V. *The Business of Empire*. Cambridge: Cambridge University Press, 2006.
Chaudhuri, K. N. *The Trading World of Asia and the English East India Company*, 1660–1760. Cambridge: Cambridge University Press, 1978.
Clarke, D. *Arthur Dobbs Esquire, 1689–1765*. London: Bodley Head, 1958.
Crouzet, F. "*Angleterre et France au XVIIIe siècle: Essai d'analyse comparée de deux croissances économiques*." *Annales: Economies, Societes, Civilisations* 21 (1966).
Crowhurst, P. *The Defence of British Trade, 1689–1815*. Folkestone: Dawson, 1977.
Cruickshanks, E. "The Political Management of Sir Robert Walpole, 1720–42." In *Britain in the Age of Walpole*, edited by J. Black, PAGE NOS (Basingstoke: Macmillan, 1984).
Davies, K. G. *The Royal African Company*. New York: Atheneum, 1970.
Davis, R. *Aleppo and Devonshire Square*. London: Macmillan, 1967.

Earle, Peter. *The Making of the English Middle Class: Business, Society and Family Life in London*, 1660–1730. London: Methuen, 1989.

Galbraith, J. S. *The Hudson's Bay Company as an Imperial Factor, 1821–1869*. Cambridge: Octagon Books, 1957.

Kaplan, H., *Russian Overseas Commerce with Great Britain during the Reign of Catherine II*. Philadelphia, PA: American Philosophical Society, 1995.

Mitchell, Matthew D. "Legitimate Commerce in the Eighteenth Century: The Royal African Company of England under the Duke of Chandos, 1720–1726." *Enterprise and Society* 14, no. 3 (2013): 544–578.

O'Brien, Patrick, "The Political Economy of British Taxation, 1660–1815." *Economic History Review* 41 (1988), Page Nos.

Parry, J. H. *Trade and Dominion: The European Oversea Empires in the Eighteenth Century*. London: Phoenix, 1974.

Pettigrew, William A. "Regulatory Inertia and National Economic Growth." In *Regulating the British Economy, 1660–1850*, edited by P. Gauci, 25–40. Farnham: Ashgate, 2011.

———. *Freedom's Debt: The Royal African Company and the Politics of the Atlantic Slave Trade, 1672–1752*. Chapel Hill: University of North Carolina Press, 2013.

Plumb, J. H. *Sir Robert Walpole, the King's Minister*. London: Cresset Press, 1960.

Porter, A., ed. *The Oxford History of the British Empire: The Nineteenth Century*. Oxford: Oxford University Press, 1999.

Rodger, N. A. M. "War as an Economic Activity in the Long Eighteenth Century." *International Journal of Maritime History* 22, no. 2 (2010): PAGE NOS.

Stern, Philip J. *The Company-State: Corporate Sovereignty and the Early Modern Foundations of the British Empire in India*. Oxford: Oxford University Press, 2011.

Sweet, R. *The English Town, 1680–1840: Government, Society and Culture*. Harlow: Longman, 1999.

Thomson, J. E. *Mercenaries, Pirates and Sovereigns: State-building and Extraterritorial Violence in Early Modern Europe*. Princeton: Princeton University Press, 1996.

Wagner, M., "Misunderstood and Unappreciated: The Russia Company in the Eighteenth Century." *Russian History* 41, no. 3 (2014): Page Nos.

———. "The Levant Company under Attack in Parliament, 1720–53." *Parliamentary History* 34, no. 3 (2015): Page Nos.

Willan, T. S. *The Early History of the Russia Company, 1553–1603*. Manchester: Manchester University Press, 1956.

Wood A., *A History of the Levant Company*. London: Frank Cass, 1935.

5

Corporate Social Responsibility and the Rise of the Non-profit Sector in America

Robert E. Wright

Businesses ignore history at their peril. Viewed through the lens of the history of corporations, the rise of the corporate social responsibility (CSR) movement in the USA over the past few decades is highly problematic. America went down the CSR road in the early nineteenth century and concluded that the only social responsibility of business corporations was to obey the laws of the land.

The essentially premodern notion that business corporations, or moneyed corporations in the parlance of the nation's early decades, owed a positive responsibility to anyone other than their shareholders and contractual counterparties was jettisoned in the early nineteenth century in favour of a system in which responsibility for social objectives was delegated to non-profits, or non-pecuniary or non-stock corporations as they were once known. In other words, before the Civil War, US business corporations came to be considered forms of private

R.E. Wright (✉)
Augustana University, Sioux Falls, United States
e-mail: Robert.Wright@augie.edu

W.A. Pettigrew and D.C. Smith (eds.), *A History of Socially Responsible Business, c.1600–1950*, Palgrave Studies in the History of Finance,
DOI 10.1007/978-3-319-60146-5_5

property, a nexus of contracts, not a social entity distinct from its owners that had moral or social responsibilities, the role taken up by non-profits.[1]

The non-profit sector continues to thrive, yet business corporations are again being sucked into the maw of direct provision of public services. The impetus for the reversal came from two distinct interests, corporate executives and statists. The former pushed adoption of the "social entity" view of the business corporation in order to better ensconce themselves in power by augmenting their discretion over corporate cash flows and their power to combat hostile takeovers.[2] The latter sought to curb the number, size, and importance of non-profits because non-profits are more difficult, politically and practically, to regulate than are for-profits. What is sometimes termed the Third Sector has been called a threat to "democracy", but what it actually challenges is oversized government, regulation, and taxation. The distinction between business and non-profit enterprise has also been blurred by attempts by the former to increase profits by partnering with non-profits on salient issues such as endangered species and child safety.[3]

The first Anglo-Dutch business corporations were monopolistic entities loathed by almost everyone, including Adam Smith. To survive under their own massive weight, Smith argued, corporations needed special legal powers denied to sole proprietorships and partnerships, privileges like monopoly rights, perpetual succession, limited liability, and eminent domain. To render themselves more palatable to lawmakers, jurists, and voters, early business corporations promised to provide public services such as the establishment of distant colonies or trading facilities, the construction of canals, or the financing of government debt.[4]

The notion that businesses that sought incorporation had to provide a public service was transplanted to colonial British North America and grew tenuous roots. Most of the few business corporations chartered in the colonies were either mutuals, like the Philadelphia Contributionship, utilities like water aqueducts, or transportation infrastructure like wharves. The two exceptions were trading companies, one of which was chartered by Pennsylvania's Lord Proprietor instead of its legislature. It quickly went bankrupt. The other had its Connecticut charter quickly revoked when it began to operate as a bank. Other early bank schemes, in Massachusetts and Pennsylvania, were also denied charters, ostensibly because the would-be bankers were not able to point to a single public service they were needed to provide given the widespread use of colony-owned and -operated land banks and loan offices that issued paper money.[5]

Late in the American Revolution, however, the federal and several state governments chartered a commercial bank called the Bank of North America. When the institution was later attacked, for among other sins not providing a public service, the bank's supporters countered that the bank provided the public with convenient forms of money, in notes and deposits readily convertible into specie, an improvement over the inconvertible government paper money then in its death throes. Moreover, the bank's supporters noted, after the war was concluded the Bank of North America was neither a de jure nor a de facto monopoly. Banks had formed in other cities, like New York and Boston, and no law prevented the formation of additional banks in Pennsylvania or even Philadelphia, though early bankers warned that banking might be a natural monopoly.[6] They were, however, soon disabused of that notion, so no one bank proved indispensable to the economy or the money supply, even the two federal banks called the Bank of the United States, which were then the only banks allowed to branch across state lines.[7]

Supporters of the Bank of North America and corporations in general also pointed out that any group of Americans was free to form a business association and apply for a charter from the appropriate legislature. Americans did so, and in prodigious numbers. Before the Civil War, over 22,000 business corporations received special acts of incorporation from their respective state legislatures and thousands of others chartered under general incorporation laws.[8] Very few charters contained monopoly privileges and legislatures extended eminent domain powers only when absolutely necessary and mostly to transportation infrastructure corporations like railroads, canals, and turnpikes, the last two of which sometimes competed against free government roads and river improvements.[9]

Most importantly for this discussion, state governments soon began to charter manufacturing, mining, and a variety of miscellaneous corporations that provided no direct public service whatsoever. Already by 1825, it was clear to the Jeffersonian political economist Thomas Cooper that business corporations were chartered on the mere "pretence of promoting the GENERAL WELFARE".[10] A few years later, John Cox made a very clear distinction between a public corporation formed to build and maintain a bridge and a toll bridge corporation that "incidentally ministered to the convenience of a portion of the public, but which originated in private speculation, and was built and kept up for the profit of the individual partners in the scheme".[11]

Realization that the main purpose of business corporations was to generate private profits led naturally to the notion of general incorporation statutes,[12] an idea that would have proliferated more rapidly after being espoused by politicians like Elbridge Gerry[13] had state policymakers not so jealously guarded the rents they earned from the special incorporation model their states had inherited from the British monarchy. The sovereign's monopoly over corporate charters, though, was warmly contested.[14] Throughout the early years of the Republic, some Americans, including Alexander Hamilton, insisted that legislative sanction was necessary only if stockholders wanted to enjoy noncontractual limited liability. Associations did not need a government charter, Hamilton and others claimed, to assert other corporate powers, even perpetual succession. In fact, many such unincorporated businesses formed and conducted business, though most eventually obtained a charter.[15] For all those reasons, the close mental links between business corporations, legal monopolies and other special privileges, and public service provision began to dissolve. Not everyone broke those mental chains overnight but they were very weak by 1840, in no small part due to the rise of the non-profit sector.[16]

Scholars have yet to count non-profit corporations as thoroughly as they have counted business corporations, but nevertheless it is clear that non-profits were extremely numerous. Until at least 1810, they outnumbered business corporations,[17] and my preliminary findings suggest that non-profits were at least as numerous as for-profit corporations up to the Civil War. "Not only do they have commercial and industrial associations in which all take part", de Tocqueville noted of Americans, "but they also have a thousand other kinds: religious, moral, grave, futile, very general and very particular, immense and very small".[18] Also around 1830, the authors of America's first legal treatise dedicated to corporations noted that

> these associations we not only find scattered throughout every cultivated part of the United States, but so engaged are they in all the varieties of useful pursuit, that we see them directing the concentration of mind and capital to the advancement of religion; to the diffusion of literature, science and the arts; to the prosecution of plans of internal communication and improvement; and to the encouragement and extension of the great interests of commerce, agriculture, and manufactures.[19]

The private sector, composed of individuals but also increasing numbers of for- and non-profit corporations, long mitigated many pressing social problems, often with no more public "aid" than a government charter, which as noted above was more of an imposition than a necessity.[20] Fearful of the potentially powerful policy implications of this fact, numerous statist scholars, including William Roy, Brian Murphy, Theda Skocpol, Johann Neem, and Peter Hall,[21] assert that "the corporation was … an extension of state power",[22] that "government … got things done by deliberately bestowing public authority on … institutions in order to … channel self-interest toward public goods and civic ends",[23] that "American voluntary groups developed in close relationship to the representative and federal institutions of the US state",[24] and that "the state's role in shaping civil society and the public sphere must now be taken seriously".[25] All ignore the view of US Supreme Court Chief Justice John Marshall, who clearly noted in his 1819 Dartmouth College decision that the corporation "is no more a state instrument, than a natural person exercising the same powers, would be".[26]

As the sole goal of business corporations became improvement of the general welfare by means of the pursuit of private profit, non-profits took up the mantle of public service. For a century and a half thereafter, with a few exceptions noted by Morrell Heald, Howard Bowen, Archie Carroll, and other early scholars of the corporate social responsibility movement,[27] the business of business was business and the business of non-profits was direct public service.[28] That division of labour lasted so long because it made good economic, legal, and political sense.

Economically, non-profits tend to be more efficient than government at many tasks because they are not compulsory monopolies, they are voluntary associations that compete for resources and are accountable to their donors and volunteers.[29] "When men are no longer bound among themselves in a solid and permanent manner", de Tocqueville observed, "one cannot get many to act in common except by persuading each of them whose cooperation is necessary that his particular interest obliges him voluntarily to unite his efforts with the efforts of all the others".[30]

The main thing that has changed since the early nineteenth century is the political scene.[31] Over time, and especially due to major wars and economic disruptions, the government assumed increasingly important economic and social roles and grew larger as a percentage of the economy, thus creating large pressure groups with a vested interest in statist ideology.[32] More recently, globalization and some serious breaches of the business corporation's responsibility to behave lawfully have re-energized long dormant anti-corporate and anti-big business sentiments throughout much of America. The financial crisis of 2008 and subsequent bailouts only made matters worse.

But perhaps even more important than the resurgence of antipathy against big business is the increasingly vehement attack on the non-profit sector. "It is not only 'big business' but also 'big philanthropy' that has an increasing influence in global development policy, particularly large philanthropic foundations … most notably the Rockefeller Foundation and the Bill & Melinda Gates Foundation".[33] So wrote Jens Martens and Karolin Seitz in a November 2015 e-pamphlet, *Philanthropic Power and Development: Who Shapes the Agenda*? That duo considers philanthropy and corporate giving an area of concern because it creates

> unintended risks and side effects … particularly the fragmentation of global governance, the weakening of representative democracy … the unpredictable and insufficient financing of public goods, the lack of

monitoring and accountability mechanisms, and the prevailing practice of applying the business logic to the provision of public goods.[34]

That attack harkens back to the early days of the Republic, when those who sought power through control of government deprecated non-profits for crowding out the state. As politician James Sullivan of Massachusetts argued in 1803, the "creation of corporate interests must have a direct tendency to weaken the powers of government".[35] The proposed charter of the Women's Prison Association of New York met opposition not because its sponsors were women but because the association "would be likely to interfere with the authority of the state over prisons".[36]

In fact, as de Tocqueville noted, non-profits in a sense "regulate the state".[37] "Among democratic peoples", the astute French observer argued, "it is only by association that the resistance of citizens to the central power can occur. Thus", he concluded, the government "never sees but with disfavor associations that are not in its hands". "A government could take the place of some of the greatest American associations", de Tocqueville conceded. "But what political power", he asked, "would ever be in a state to suffice for the innumerable multitude of small undertakings that American citizens execute every day with the aid of an association?"[38]

Some Jeffersonians and Jacksonians were willing to risk the loss of those small undertakings out of fear that "a system of corporations ... calculated to deprive the people of their power and rightful influence in government" could threaten the existence of the Republic by means of a "monied aristocracy" that could control markets and politics through both business and non-profit corporations.[39] In 1830, Anti-Masonic Party stalwart Amasa Walker singled out non-profits as the bigger threat. "Voluntary associations have become the great instruments of power in the nineteenth century", he wrote, arguing that, "they move and direct the world, though often with an unseen and mysterious hand".[40] His fear was that the Masons, in particular, could "prove a most powerful engine against the state, or be devoted to purposes subversive of the public good".[41]

Some unascertainable percentage of the considerable bluster against non-profits[42] came from political leaders who saw voluntary associations as a threat to their personal power rather than as a bona fide threat to the public, or the Republic. Thomas Jefferson remained fearful of private associations his entire adult life[43] because they inhabited a space outside of "regular government".[44] So, too, did institutions like the family, but Jeffersonians worried more about non-profits because they offered a viable alternative form of governance that was more fraternal than hierarchical and hence less subject to elite, slaveholder control. As economist Edward Stringham has argued, "voluntary associations can meet many objects for creating a civil society, one of them being the creation of rules through private governance".[45]

The historian Peter Hall claimed that "eighteenth-century Americans were profoundly uncomfortable" with non-profits "because neither experience nor existing political theory provided a rationale for voluntary organizations".[46] In fact, early Americans had several powerful ways of thinking about non-profits. Outright outlawing non-profits proved legally impossible due to the broad interpretation of the First Amendment,[47] which was itself rooted in John Locke's ideal of voluntary association,[48] which was so broad that it allowed even married women the right to organize and run non-profits.[49] Of additional aid was the very English notion, perhaps put most eloquently by financier Robert Morris, that it was "inconsistent with the principles of liberty to prevent a man from the free disposal of his property on such terms and for such considerations as he may think fit".[50] Marshall asserted much the same thing in the Dartmouth case when he mentioned "the power every one has to dispose, direct, and regulate his own property". As British statesman Edmund Burke made clear, "liberty is a good to be improved, and not an evil to be lessened" so government should err on the side of allowing too much of it rather than too little.[51] Early abolitionist John Ady also noted that Anglo-America was "generally characterized by its attachment to civil and religious liberty".[52]

Contemporaries also noted that government tended to be paternalistic, while non-profits were more fraternalistic. (Some, of course, were even called fraternal societies.) "Our institutions are not of the nature of those paternal governments which assume all their subjects to be in a state of pupilage, and will not suffer them to act for fear of their acting amiss", Bostonian Samuel Eliot explained:

> Our civil polity partakes more of the character of another family relation … and may be called the fraternal government. The true idea of a government of the people is that of an association, the members of which are ready to aid each other not merely in the attainment of those objects in which they have a common interest, but also to reach such as may be particularly desirable to only one or two of the number.[53]

A firm and widespread belief in the power of pluralist competition also protected business and non-profit corporations from the wrath of political enemies. As the important early policymaker Tench Coxe explained, "many separate boards of directors, selected for the service on account of their property, integrity, talents, and attention to business, and whose primary duties are the legal, discreet, and beneficial execution of their trust", were unlikely to "deviate, in a dangerous degree, from their proper walk, into the ground of political combination and intrigue".[54] Indeed, non-profits often checked each other's excesses, as in the 1850s when the American Wine Growers Association successfully refuted the claims of teetotaller temperance societies then calling for the prohibition of all alcohol.[55]

Adam Smith argued for free entry for churches on similar pluralist and competitive grounds. Societies that allowed the formation of numerous religious organizations, Smith argued, would be free from religious zeal because the organizations would check each other, keeping any one of them from growing "considerable enough to disturb the public tranquility". Smith cited Pennsylvania as a prime example of the "good temper and moderation" induced by the fact that, although "the Quakers happen to be the most numerous, the law in reality favours no one sect more than another".[56] Many Americans clearly understood and accepted Smith's view of religious pluralism. "Thus it is that the rivalry even of religious sects, which seems at first view to produce nothing but that apparent hostility which is on the surface", wrote Eliot in 1845, "really causes an unseen under-current of kindness and active benevolence".[57]

Although always wary of the large agency costs inherent in large institutions, Smith also advocated the benefits of secular non-profits, including charities and private educational institutions.[58] In fact, according to Smith's student Dugald Stewart, "a large proportion of his annual savings was allotted to offices of secret charity".[59] And although Smith argued that "the expense of the institutions for education and religious instruction, is likewise, no doubt, beneficial to the whole society, and may, therefore, without injustice, be defrayed by the general contribution of the whole society", he also noted that

> this expense, however, might perhaps with equal propriety, and even with some advantage, be defrayed altogether by those who receive the immediate benefit of such education and instruction, or by the voluntary contribution of those who think they have occasion for either the one or the other.[60]

Smith, after all, was a keen observer of government. He realized that although the government could occasionally run a successful business, like the loan office in Pennsylvania, the public pawnshop in Hamburg, and various postal systems, government businesses often failed because of "slothful and negligent profusion" and "thoughtless extravagance".[61] Most public services, therefore, were best left to the private sector, including, when appropriate, non-profit corporations. Eliot also argued that non-profits did "many things far better than any government could possibly do them".[62]

While some non-profits, like their for-profit cousins, proved inept, others provided valuable services that supplemented or even supplanted government efforts, including law enforcement, education, and care for the poor and sick. Some even endeavoured to make government enforce its own laws regarding swearing, Sabbath-breaking, and building codes.[63]

Sometimes success or failure came down to the non-profit's ability to find outstanding leaders like Jacob Morris or Thomas Cope,[64] both of Philadelphia, ground zero in the development of America's non-profit sector.[65] Other times, the nature of the institution itself was a key. Hospitals for the insane, for example, found it easier, *ceteris paribus*, to raise funds than other charities did. "The difficulty which is to be met in so many other walks of charity is not here to be encountered", explained Eliot, "namely, to guard against offering an inducement to take advantage of the provision unnecessarily. No one becomes insane voluntarily, and there is little danger of delusion or deception. Too much, therefore, can hardly be done for the comfort, or the recovery, of those who may stand in need of the charity".[66] According to Eliot, there were simply too many charities so "nearly all our permanent benevolent institutions are sadly ... crippled for want of means. They cannot do all that they are called upon, and designed, to do" even though it was "a fact, that a much larger amount has been distributed by the individual inhabitants of Boston than by the City government ... This is done freely, voluntarily, by no compulsion of any sort".[67]

Unable to quash its prolific non-profit rivals on legal or economic grounds, the government settled instead for "overseeing and regulating" them.[68] It is through the power of regulation that some dyed-in-the-wool statists wish to reduce the influence of non-profits and thus, it is hoped, expand the purview of government.[69] Non-profits, however, are difficult to control due to the widespread support the sector elicits. Far from waning after de Tocqueville's tour of America, for-profits grew both larger and more numerous. In 1940, 12,500 secular charitable tax-exempt organizations were in operation.[70] That "vast network of clubs and organizations", writer Charles Abrams claimed, constituted "one of the remarkable phenomena of the American political and social scheme. ... There is", he noted, "hardly a cause in American life, from a universal language to the preservation of barber shop quartets, that sooner or later does not spawn an organization to sponsor it".[71] In 1950, more than 12 million Americans owned interests in consumer cooperatives, almost more than twice the number that owned common stocks directly.[72] By 1999, non-profits had operating expenditures of $500 billion.[73] In 2008, the total number of all American non-profits stood at about 700,000.[74] That year, some 48,000 cooperatives counted more than 120 million Americans as members. Farmer-owned cooperatives numbered about 3400 and 6400 housing cooperatives aided more than 1 million households. About 36 million Americans received electricity from almost 1000 rural electric co-ops and 250 purchasing cooperatives helped over 50,000 small businesses. Credit unions, cooperative depository institutions, banked 84 million Americans.[75] By 2014, over 86,000 foundations were registered in the USA and their total annual giving in 2013 was an estimated $54.7 billion.[76]

The confused jumble of ideas concerning the development of the corporation has already proved costly. As Oliver Williamson argued decades ago, the "failure to understand the main purposes of the corporation has been the source of much confusion and ill-conceived public policy".[77] Business historians need to set the record straight so that no more costs, essentially deadweight losses, are incurred trying to twist business and non-profit corporations into something they aren't, and weren't meant to be. Since the nation's early years, business corporations were to sell goods to customers and provide employment for the sole purpose of generating profits for stockholders. Aside from obeying the law, they had no direct social responsibility to employees, including corporate officers, or other elements of society. At the same time, non-profits provided public services that government would not provide at all, or could not provide as efficiently.

Notes

1. William T. Allen, "Our Schizophrenic Conception of the Business Corporation", *Cardozo Law Review* 14, no. 2 (1992): 264–65.
2. History of Corporate Responsibility Project, *Corporate Social Responsibility: The Shape of a History, 1945–2004* (Center for Ethical Business Cultures, 2010), 6; Allen, "Our Schizophrenic Conception of the Business Corporation", 273–77.
3. Richard Steckel, Robin Simons, Jeffrey Simons, and Norman Tanen, *Making Money While Making a Difference: How to Profit with a Nonprofit Partner* (Homewood, IL: High Tide Press, 1999), 5.
4. History of Corporate Responsibility Project, *Corporate Social Responsibility*, 4.
5. Mary Schweitzer, *Custom and Contract: Household, Government, and the Economy in Colonial Pennsylvania* (New York: Columbia University Press, 1987).
6. Anna Schwartz, "The Beginning of Competitive Banking in Philadelphia, 1782–1809", *Journal of Political Economy* 55 (1947): 417–31.

7. Robert E. Wright, *The First Wall Street: Chestnut Street, Philadelphia, and the Birth of American Finance* (Chicago: University of Chicago Press, 2005).
8. Robert E. Wright, *Corporation Nation* (Philadelphia, PA: University of Pennsylvania Press, 2015).
9. John L. Brooke, *The Heart of the Commonwealth: Society and Political Culture in Worcester County, Massachusetts, 1713–1861* (Amherst: University of Massachusetts Press, 1989), 280.
10. As quoted in Herbert Hovenkamp, *Enterprise and American Law, 1836–1937* (Cambridge: Harvard University Press, 1991), 36.
11. John Cox, *On the Argument, in Reference to the Bridge Bill, Prepared by Judge Cranch and Doctor May* (Washington? 1832), 2–3.
12. Brooke, *Heart of the Commonwealth*, 281.
13. Johann Neem, *Creating a Nation of Joiners: Democracy and Civil Society in Early National Massachusetts* (Cambridge, MA: Harvard University Press, 2008), 75.
14. Brooke, *Heart of the Commonwealth*, 285.
15. Shaw Livermore, *Early American Land Companies: Their Influence on Corporate Development* (New York: Commonwealth Fund, 1939).
16. Peter Dobkin Hall, *Inventing the Nonprofit Sector and Other Essays on Philanthropy, Voluntarism, and Nonprofit Organizations* (Baltimore, MD: The Johns Hopkins University Press, 1992), 3.
17. Jason Kaufman, "Corporate Law and the Sovereignty of States", *American Sociological Review* 73 (2008): 413–17.
18. Tocqueville, *Democracy in America*, 489.
19. Joseph K. Angell and Samuel Ames, *A Treatise on the Law of Private Corporations Aggregate* (Boston, MA, 1832).
20. See, for example, Robert E. Wright, "The Pivotal Role of Private Enterprise in America's Transportation Age, 1790–1860", *Journal of Private Enterprise* 29, no. 2 (2014): 1–20.
21. Hall, *Inventing the Nonprofit Sector*, 16–21.
22. William G. Roy, *Socializing Capital: The Rise of the Large Industrial Corporation in America* (Princeton: Princeton University Press, 1997), xiv.
23. Brian Murphy, *Building the Empire State: Political Economy in the Early Republic* (Philadelphia: University of Pennsylvania Press, 2015), 7.
24. Theda Skocpol, Marshall Ganz, and Ziad Munson, "A Nation of Organizers: The Institutional Origins of Civic Voluntarism in the United States", *American Political Science Review* 94 (2000): 527–46.
25. Neem, *Creating a Nation of Joiners*, 4.

26. *Trustees of Dartmouth College* v. *Woodward*, 17 US 4 Wheaton, 518 (1819), at 636.
27. History of Corporate Responsibility Project, *Corporate Social Responsibility*, 9–10.
28. Steckel et al., *Making Money While Making a Difference*, 5–6.
29. Edward Stringham, *Private Governance: Creating Order in Economic and Social Life* (New York: Oxford University Press, 2015), 30; De Tocqueville, *Democracy in America*, 490; Robert E. Wright, "On the Economic Efficiency of Organizations: Toward a Solution of the Efficient Government Enterprise Paradox", *Essays in Economic and Business History* 25 (2007): 143–54.
30. De Tocqueville, *Democracy in America*, 493.
31. For a recent critique of government service provision, see Peter H. Schuck, *Why Government Fails So Often and How It Can Do Better* (Princeton: Princeton University Press, 2014).
32. Robert Higgs, *Crisis and Leviathan: Critical Episodes in the Growth of American Government* (New York: Oxford University Press, 1989).
33. Jens Martens and Karolin Seitz, *Philanthropic Power and Development: Who Shapes the Agenda*? (Bonn: Global Policy Forum, 2015), 5.
34. Ibid., 214.
35. As quoted in Hall, *Inventing the Nonprofit Sector*, 22.
36. As quoted in Lori D. Ginzberg, *Women and the Work of Benevolence: Morality, Politics, and Class in the Nineteenth-Century United States* (New Haven, CT: Yale University Press, 1990), 48.
37. De Tocqueville, *Democracy in America*, 499.
38. Ibid., 490–91.
39. As quoted in Brooke, *Heart of the Commonwealth*, 311.
40. As quoted in ibid., 311.
41. As quoted in ibid., 327.
42. Neem, *Creating a Nation of Joiners*, 4.
43. Ibid., 5.
44. As quoted in Ibid., 5.
45. Stringham, *Private Governance*, 26.
46. Hall, *Inventing the Nonprofit Sector*, 20.
47. Arthur Selwyn Miller, *The Supreme Court and American Capitalism* (New York: Free Press, 1968), 146–48.
48. Brooke, *The Heart of the Commonwealth*, 81.

49. Anne Scott, *Natural Allies, Women's Associations in American History* (Chicago: University of Illinois Press, 1992), 19, 26.
50. As quoted in Robert A. East, *Business Enterprise in the American Revolutionary Era* (New York: Columbia University Press, 1938), 205.
51. Edmund Burke, "A Letter from Mr. Burke, to John Farr and John Harris, Esqrs., Sheriffs of the City of Bristol, on the Affairs of America", in *On Empire, Liberty, and Reform: Speeches and Letters*, ed. David Bromwich (New Haven, CT: Yale University Press, 2000), 170.
52. John Ady, *The Case of our Fellow-Creatures, the Oppressed Africans* (London, 1784), 7.
53. Samuel Atkins Eliot, "Public and Private Charities in Boston", *North American Review* (1845), 139.
54. Tench Coxe, *A View of the United States of America, in a Series of Papers* (Philadelphia, 1794), 354.
55. Jed Dannenbaum, *Drink and Disorder: Temperance Reform in Cincinnati from the Washingtonian Revival to the WCTU* (Chicago: University of Illinois Press, 1984), 135–36, 147.
56. Adam Smith, *Wealth of Nations*, Book V, Chap. 1, Part III, Article 3 "On the Expense of the Institutions for the Instruction of People of All Ages".
57. Eliot, "Public and Private Charities in Boston", 149.
58. Adam Smith, *Wealth of Nations*, Book V, Chap. 1, Part II, Article 1 "Of the Public Works and Institutions Which Are Necessary for Facilitating Particular Branches of Commerce".
59. Dugald Stewart, "Account of the Life and Writings of Adam Smith, LL.D". in *Adam Smith: Essays on Philosophical Subjects* ed. W. P. D. Wightman and J. C. Bryce (Indianapolis, IN: Liberty Fund, 1982), 326.
60. Adam Smith, *Wealth of Nations*, Book V, Chap. 1, Part IV, "Of the Expense of Supporting the Dignity of the Sovereign".
61. Ibid., Book V, Chap. 2, Part I, "Of the Funds or Sources of Revenue Which May Peculiarly Belong to the Sovereign or Commonwealth".
62. Eliot, "Public and Private Charities in Boston", 155.
63. Richard D. Brown, "The Emergence of Urban Society in Rural Massachusetts, 1760–1820", *Journal of American History* 61 (1974): 38–39.
64. Robert E. Wright, "Specially Incorporated For- and Non-Profit Corporations in America, 1607–1860", in *Research Handbook*

on the *History of Corporate and Company Law*, ed. Harwell Wells (Northampton, MA: Edward Elgar Press), forthcoming.

65. Jessica Choppin Roney, *Governed by a Spirit of Opposition: The Origins of American Political Practice in Colonial Philadelphia* (Baltimore: Johns Hopkins University Press, 2014), 4–5.
66. Eliot, "Public and Private Charities in Boston", 138–39.
67. Ibid., 149, 150, 155.
68. De Tocqueville, *Democracy in America*, 658.
69. Hall, *Inventing the Nonprofit Sector*, 15.
70. John Curl, *For All the People: Uncovering the Hidden History of Cooperation, Cooperative Movements, and Communalism in America* (Oakland, CA: PM Press, 2009), 13.
71. Charles Abrams, *Forbidden Neighbors: A Study of Prejudice in Housing* (New York: Harper & Brothers, 1955), 181.
72. Janice M. Traflet, *A Nation of Small Shareholders: Marketing Wall Street After World War II* (Baltimore, MD: Johns Hopkins University Press, 2013), 75.
73. Steckel et al., *Making Money While Making a Difference*, 5.
74. Curl, *For All the People*, 13.
75. Ibid., 1.
76. Martens and Seitz, *Philanthropic Power and Development*, 9, 13.
77. Oliver Williamson, "The Modern Corporation: Origins, Evolution, Attributes", *Journal of Economic Literature* 19, no. 4 (1981): 1537–68.

References

Abrams, Charles. *Forbidden Neighbors: A Study of Prejudice in Housing*. New York: Harper & Brothers, 1955.

Ady, John. *The Case of our Fellow-Creatures, the Oppressed Africans*. London, 1784.

Allen, William T. "Our Schizophrenic Conception of the Business Corporation." *Cardozo Law Review* 14, no. 2 (1992): 261–81.

Angell, Joseph K., and Samuel Ames. *A Treatise on the Law of Private Corporations Aggregate*. Boston, MA, 1832.

Brooke, John L. *The Heart of the Commonwealth: Society and Political Culture in Worcester County, Massachusetts, 1713–1861*. Amherst: University of Massachusetts Press, 1989.

Brown, Richard. "The Emergence of Urban Society in Rural Massachusetts, 1760–1820." *Journal of American History* 61 (1974): 29–51.

Burke, Edmund. "A Letter from Mr Burke, to John Farr and John Harris, Esqrs., Sheriffs of the City of Bristol, on the Affairs of America." In *On Empire, Liberty, and Reform: Speeches and Letters*, edited by David Bromwich, 138–83. New Haven, CT: Yale University Press, 2000.

Cox, John. *On the Argument, in Reference to the Bridge Bill, Prepared by Judge Cranch and Doctor May* [Washington?], 1832.

Coxe, Tench. *A View of the United States of America, in a Series of Papers*. Philadelphia, 1794.

Curl, John. *For All the People: Uncovering the Hidden History of Cooperation, Cooperative Movements, and Communalism in America*. Oakland, CA: PM Press, 2009.

Dannenbaum, Jed. *Drink and Disorder: Temperance Reform in Cincinnati from the Washingtonian Revival to the WCTU*. Chicago: University of Illinois Press, 1984.

De Tocqueville, Alexis. *Democracy in America*. Translated by Harvey C. Mansfield and Delba Winthrop. Chicago, IL: University of Chicago Press, 2000.

East, Robert. *Business Enterprise in the American Revolutionary Era*. New York: Columbia University Press, 1938.

Eliot, Samuel Atkins. "Public and Private Charities in Boston." *North American Review*. July 1845.

Ginzberg, Lori D. *Women and the Work of Benevolence: Morality, Politics, and Class in the Nineteenth-Century United States*. New Haven, CT: Yale University Press, 1990.

Hall, Peter Dobkin. *Inventing the Nonprofit Sector and Other Essays on Philanthropy*, Voluntarism, and Nonprofit Organizations. Baltimore, MD: Johns Hopkins University Press, 1992.

Higgs, Robert. *Crisis and Leviathan: Critical Episodes in the Growth of American Government*. New York: Oxford University Press, 1989.

History of Corporate Responsibility Project, *Corporate Social Responsibility*: The Shape of a History, 1945–2004. Center for Ethical Business Cultures, 2010.

Hovenkamp, Herbert. *Enterprise and American Law, 1836–1937*. Cambridge, MA: Harvard University Press, 1991.

Kaufman, Jason. "Corporate Law and the Sovereignty of States." *American Sociological Review* 73 (2008): 413–17.

Livermore, Shaw. *Early American Land Companies: Their Influence on Corporate Development*. New York: Commonwealth Fund, 1939.
Martens, Jens, and Karolin Seitz. *Philanthropic Power and Development: Who Shapes the Agenda?* Bonn: Global Policy Forum, 2015.
Miller, Arthur Selwyn. *The Supreme Court and American Capitalism*. New York: Free Press, 1968.
Murphy, Brian. *Building the Empire State: Political Economy in the Early Republic*. Philadelphia: University of Pennsylvania Press, 2015.
Neem, Johann. *Creating a Nation of Joiners: Democracy and Civil Society in Early National Massachusetts*. Cambridge, MA: Harvard University Press, 2008.
Roney, Jessica Choppin. *Governed by a Spirit of Opposition: The Origins of American Political Practice in Colonial Philadelphia*. Baltimore, MD: Johns Hopkins University Press, 2014.
Roy, William G. *Socializing Capital: The Rise of the Large Industrial Corporation in America*. Princeton: Princeton University Press, 1997.
Schuck, Peter H. *Why Government Fails So Often and How It Can Do Better*. Princeton: Princeton University Press, 2014.
Schwartz, Anna. "The Beginning of Competitive Banking in Philadelphia, 1782–1809." *Journal of Political Economy* 55 (1947): 417–31.
Schweitzer, Mary. *Custom and Contract: Household, Government, and the Economy in Colonial Pennsylvania*. New York: Columbia University Press, 1987.
Scott, Anne. *Natural Allies, Women's Associations in American History*. Chicago: University of Illinois Press, 1992.
Skocpol, Theda, Marshall Ganz, and Ziad Munson. "A Nation of Organizers: The Institutional Origins of Civic Voluntarism in the United States." *American Political Science Review* 94 (2000): 527–46.
Steckel, Richard, Robin Simons, Jeffrey Simons, and Norman Tanen. *Making Money While Making a Difference: How to Profit with a Nonprofit Partner*. Homewood, IL: High Tide Press, 1999.
Stewart, Dugald. "Account of the Life and Writings of Adam Smith, LL.D." In *Adam Smith: Essays on Philosophical Subjects*, edited by W. P. D. Wightman and J. C. Bryce, 269–351. Indianapolis, IN: Liberty Fund, 1982.
Stringham, Edward. *Private Governance: Creating Order in Economic and Social Life*. New York: Oxford University Press, 2015.
Traflet, Janice M. *A Nation of Small Shareholders*: Marketing Wall Street After *World War II*. Baltimore, MD: Johns Hopkins University Press, 2013.

Williamson, Oliver. "The Modern Corporation: Origins, Evolution, Attributes." *Journal of Economic Literature* 19, no. 4 (1981): 1537–68.

Wright, Robert E. *The First Wall Street: Chestnut Street, Philadelphia*, and the Birth of American Finance. Chicago, IL: University of Chicago Press, 2005.

———. "On the Economic Efficiency of Organizations: Toward a Solution of the Efficient Government Enterprise Paradox." *Essays in Economic and Business History* 25 (2007): 143–54.

———. "The Pivotal Role of Private Enterprise in America's Transportation Age, 1790–1860." *Journal of Private Enterprise* 29, no. 2 (2014): 1–20.

———. *Corporation Nation*. Philadelphia: University of Pennsylvania Press, 2015.

———. "Specially Incorporated For- and Non-Profit Corporations in America, 1607–1860." In *Research Handbook on the History of Corporate and Company Law*, edited by Harwell Wells (Northampton, MA: Edward Elgar Press), forthcoming.

6

Local Concerns, Global Impact: The Social Structures and Influence of Early Anglo-American Firms at Home and Abroad, 1815–1840

Emily Buchnea

The subject of globalization, multinational corporations, and the impact of developing economies is one that remains at the forefront of discussions within international business and corporate social responsibility literature. The history of multinationals and early international business gained momentum in the later decades of the twentieth century, with scholars such as Mira Wilkins and Geoffrey Jones making a significant contribution.[1] A recent special issue of *Business History Review* demonstrates that there is still much left unsaid about the activity of multinationals, in particular early multinationals, and their place within the expanding global economy.[2] In this issue, Wilkins argues that the "general and multipole roles of the multinational still need to be understood."[3] What was the impact of early multinationals and internationally focused trading firms on the locations in which they extended their reach? The roles they undertook need to be understood in a societal rather than a purely economic sense. While merchants displayed a

E. Buchnea (✉)
Newcastle Business School, Northumbria University,
Newcastle upon Tyne, UK
e-mail: Emily.Buchnea@northumbria.ac.uk

W.A. Pettigrew and D.C. Smith (eds.), *A History of Socially Responsible Business, c.1600–1950*, Palgrave Studies in the History of Finance,
DOI 10.1007/978-3-319-60146-5_6

genuine concern for community welfare, especially that of the business community, their activities had far-reaching consequences. At a local level, their role in politics and in charitable societies often hinted of self-interest; they lobbied Parliament for self- or community-serving aims, they networked with other merchants in benevolent and learned societies, and seldom wrote of the people and environments of the distant locales in which they conducted business.

This chapter examines the transnational networks of early Anglo-American "multinational" merchant firms and the variegated social impact they had upon England, the USA, Canada, Caribbean, and Central and South America: from the financial sector and transportation networks to mining and land acquisition in distant locations.[4] These firms were not often formalized corporations, but loosely governed partnerships. They succeeded across national borders because of their ability to develop networks of agents in different societies. As unchartered entities, they enjoyed some freedom from state regulations during this crucial period for multinational enterprises—the first half of the nineteenth century. Yet they were influenced by broader cultural expectations that they act sensitively toward the local communities with which they interacted. They acted as lobbyists for various social causes, and some of them engaged with the campaign to abolish slavery. While they were careful to nurture a socially responsible profile locally, beyond the need to cultivate overseas agents for their businesses, they neglected the social constituencies of their overseas trading hinterlands. So these institutions pioneered structures for unregulated, unchartered multinational enterprise, and in doing so began to expose the challenges of acting socially in their global as well as local constituencies.

Early conceptions of corporate social responsibility (CSR) have been explained by scholars as having a largely local, communal focus driven by local company leaders. As industrial centers grew, the manufacturing sector in particular experienced a growth in awareness of working conditions and worker welfare which resulted in the creation of a number of charities.[5] Bryan Husted argues that particular industrialists spearheaded CSR during the Industrial Revolution by showing growing concern for the welfare of their employees and, as a result, created old-age pensions, facilities for workers' children, and improvements in employee training.[6] More general concerns regarding air pollution and the environmental impact of manufacturing centers can be seen in the Garden city movement in the late nineteenth century.[7] Active engagement in what can be seen as early forms of corporate social responsibility came, in many of these instances, directly from the factory or company owner. Maritime industries also had a long-running tradition of supporting mariner relief charities, mission societies, and sailors' hospitals. These institutions were supported more widely by the community as well as the commercial elite. John Press argued that Victorian Christian virtues led to the development and support of many of these institutions in port cities around Britain, such as the Liverpool Sailors' Home and the Shipwrecked Fishermen and Mariners' Royal Benevolent Society.[8] While Press comments that shipowners demonstrated a degree of indifference to their sailors' welfare, some merchants were involved in supporting these institutions. The charitable work of merchants and their associated firms was, to an extent, truly philanthropic; however, due to the extensive interconnection between social and economic life, participation in charities was in itself an act of self-promotion and business networking.

That said, merchants seemed to display a concern for the well-being of their town or the city of residence and their community of peers. Avner Greif presents the idea of CRS (community responsibility system), which may be a good way of viewing how merchant firms conceived of their responsibility to the public.[9] While Greif had in mind self-governed *communes*, port cities were at times reflective of a community that possessed a high level of coercive power over government and were relatively independent in terms of business practices. Places such as Liverpool carried a collective reputation which, in belonging to the city, trickled down to businesses operating within. Thus firms within the city had an incentive to protect and uplift the business community and wider inhabitants. Thus, Grief's idea of CRS could be a good way of explaining merchant involvement in charities and political lobbying beyond self-interest and evangelical motivations. The examples in this chapter suggest how much of a challenge the increasingly global ambitions of these firms presented to such a system of responsibility.

One first needs to identify what constitutes a multinational enterprise (MNE) at this time, to understand the dynamics of their business abroad. Peter Buckley and Mark Casson define the MNE as an "enterprise which owns and controls activities in different countries."[10] Another definition from Dunning and Lundan defines a multinational or transnational enterprise as "*an enterprise* that engages in *foreign* direct investment (FDI) and *owns* or, in some way, *controls* value-added *activities* in more than one *country*."[11] Both of these definitions could encompass an assessment of firms' social enterprises in local and transnational contexts. The firms examined in this chapter had a domestic base in either Britain or the USA (and on occasion in additional locations). They sent members or associates abroad who acted on behalf of the firm and who, ideally, reported back to the firm on a regular basis. These individuals set up either branch houses or sister houses or were deemed "special resident agents."[12] Who these members were and how they were linked to the firm was far more informal than modern notions of headquarters, subsidiaries, and formal, rigid organisational structure in general; however, the fundamentals and reasons for going abroad were generally the same: opportunity, resources, and closer control over activity in regional and local markets. Within these international locations, they played different roles. Some used one location to springboard business activities into adjacent regions and thus had loose connections to many locales. Others were agents of British or American firms as well as permanent residents abroad and thus had a vested interest in the locations in which they conducted business (i.e., they were active members of those communities).

With the importance of international networks to the business of these firms, business historians and scholars of international business still need to question what the limits of the firm were and, through this, gain an understanding of the true impact of individual firms, both socially and otherwise.[13] Some might argue, for example, that the Barings who were heavily reliant on resident agents were not multinationals because they did not possess a branch house. However, their business was so reliant upon these individual agents that one perhaps needs to ask: How much control did they have over these individuals? To what extent were the actions of these individuals reflected back on the firm, and what were the implications of their failure for the principal firm? If a firm's legitimacy, reputation, and interests are protected by a resident agent, then should we not consider this individual as an extension of the firm rather than merely a networked associate? What effects did these more loosely configured businesses have on the local reputations and social impacts of these firms?

A strong commercial link between Britain and the USA was present in the eighteenth century, first through a colony-metropole arrangement and later because firms on each side benefited from access to diverse commodities and the availability of credit. The commercial links between Britain and the American colonies (later the United States) were controlled by private partnerships; these firms became embedded in large networks of exchange and information, which extended into multiple geographical regions and industries. While the character and nature of nineteenth-century transactions remained the same, the scope and scale increased exponentially, for some locations in particular (Table 6.1).

The Liverpool–New York trade link underwent significant growth in the early decades of the nineteenth century, greater than any other Anglo-American trade route. The reasons for this are many but fundamentally came down to the availability of manufactured goods and credit through Liverpool and New York's booming coastal trade which made the American port a springboard to other locations in North, Central, and South America.[14] The scale and value of many merchants' businesses increased, the regions in which they dealt multiplied, and with this the risks increased. This made the networks to which they belonged far more crucial. By the second decade of the nineteenth century, although the number of firms involved in this trade had decreased, the volume of trade and credit had increased, signifying that there was greater wealth and the scale of business concentrated in fewer hands. The number of firms deemed to be multinational also increased. The rise of these firms in this era seems to be rooted in two explanations: First, they needed to place trusted members abroad to protect their interests, and second, they needed a representative abroad who could embed themselves in local and regional networks to access resources and opportunities more effectively. These firms cultivated an international reputation. Liverpool and New York newspapers reported constantly on

Table 6.1 Examples of Anglo-American Firms operating between Liverpool and New York, 1815–1850

Firms (base)	Firm (Branch/Resident Agent)	Origins	Principal business
Bolton, Ogden & Co. (Liverpool)	Ogden, Ferguson & Co. (Ferguson, Day & Co.) (New York)	Bolton & Ogden both from West Yorkshire—Ogden immigrated to New York in 1790s	Commodities Trade (Cotton, Manufactures)
Brown Brothers & Co. (New York)	W. & J. Brown & Co. (Liverpool) Later Brown, Shipley & Co.	Alexander Brown—Baltimore—1800	Finance
Baring Bros & Co. (London)	Baring Bros & Co. (Liverpool) Joshua Bates (partnered with John Baring from 1820 s, based between London and Boston) Thomas Ward (resident agent—Boston and other locations)	London Commission merchant house founded in 1763, set up branch in Liverpool in 1832	Finance
Phelps & Peck (later, Phelps Dodge & Co.—New York)	Peck & Phelps (later Phelps, James & Co.—Liverpool)	Both Peck and Phelps merchants from Connecticut, Peck sent to Liverpool in 1815	Metal trade
Chares Tayleur & Co. (Liverpool)	C. Tayleur, Son & Co. (USA and South America)	Originated in north west England, manufacturing ventures there. Also houses in New Orleans, Mexico and Buenos Aires	Commission merchants
Wildes Pickersgill & Co. (Liverpool)	Pickersgill & Co. (New York)	Formed in 1835, first in London and then Liverpool and New York	Finance

(continued)

Table 6.1 (continued)

Firms (base)	Firm (Branch/Resident Agent)	Origins	Principal business
Prime, Ward & King (New York)	Gracie & King (Liverpool) (also several other related firms)	Formed in 1808, members occasionally sent to Liverpool to be resident there (King in particular)	Finance
Dennistoun, Mackie & Co. (Glasgow & Liverpool)	Mackie, Milne & Co. (New York)	Scottish merchants from Glasgow, Dennistoun was based in Liverpool, Mackie in New York and Milne in Charleston	Commission merchants
Grinnell, Minturn & Co. (New York)	Cearns, Fish and Crary (Liverpool) and other related firms	E. Cearns based in Liverpool; the rest of the firm appears to be originally from the USA	Commission Merchants
Abraham Bell & Co. (New York)	Malcolmson, Bell & Co. (Liverpool)		Commission Merchants

Sources Stanley Chapman, *Merchant Enterprise in Britain: From the Industrial Revolution to World War I* (Cambridge: Cambridge University Press, 2004). Carlos A. Schwantes, *Vision and Enterprise: Exploring the History of Phelps Dodge Corporation* (Phoenix: University of Arizona Press, 2000). Colm Brogan and James Finlay, *James Finlay & Company Limited: Manufacturers and East India merchants 1750–1950* (Glasgow: Jackson, 1951). John Crosby Brown, *A Hundred Years of Merchant Banking* (New York: J. C. Brown, 1909). Walter Barrett, *The Old Merchants of New York City* (New York, 1863), Baring Archive, ING; Ogden, Ferguson, Day & Co. (Ferguson, Day & Co.), Business Correspondence, 1797–1837, MS 466; Abraham Bell & Co. Records (1821–1910), Col. 194, Baring North America Correspondence, Baring Archive, ING news from every corner of the globe, streets, and docks were named for distant locations, and both goods and populations were become increasingly diverse as the shipping links brought migrants to their shores.

These early multinationals formed loose relationships with various constituencies within the societies in which they operated. These relationships helped the firms to succeed commercially and suggested a particular kind of relationship between firms and their various domiciled societies. The firms active in the Liverpool–New York trade network were comprised of between two and five members with additional clerks and agents. Firms were often formed within family networks, like the Brown Brothers, but this was not always the case. Local, ethnic, and religious ties also played a role, and long-standing associations or friendships could create family-like ties, also known as "fictive kin."[15] Occasionally, once partnerships were formed, sons, daughters, brothers, and sisters of the merchant partners married, further cementing ties, and in some instances, this insured the longevity of the firm.[16]

Firms built informal, transnational social networks to facilitate their businesses. In an era before limited liability, natural hazards, moral hazards such as fraud, and crises of many kinds were incurred by individual firms. To prevent at least some of these (namely moral hazards), firms transacted with individuals and partnerships they knew and trusted to behave in a particular way. Thus, firms became linked in intricate networks in which credit was extended, commodities were bought and sold, and reputations and relevant information were communicated. These networks developed their own informal behavioral codes that operated outside of formal institutions (although there was some form of bankruptcy law in place in both Britain and the USA), which also resulted in business transactions occurring entirely independent of regulation and control other than through the custom house in a given location.[17] Multinational firms were established within these networks, and it was because of these networks that their activity usually stretched far beyond their locales, and they were able to vary the types of businesses in which they were involved. For example, the Barings had branch houses in London and Liverpool, and special agents in a number of American port cities, but their activities and networks stretched well beyond these. The Barings pursued business in many locations in

North and South America; however, they never set up a branch house outside of Britain, relying mainly on the assistance of resident agent merchants. Thus, despite the Barings being resident in London and Liverpool, their business impacted on a number of cities, towns, and regions in which they often held only an economic interest. Firms such as Barings had roots in a community, whether London, Liverpool, or New York; however, their business interests touched many other communities, port cities, agricultural regions, and industrial districts across the globe. While the majority of firms constantly communicated information about international markets, their concern lay in the protection of their business interests and those of the local business community.

How did these firms impact upon a society? Did they, for instance, dictate the development of local infrastructure or the establishment of charitable or benevolent societies? What role did they play in politics? The answer, at least in nineteenth-century Anglo-American commercial centers, is that they made a major contribution to many of these areas of society. Especially in Liverpool, many individuals from established merchant and merchant-banking firms became involved in politics, and lobbied the government on issues such as trade embargos, the cessation of the East India Company's trading activities (1833), the repeal of the Corn Laws (1840s), and the limited liability debate (1850s).[18] For example, in 1812, Liverpool merchants gave evidence in Parliament regarding the devastation to trade caused by the Orders-in-Council which restricted trade with the USA.[19] Alexander Baring, who had been brought up in the Barings' merchant firm and later conducted business in the USA on behalf of Hope & Co. (which later merged with the Baring Brothers), entered politics in his later life. Through this political conduit, Baring on numerous occasions represented the interests of British merchants, for example, he actively fought for the repeal of the Corn Laws, which hampered many merchants who traded in foreign corn.[20]

It certainly appears that any political activism on the behalf of Anglo-American merchant firms was aimed to protect business interests and the economic prosperity of the communities in which their businesses were based. Perhaps the only exception in this period was the active campaign for the abolition of the transatlantic slave trade and later slavery in the British colonies. This appears to be an astonishing case of compartmentalization, in that Quaker merchants motivated by the values of their religion fervently opposed the practice of a trade in human beings and their enslavement yet traded frequently in slave-produced goods, namely cotton, tobacco, and naval stores.[21] As Seymour Drescher has argued, the early national abolition movement of the 1780 s did not affect Liverpool's trade activity.[22] Those investing in the trade directly, such as John Tarleton and Thomas Golightly, opposed the abolition of the slave trade.[23] That said, individuals not participating in the slave trade but active in the trade in slave-produced goods were instrumental in the founding of political organizations that promoted the abolition of the British slave trade.[24] Rathbone Brothers & Co., perhaps the most notable Quaker merchants in Liverpool, were founding members of the Liverpool Committee for the Abolition of the Slave Trade; similar movements in New York were also supported by Quaker merchants.[25] However, despite active involvement in abolition, letters between Liverpool and New York merchants seem to convey no conversation of the imminent bill, signifying that they felt the ending of the British slave trade would have no impact on their business, or they sought to keep that part of their consciousness entirely separate from their transnational business interests. Either way, during the early nineteenth century, this appears the only instance in which merchants of this community engaged in distant political and social movements that impacted societies and practices outside of their own business interests and local communities.

In terms of more local concerns, many partners in Anglo-American firms were actively involved in charities and benevolent societies in their towns or cities of residence. The charitable work conducted by merchants and their families was articulated by William Rathbone Jr, whose treatise *Social Duties Considered with Reference to the Organization of Effort in Works of Benevolence and Public Utility* encouraged involvement in charity beyond monetary donations and encapsulated Victorian values of benevolence and philanthropy.[26] For the early nineteenth century, there is much evidence of merchant involvement in organizations that benefited the local public goods, and it was the so-called elite (who were often merchants in the case of port cities) who became "stewards" of such organizations.[27] For example, in the eighteenth century, the governors and trustees of the Blue-Coat Hospital in Liverpool were mainly merchants.[28] In 1819, merchants James Cropper and Samuel Hope established the

Charitable Institution House, which provided a meeting place for the committees of charities in Liverpool.[29] However, local charitable activity was motivated not only by Christian values, but by a desire (or need) to build one's reputation.[30] The intersection of the social, the religious, and the economic led to charitable activities having a distinct personal benefit, and thus, merchant involvement in these activities was motivated by both faith and business.[31] In terms of the wider world, these merchants took a more pragmatic view, investing in particular locations and industries without questioning the positive or negative impact on those societies, industries, and associated populations.

The international scope of these firms' businesses and investments informed the wider implications and societal transformations that resulted from their activities. The structure and operation of banking systems in Britain and the USA came largely through the activities of merchants, specifically those of merchant bankers—or, as they have recently been described, "hybrid trading companies."[32] Like the merchant banks of the twentieth century, their focus was largely on international business. For much of the nineteenth century, large British merchant bankers had a hand in American business and, for multinationals in particular, it made sense to get involved in credit extension since they were able to monitor their investments at a local level. The Barings, although involved in many industries, were primarily merchant bankers, and their banking legacy continued until their fall from grace in the 1990 s. The Barings' financial activities in Central, North, and South America extended to many industries and newly independent governments which altered the growth, landscape, and demographics of particular countries and regions.[33] Finance touched many industries and in that sense, many merchant-banking firms remained connected to a range of sectors within local economies. The transformation of New York from a port economy to a service economy is irrevocably linked to its involvement in international trade and credit networks.

International firms also played a central part in the creation of transport infrastructure. In Anglo-American trade, ships were either owned by individual merchant firms or part-owned by clusters of merchants. For example, the Black Ball Line, the first regular packet line between England and the USA (Liverpool–New York specifically), was started by a group of merchants involved in the Yorkshire woolen trade.[34]

These Liverpool merchants had a particular interest in American markets and in particular New York, having traded with the port and merchants there for over two decades before founding the packet. Thus, it was through embedded networks that these sorts of ventures could be undertaken. As migration and trade to the USA increased through the nineteenth century, clusters of merchants continued to invest in regular packet lines. For example, packet lines were also started from Baltimore–Liverpool and Philadelphia–Liverpool, aided by the Browns on the Liverpool side and the Browns and Thomas Cope on the other.[35] These early ventures charted a course for mass Anglo-American shipping networks that would impact greatly on the movement of peoples into the late nineteenth century by dictating entry points of mass European migration to the USA. Early multinationals and internationally focused firms were also involved in the extension of American rail networks, typically by two means: investment through shares in railway companies and the provision of materials (usually manufactured or part-finished good) to aid in the completion of railways.[36] For example, Bolton, Ogden & Co. was involved in the Boston & Providence rail company (incorporated in 1831) and the Pontchartrain Railroad Co. , which connected New Orleans to the cotton-producing hinterland.[37]

Another sector in which multinational firms played a role, potentially more apparent in physical and regional terms, is the extractive industries and, to a degree, land acquisition. Some, such as Peck & Phelps or Phelps, Dodge & Co., moved gradually from trading to manufacturing to mining. Through their land acquisitions, manufacturing towns and mines, Phelps, Dodge & Co. had a significant impact on the creation of productive centers in the American west. The Barings were similarly influential in extending their networks into new mining regions. In the 1820 s, they held investments in the Viva mine in Lima, Peru, and later copper mines in Chile.[38] In 1832, the Barings were consulted by Edward Stopford regarding the potential for profitable mines in Venezuela and asked for help in financing this new venture.[39] Later in the century, they became involved in El Callao gold mine in Venezuela worked mainly by immigrants from the British Caribbean which served to transform the demographics and culture of the region.[40] Emergent mining industries shaped the landscape and the towns that developed because of them, and much of this was down to investment from foreign firms.

Additionally, many firms, especially the Barings, were involved in government loans and financing land purchases for development in the central states (such as Alabama and Louisiana), which occurred as a result of growing British interests and networks in the American cotton trade.

The purchasing of land, financing of a South American mine, or extension of credit to an agricultural area initiated by the firms discussed here shaped regions, markets, and populations. At a local level, the partners in these firms demonstrated concern for their neighbors, associates, and the communities in which they resided. Funding and philanthropic work on the boards of hospitals, orphanages, and learned societies demonstrate an interest in uplifting their society and, at times, themselves. Activity in government shows a concern for the prosperity of their business community perhaps motivated by Greif's community responsibility system. However, beyond the borders where their business interests resided, merchants appeared merely as rent seekers with little concern for the societies and populations affected by their pursuit of wealth. This chapter opens an opportunity to explore further the private partnership, whose informality, pragmatism, and perhaps lack of accountability give an interesting insight into opaque private organizations. Between the government-supported trading companies of the seventeenth century and centralized corporations of the early twentieth century, there was a period of relatively free economic movement controlled by transnational firms that greatly impacted on the development of the American continents while seemingly answering to no one except their own business communities.

Notes

1. Geoffrey Jones, *Merchants to Multinationals: British Trading Companies in the Nineteenth and Twentieth centuries* (Oxford: Oxford University Press, 2000); Mira Wilkins, *The Emergence of Multinational Enterprise: American Business Abroad from the Colonial Era to 1914* (Cambridge, MA: Harvard University Press, 1970).
2. Mira Wilkins, "The History of Multinationals: A 2015 View," *Business History Review* 89, no. 3 (2015): 405–14.
3. Wilkins, "History of Multinationals," 409.

4. Wilkins, *Emergence of Multinational Enterprise.*
5. Bryan W. Husted, "Corporate Social Responsibility Practice from 1800–1914: Past Initiatives and Current Debates," *Business Ethics Quarterly* 25, no. 1 (2015): 125–41.
6. Husted, "Corporate Social Responsibility Practice from 1800–1914," 125–41.
7. Lee D. Parker, "Corporate Social Accountability Through Action: Contemporary Insights from British Industrial Pioneers," *Accounting, Organizations and Society* 39, no. 8 (2014): 632–59.
8. Jon Press, "Philanthropy in the British Shipping Industry, 1815–1860," *International Journal of Maritime History* 1 (1989): 107–27.
9. Avner Greif, "Institutions and Impersonal Exchange: From Communal to Individual Responsibility," *Journal of Institutional and Theoretical Economics* 158, no. 1 (2002): 168–204.
10. Peter J. Buckley and Mark Casson, *Future of the Multinational Enterprise* (London: Macmillan, 1976).
11. John H. Dunning and Sarianna M. Lundan, *Multinational Enterprises and the Global Economy* (Cheltenham: Edward Elgar Publishing, 2008).
12. Ralph W. Hidy, "The Organization and Functions of Anglo-American Merchant Bankers, 1815–1860," *Journal of Economic History* 1 (1941): 53–66.
13. Mira Wilkins, "Defining a Firm: History and Theory," *Transnational Corporations: A Historical Perspective* 2 (1993): 206.
14. Emily Buchnea, "Transatlantic Transformations: Visualizing Change Over Time in the Liverpool–New York Trade Network, 1763–1833," *Enterprise & Society* 15, no. 4 (2015): 687–721; Peter Maw, "Yorkshire and Lancashire Ascendant: England's Textile Exports to New York and Philadelphia, 1750–1805," *Economic History Review* 63 (2010): 734–68; Liverpool Custom Bills of Entry, 1820, Liverpool Record Office.
15. Craig Muldrew, *The Economy of Obligation: The Culture of Credit and Social Relations in Early Modern England* (Basingstoke: Palgrave Macmillan, 1998); Ann Prior and Maurice Kirby, "The Society of Friends and the Family Firm, 1700–1830," *Business History* 35, no. 4 (1993): 66–85; Geoffrey Jones and Mary B. Rose, "Family Capitalism," *Business History* 35, no. 4 (1993): 1–16.
16. Susan Migden Socolow, "Marriage, Birth, and Inheritance: The Merchants of Eighteenth-Century Buenos Aires," *Hispanic American Historical Review* 60, no. 3 (1980): 387–406.
17. Sebouh Aslanian, "Social Capital,'Trust'and the Role of Networks in Julfan Trade: Informal and Semi-formal Institutions at Work," *Journal of Global History* 1, no. 3 (2006): 383–402; Xabier Lamikiz, *Trade and*

Trust in the Eighteenth-century Atlantic World: Spanish Merchants and their Overseas Networks (Woodbridge: Boydell Press, 2013); Robin Pearson and David Richardson, "Social Capital, Institutional Innovation and Atlantic Trade Before 1800," *Business History* 50, no. 6 (2008): 765–80; Charles Tilly, "Trust Networks in Transnational Migration," *Sociological Forum* 22, no. 1 (2007): 3–24; Sheryllynne Haggerty, "Risk and Risk Management in the Liverpool Slave Trade," *Business History* 51, no. 6 (2009): 817–34.

18. Patrick K. O'Brien, and Geoffrey Allen Pigman, "Free Trade, British Hegemony and the International Economic Order in the Nineteenth Century," *Review of International Studies* 18, no. 2 (1992): 89–113.
19. Minutes of evidence, taken before the Committee of the Whole House...to consider of the several petitions...relating to the orders in council (25 May 1812), House of Commons Parliamentary Papers.
20. Donald Grove Barnes, *A History of English Corn Laws: From 1660–1846* (London: Routledge, 2013).
21. David B. Davis, "James Cropper and the British Anti-Slavery Movement, 1823–1833," *Journal of Negro History* 45, no. 3 (1961): 154–73; Florence Baggett, "The Slaving Capital in the Era of Abolition: Liverpool's Silent Rejection of the Slave Trade, 1787–1807" (unpublished master's thesis, Victoria University of Wellington, 2013).
22. Seymour Drescher, "The Slaving Capital of the World: Liverpool and National Opinion in the Age of Abolition," *Slavery and Abolition* 9, no. 2 (1988): 128–43.
23. Leonardo Marques, "Slave Trading in a New World: The Strategies of North American Slave Traders in the Age of Abolition," *Journal of the Early Republic* 32, no. 2 (2012): 233–60; Robert J. Bennett, *Local Business Voice: The History of The Chamber of Commerce in Britain, Ireland and Revolutionary America, 1760–2011* (Oxford: Oxford University Press, 2011), 390.
24. Brian Howman, "Abolitionism in Liverpool", in *Liverpool and Transatlantic Slavery*, ed. David Richardson, Anthony Tibbles and Suzanne Schwarz (Liverpool: Liverpool University Press, 2007), 77–96.
25. John R. Oldfield, *Popular Politics and British Anti-Slavery: The Mobilisation of Public Opinion Against the Slave Trade, 1787–1807* (London: Routledge, 1998), 53.
26. William Rathbone, *Social Duties Considered with Reference to the Organization of Effort in Works of Benevolence and Public Utility* (London, 1867).
27. Howard M. Wach, "Unitarian Philanthropy and Cultural Hegemony in Comparative Perspective: Manchester and Boston, 1827–1848," *Journal of Social History* 26 (1993): 539–57.

28. Richard Brooke, *Liverpool as it was During the Last Quarter of the Eighteenth Century. 1775 to 1800* (Liverpool, 1853).
29. Benjamin Smith, *Smith's Strangers' Guide to Liverpool, its Environs, and part of Cheshire, for 1843* (Liverpool, 1843).
30. Wach, "Unitarian Philanthropy," 539–57.
31. Jon Stobart, "Information, Trust and Reputation: Shaping a Merchant Elite in early Eighteenth-century England," *Scandinavian Journal of History* 30, no. 3–4 (2005): 298–307.
32. Jones, *Merchants to Multi-Nationals*; Llorca-Jana, "Shaping Globalization," 469–95.
33. Share Certificates, House Correspondence, Latin and Portuguese Latin American, HC 4, Baring Archive, ING.
34. Chapman, *Merchant Enterprise in Britain*.
35. John Killick, "An Early Nineteenth-Century Shipping Line: The Cope Line of Philadelphia and Liverpool Packets, 1822–1872," *International Journal of Maritime History* 12, no. 1 (2000): 61–88.
36. Liverpool-New York Trade Database, 1837.
37. John Ogden correspondence, Ogden collection, NYHS, 1830–1837.
38. Share Certificates, House Correspondence, Latin and Portuguese Latin American, HC 4, Baring Archive, ING
39. Stopford to Barings, July 6, 1832, House Correspondence, Latin and Portuguese Latin American, HC 4, Baring Archive, ING.
40. 1883, Bolivar, Venezuela, House Correspondence, Latin and Portuguese Latin American, HC 4, Baring Archive, ING.

References

Archives

Abraham Bell & Co. Records (1821–1910), Col. 194.

Baring Archive, ING: Ogden, Ferguson, Day & Co. (Ferguson, Day & Co.), Business Correspondence, 1797–1837, MS 466.

Baring Archive, ING: Baring North America Correspondence.

Baring Archive, ING: Share Certificates, House Correspondence, Latin and Portuguese Latin American, HC 4.

Baring Archive, ING: Stopford to Barings, July 6, 1832, House Correspondence, Latin and Portuguese Latin American, HC 4.

Baring Archive, ING: 1883, Bolivar, Venezuela, House Correspondence, Latin and Portuguese Latin American, HC 4.
John Ogden correspondence, Ogden collection, NYHS, 1830–1837.
Liverpool Record Office: Liverpool Custom Bills of Entry, 1820.

Primary published material and calendars

Brooke, Richard. *Liverpool as it was During the Last Quarter of the Eighteenth Century. 1775 to 1800*. Liverpool, 1853.
House of Commons Parliamentary Papers. Minutes of evidence, taken before the Committee of the Whole House...to consider of the several petitions... relating to the orders in council (May 25, 1812).
Rathbone, William. Social Duties Considered with Reference to the Organization of Effort in Works of Benevolence and Public Utility. London, 1867.
Smith, Benjamin. *Smith's Strangers' Guide to Liverpool, its Environs, and part of Cheshire, for 1843*. Liverpool, 1843.

Secondary literature

Aslanian, Sebouh. "Social Capital, 'Trust'and the Role of Networks in Julfan Trade: Informal and Semi-formal Institutions at Work." *Journal of Global History* 1, no. 3 (2006): 383–402.
Baggett, Florence. "The Slaving Capital in the Era of Abolition: Liverpool's Silent Rejection of the Slave Trade, 1787–1807." Unpublished master's thesis, Victoria University of Wellington, 2013.
Brian Howman, "Abolitionism in Liverpool", in David Richardson, Anthony Tibbles and Suzanne Schwarz (eds), *Liverpool and Transatlantic Slavery* (Liverpool: Liverpool University Press, 2007).
Barnes, Donald Grove. *A History of English Corn Laws: From 1660–1846*. London: Routledge, 2013.
Barrett, Walter. *The Old Merchants of New York City*. New York, 1863.
Bennett, Robert J. *Local Business Voice: The History of The Chamber of Commerce in Britain, Ireland and Revolutionary America, 1760–2011*. Oxford: Oxford University Press, 2011.
Brogan, Colm, and James Finlay. *James Finlay & Company Limited: Manufacturers and East India merchants 1750–1950*. Glasgow: Jackson, 1951.

Brown, John Crosby. *A Hundred Years of Merchant Banking*. New York: J. C. Brown, 1909.

Buchnea, Emily. "Transatlantic Transformations: Visualizing Change Over Time in the Liverpool–New York Trade Network, 1763–1833." *Enterprise & Society* 15, no. 4 (2015): 687–721.

Buckley, Peter J., and Mark Casson. *Future of the Multinational Enterprise*. LOCATION?: Springer, 1976.

Chapman, Stanley. *Merchant Enterprise in Britain: From the Industrial Revolution to World War I*. Cambridge: Cambridge University Press, 2004.

Davis, David B. "James Cropper and the British Anti-Slavery Movement, 1823–1833." *Journal of Negro History* 46, no. 3 (1961): 154–73.

Drescher, Seymour. "The slaving capital of the world: Liverpool and national opinion in the age of abolition." *Slavery and Abolition* 9, no. 2 (1988): 128–43.

Dunning, John H., and Sarianna M. Lundan. *Multinational Enterprises and the Global Economy*. Cheltenham: Edward Elgar Publishing, 2008.

Greif, Avner. "Institutions and impersonal exchange: from communal to individual responsibility." *Journal of Institutional and Theoretical Economics* 158, no. 1 (2002): 168–204.

Haggerty, Sheryllynne. "Risk and risk management in the Liverpool slave trade." *Business History* 51, no. 6 (2009): 817–834

Hidy, Ralph W. "The organization and functions of Anglo-American merchant bankers, 1815–1860." *The Journal of Economic History* 1, no. S1 (1941): 53–66.

Husted, Bryan W. "Corporate Social Responsibility Practice from 1800–1914: Past Initiatives and Current Debates." *Business Ethics Quarterly* 25, no. 1 (2015).

Jones, Geoffrey, and Mary B. Rose. "Family capitalism." *Business History* 35, no. 4 (1993): 1–16.

Jones, Geoffrey. *Merchants to multinationals: British trading companies in the nineteenth and twentieth centuries* (Oxford: Oxford University Press, 2000).

John R. Oldfield, *Popular Politics and British Anti-Slavery: The Mobilisation of Public Opinion against the Slave Trade, 1787–1807* (London: Routledge, 1998)

Killick, John. "An Early Nineteenth-Century Shipping Line: The Cope Line of Philadelphia and Liverpool Packets, 1822–1872." *International journal of maritime history* 12, no. 1 (2000): 61–88.

Lamikiz, Xabier. *Trade and trust in the eighteenth-century Atlantic world: Spanish merchants and their overseas networks* (Woodbridge, Boydell Press, 2013).

Marques, Leonardo. "Slave Trading in a New World: The Strategies of North American Slave Traders in the Age of Abolition." *Journal of the Early Republic* 32, no. 2 (2012): 233–60.

Muldrew, Craig. *The Economy of Obligation: The Culture of Credit and Social Relations in Early Modern England* (Basingstoke: Palgrave Macmillan, 1998).
O'Brien, Patrick K., and Geoffrey Allen Pigman. "Free trade, British hegemony and the international economic order in the nineteenth century." *Review of International Studies* 18, no. 2 (1992): 89–113.
Peter Maw, "Yorkshire and Lancashire Ascendant: England's textile Exports to New York and Philadelphia, 1750–1805", *Economic History Review* 63 (2010), 734–68.
Parker, Lee D. "Corporate social accountability through action: Contemporary insights from British industrial pioneers." *Accounting, Organizations and Society* 39, no. 8 (2014): 632–659.
Pearson, Robin, and David Richardson. "Social capital, institutional innovation and Atlantic trade before 1800." *Business History* 50, no. 6 (2008): 765–780
Press, Jon. "Philanthropy in the British Shipping Industry, 1815–1860 International Journal of Maritime History, Vol. I (1989), 107–27." *International Journal of Maritime History* 1 (1989): 107–27.
Prior, Ann, and Maurice Kirby. "The Society of Friends and the family firm, 1700–1830." *Business History* 35, no. 4 (1993): 66–85.
Schwantes, Carlos A. *Vision & Enterprise: Exploring the History of Phelps Dodge Corporation* (Tucson: University of Arizona Press, 2000).
Socolow, Susan Migden. "Marriage, Birth, and Inheritance: The Merchants of Eighteenth-Century Buenos Aires." *The Hispanic American Historical Review* 60, no. 3 (1980): 387–406.
Tilly, Charles. "Trust networks in transnational migration." In *Sociological Forum*, vol. 22, no. 1, 3–24.
Wach, Howard M. "Unitarian philanthropy and cultural hegemony in comparative perspective: Manchester and Boston, 1827–1848." *Journal of Social History* (1993): 539–557.
Wilkins, Mira. *The emergence of multinational enterprise: American business abroad from the colonial era to 1914* (Cambridge, MA: Harvard University Press, 1970).
———, "Defining a firm: History and Theory." *Transnational Corporations: A Historical Perspective* 2 (1993).
———, "The History of Multinationals: A 2015 View." *Business History Review* 89, no. 3 (2015).

7

The Distant Shareholder: Attenuated Investment and the Diffusion of Social Concerns

Janette Rutterford

In *A Man of Property* (1906), the first novel of the *Forsyte Saga* which charts the fortunes and misfortunes of the Forsyte family, John Galsworthy commented:

> The historian of the English eighties and nineties will, in good time, depict the somewhat rapid progression from self-contented and contained provincialism to still more self-contented if less contained imperialism—in other words, the "possessive" instinct of the nation on the move.[1]

That "possessive" instinct—the instinct to know the value of everything and to acquire only that which would provide a decent return on investment—was demonstrated most strongly by the middle class in relation to the ownership of possessions, whether house property, works of art, stocks, or shares. This paper concentrates on the latter, for it was in

J. Rutterford (✉)
Open University, Milton Keynes, UK
e-mail: janette.rutterford@open.ac.uk

W.A. Pettigrew and D.C. Smith (eds.), *A History of Socially Responsible Business, c.1600–1950*, Palgrave Studies in the History of Finance,
DOI 10.1007/978-3-319-60146-5_7

the final decades of the nineteenth century that Britain became what Robb has termed a "nation of shareholders"—in the process of which the "possessive" instinct expanded from a regional and provincial to a national if not international scope of operations.[2] The kinds of shares held by investors, the kinds of companies in which they invested, and the kinds of individuals involved in such investments are the key elements in understanding the constituent elements of the rise of Britain as a shareholder nation.

Here, I explore these issues through the lens of geography, focusing on the relationship between distance, shareholding, and supply and demand for securities, both domestic and overseas. I examine the significance of shareholding in the population at large, and then look at what these investors bought—domestic, colonial, and foreign securities. Finally, I explore some of the implications that the geography of shareholding raises for understanding both individual investor behaviour and its impact on corporate governance.

To do this, I turn to two samples of shareholders, one derived from shareholder records, and covering more than 30,000 shareholders sampled from 223 share records of forty-seven companies registered in England over the period 1870 to 1935. The sample included seven companies with foreign operations, seven with colonial operations, and the remainder with domestic operations. The second sample is derived from the IR19 series on the valuation of property for the purposes of paying legacy, succession and estate duties levied at the time of death collected as part of an ESRC research project. The Residuary Accounts for the assessment of this tax that have survived provide detailed information on an individual's personal wealth at death.[3] The sample is a 100% sample of the 1446 individuals whose Residuary Accounts have been preserved and who died in England and Wales between 1870 and 1902.[4] Of the 1446, 515 held financial assets, of whom 508 had portfolios that could be analysed, as the files included descriptions of the investments held at death.[5]

Evidence of the growing significance of shares in wealth portfolios from the 1870s can be seen from a detailed analysis of the value of personal estates assessed for death duties from the 1870s to the 1900s, together with aggregate figures from 1901 drawn from Inland Revenue returns of estate duty. [6] The figures support Ranald Michie's assessment that, between 1850 and 1913, financial assets (albeit including mortgages, bank deposits, trade credit, and government and corporate debt as well as shares) rose from an estimated 39% to 64% of all assets owned by British people.[7] The increasing significance of financial securities, which rose from about 27% to 47% by value of all assets between the 1870s and 1890s, matched the rapid growth in the value of issued capital traded on the London Stock Exchange.[8]

The growing importance of financial securities within individual wealth portfolios and the increasing numbers of persons who held shares as part of their personal estate hint at a growing body of shareholders in the population at large. However, there is no agreement as to the number of shareholders at any point in this period. Early rough estimates of the number of "serious shareholders" in securities in the UK are 250,000 in 1870 and 1 million in 1914.[9] Clapham suggests that there were 900,000 railway and 300,000 bank shareholders by 1914.[10] However, there were no contemporary estimates of shareholder numbers in the UK. Company directors did, though, note their significant shareholder numbers. J. P. Coats had 25,000 shareholders as early as 1896. At the first annual general meeting of Thomas J. Lipton Limited, the tea company, in 1888, the chairman announced that there had been an enormous number of applications for shares, "as evidenced by the fact that there are now 74,000 shareholders". He believed "that this was the largest number of shareholders of any British industrial company".[11] Hannah estimates that circa 1900 for the UK, in addition to large industrial and commercial companies, four British banks and ten British railway companies already had more than 10,000 shareholders.[12]

The increase in the number of shareholders reflected several factors. First, there was the mere fact of demographic growth—the population of England and Wales increased by 10 million to 32 million between 1871 and 1901. Second, there was an improvement in the material standard of living and the availability of surplus capital for larger numbers of individuals. Until the inflationary pressures of the World War I, the retail price index hardly changed between 1870 and 1914 despite an overall increase in national income.[13] Third, from the later decades of the nineteenth century, the decline in middle-class family size—a feature that John Galsworthy in the *Forsyte Saga* rightly or wrongly linked to the falling rate of return on investments—meant that households had more income to invest across the life course.[14]

This increase is also consistent with what we know about supply side issues concerning the growth of opportunities to invest in shares. The early nineteenth-century Companies Acts facilitated company formation, and the introduction of general registration with limited liability through the Joint Stock Companies Act of 1856 made the possibility of investment in company shares less risky and hence more attractive. The dispersal of ownership, if not necessarily of control, was further encouraged by the Stock Exchange stipulation that, for securities to be quoted in the Official List, two-thirds had to be in public hands.[15] The wider dispersion of shareholding was further encouraged by the growing national integration of the securities market via the expansion of provincial stock exchanges, and the introduction of the telegraph and later of the telephone, all of which were accompanied by large increases in the volume of securities traded.[16] In addition, when limited liability became widespread in the banking system after the spectacular failure of the City of Glasgow Bank in 1878, the effect was to encourage a much wider set of mainly less-wealthy investors in bank shares.[17] Shares became available in lower denominations and hence more accessible to less affluent investors: between 1856 and 1866 nominal values of around £10 per share were common, but by 1900 a £1 nominal value was quite normal.[18] There were also important changes in the classes of shares that were offered. Preference shares and debenture stock, providing lower-risk alternatives to ordinary shares, were increasingly available. Between 1885 and 1895, Ann Essex-Crosby estimated that the importance of preference shares nearly doubled—rising from 12.2% to 22.4% of total capital, a trend maintained to the beginning of the twentieth century.[19] By 1900, the average capital structure for all companies listed in Burdett's Official Intelligence was only one-half the riskier ordinary shares, and the rest was in relatively low-risk preference shares or debentures. [20]

One example of the importance of women investors by the early twentieth century is that of Spratt's Patent whose chairman, at the 1903 annual general meeting, noted that, of the 1482 shareholders, there were 585 "ladies, who were generally investors and who were therefore, as a rule, preferable to those who bought the shares merely as a speculation".[21] Women as well as men attended annual general meetings and were not afraid of asking critical questions about the share price or dividend performance: "It is said that where women are serious investors, they are generally conscientious shareholders, attending the meetings of companies in which they are interested, taking intelligent interest in reports, and faithful in using their votes".[22] Women were also allowed to vote at AGMs, a privilege not accorded to any British women with regard to parliamentary voting until 1918. As Barbara Bodichon, George Eliot's closest female friend wrote: "a woman can take part in the government of a great empire by buying East India Stock".[23]

Rutterford et al. have documented the rise in importance of women investors in the nineteenth and twentieth centuries. In a study of 223 share registers of 47 UK-registered companies between 1870 and 1935, they found that women represented 15% by number and 5% by value in the 1870s, rising to over 45% by number and over 33% by value by the 1930s.[24] There are a number of reasons for this rise. First, there were a large number of single women, sometimes called "surplus" or "redundant" women, first noted in the census of 1851 and particularly prevalent in the upper classes, where primogeniture, and the use of trusts for intergenerational transfer of wealth, left many upper-class women lacking a sufficient dowry to tempt younger sons.[25] Marriage to someone of lower-social rank would have deprived such women of the social status to which they were accustomed. And many such women preferred to live from investment income rather than "engage in trade or business".[26] Second, the Married Women's Property Acts, passed in 1870 and 1882, gave married women similar rights to those of single women with regard to holding assets—including financial securities—in their own names. Before that, married women had been forced to hold securities through marriage settlements, with trustees in charge of investment decision-making, often investing only in so-called trustee stocks, which by 1900 consisted primarily of UK government and municipal securities, some railway fixed interest securities, and low-risk colonial stocks.[27]

Observers gradually became aware, as individuals increased their investment in stocks and shares, of the so-called democratisation of investors over this period. As Alexander Cairncross argued, early gentlemen and aristocratic investors in limited companies had, by the end of the nineteenth century, been joined by "retailers, professional men, skilled workers and women".[28] Ellis Powell, writing in 1919, commented on the characteristics of the early shareholders of Alamillos Company Ltd, incorporated in 1864. He found that the list consisted, except for one or two exceptions, of "very substantial holdings" by persons of "some position". He compared this list with the more dispersed list of the newly opened department store, Selfridge's. In the store's 1910 register, he found that shareholders included "a cabinet maker, a gas collector, a clerk, a nurse, a housekeeper, a school mistress and a governess", each of whom represented "a class of the community to whom investment was a word of unknown meaning and the process itself an unprobed mystery fifty years ago".[29] He argued that the change was due to education which "has been the radical influence, and a cheap press the main method of its operation".[30] As Dilwyn Porter has noted, the number of financial periodicals grew—from 19 in 1874 to 109 in 1914—boosted by cable communication, the growth in the number of limited liability companies, and the increased demand for prospectus advertising.[31] One new issue in 1899, for preference shares and debenture stock in a Thames shipbuilding company, received comment from no fewer than 48 national and regional newspapers.[32]

However, potential investors were not just targeted via the press. Numerous investment texts were aimed at the would-be investor.[33] In 1870, Chadwicks, a firm of accountants based in Manchester, began a monthly newsletter to prospective investors in envelopes marked "private and confidential", inviting "friends" to subscribe to the new issues discussed. By 1878, it is estimated that Chadwicks had 5000 contacts.[34] Company promoters in the 1880s and 1890s were able to use the services of professional mailing services. The first British mail order firm of G. Smith Dalby-Welch Limited, founded in 1868, listed 510,000 individual investors in Britain in its pamphlet *Finding the Buyer*, published in 1911.[35] The company compiled and collated *The Investors' Register* and was able to provide companies with lists of investors in different categories of companies, such as theatres and music halls or home railways. They were able to do this as companies were required to provide annual lists of shareholders to the Registrar of Companies, and these were available for public inspection. The names on the shareholder lists represented the "modern investing public, its personnel numbered by hundreds of thousands, and representing every class of society except the absolutely destitute".[36]

I now turn to the types of securities bought by investors, in particular, international securities. There was ample supply. The total nominal value of securities quoted on the London Stock Exchange increased by a factor of 4 from £2.2 billion to £8.8 billion in the thirty years to 1903, with government and municipal bonds representing 50%, railways a further 35% and other securities 15%.[37] At the same time, increasing numbers of foreign and colonial companies, in sectors such as rubber, gold mining, railways, and utilities were being registered in London and listed on the London Stock Exchange. By 1903, foreign bonds represented 33% of all issued capital, British bonds 12% and colonial bonds 5%. Foreign railways represented 19% of total issued capital and British railways a further 12%.

Overseas securities could appear more attractive as an alternative to safe British securities, such as trustee stocks. For example, the yield on Consols hovered close to 3% in the second half of the nineteenth century, dipping below 2.5% in 1894, and British railway debenture stock yielded around 3–4%, whereas empire and foreign fixed interest securities could yield 5% and, in many cases, much more.[38] Indian government bonds, in comparison, were considered to be as low risk as home government bonds, but offered a higher return. "The security of the Indian Government is scarcely, if at all, inferior to that of the British government itself; for where would be the prestige of the British name were we to allow our Indian empire to be wrested from us by any power whatever?"[39] Investors clearly agreed. Cairncross estimated that, as early as 1870, there were 50,000 investors in Indian Guaranteed railway securities, holding an average of nearly £1800 each.[40] As Daniel Thorner put it, "the capital which moved from England to India" under the guaranteed railway contract of 1849 "formed the largest single unit of international investment in the nineteenth century".[41] Other overseas government and municipal bonds were clearly riskier than British or colonial bonds, but offered highly attractive rates. For example, *Chadwicks* reported among new foreign issuers in London in 1870 the City of Boston, Massachusetts, offering 5% coupon at a price of 87% of par, Russia offering 5% at 80, and the Mississippi Bridge financing paying 7% and offered at 90; Japan came to the market for the first time in that year, with a 9% offering at 98.[42] Because all these bonds were priced *below* par, the effective yields were higher than the announced coupons. Such offers were very attractive in yield terms compared to British government bonds. They also offered investors the reassurance of fixed, regular payments. The only way to enhance return by buying domestic securities was to buy ordinary shares, which did not offer a fixed return and were liable to capital loss.

As these yield differentials widened towards the end of the century, investors sought alternative sources of income from other types of securities.[43] The range of such opportunities expanded rapidly between the 1870s and 1890s, as new parts of the world were being opened up for investment. For example, there were a series of mining booms in South America, India, and Australia, the last alone resulting in the formation of 500 new companies between 1886 and 1887.[44] During the early 1880s, and again between 1897 and 1909, returns on overseas companies generally outperformed those of domestic concerns.[45] Despite the greater risks involved in some of these ventures, there was enormous enthusiasm for such investments and by 1914, Britain's overseas lending of £20,000 million represented around 44% of total overseas investment worldwide.[46] Such internationalisation of investment was not confined to larger investors. Powell noted, in 1919, how "the small investor ventures, as he does now in ever-increasing numbers, into foreign bonds, colonial municipal securities, and even American public utility stocks".[47] And there was another reason for investing overseas: domestic politics. In 1908, a year before the People's Budget imposed a higher rate of tax on unearned income relative to earned income, Hartley Withers, future editor of the *Economist*, wrote in the *Financial Review of Reviews*: "Indeed, today, there is no section of the globe in which invested capital stands in such imminent peril as it does in England. In the present Parliament legislation has been largely confined to efforts to dis-endow the property-holder and to endow labour at capital's expense".[48]

The ability to invest a relatively small amount in each security through lower nominal values, and the increasing variety of securities available on the LSE as well as on provincial exchanges, allowed investors to improve yield, without increasing risk, by holding a portfolio of different securities—so-called diversification. In particular, commentators encouraged the inclusion of a number of foreign and colonial securities in British investor portfolios. For example, after acknowledging the British investor's preference for none but British securities, *Chadwicks' Investment Circular* argued, as early as 1870:

> We are now too much alive to our own interests to place our trust in Consols alone; for indeed the British government funds cannot accommodate a tithe of the money that is always pressing forward for investment. Moreover, railways, and even foreign stocks, have been found to pay better in the long run. We hold that, by a careful selection from the various media of investment, very remunerative returns in the shape of interest may be obtained; while, by a proper division of risks, not only may the *security* for the principal be rendered perfectly satisfactory, but there may be a good prospect that the invested capital will steadily increase in value.[49]

Similar advice was also offered in *Beeton's Guide to Investing Money with Safety and Profit*, published in the same year. "If an investor wishes to secure a high rate of interest, he should divide his capital among a number of stocks that can be bought to pay a high rate of interest—the more the better. Supposing he has £500 to invest, let him invest £100 in each of the following—Turkish, Italian, Spanish, Egyptian, Guatemalan, or Argentine. By dividing his capital in this way, the investor reduces risk to a minimum, as it is unlikely that all these countries could stop paying their interest, although it is not unlikely that any one might do so". Although appearing to limit investor choice to government bonds, *Beeton's Guide* allowed choice from a wide range of countries and types of security. The key point was that "it is only necessary to invest a small portion of the whole in a high dividend-paying stock to bring the rate up to 5% and that the greater part is invested in perfectly safe securities. The more the capital is divided the better, so that there may be a smaller amount in each security".[50]

A key development by 1900 was a more "scientific" approach to global portfolio diversification. Instead of adding as many risky securities as needed to generate the required yield, some investors began to realise that a more top-down approach to portfolio construction was desirable, targeting a particular level of yield, and minimising capital risk through the choice of relatively uncorrelated securities. This type of diversification was called Scientific Investment and was heavily promoted by the *Financial Review of Reviews*, a monthly magazine first published in 1905, and in textbooks such as *Investment: An Exact Science*, written by the magazine's editor, Henry Lowenfeld. Lowenfeld encouraged *full* global diversification by splitting the world into nine regions—British, British Colonial, North Europe, South Europe, Asia, Africa, North America, Central America, South America—as well as adding an "international" grouping made up of companies operating on a global scale: international trusts, shipping, telegraph, marine insurance, etc. Such proposals recommended investing in each region of the world, and in a variety of types of security in each region should funds permit, although preference shares and debentures were preferred to ordinary shares, the latter deemed more exposed to market volatility.[51]

The thinking behind full global coverage was that, overall, the global population was growing, as was international trade. A global portfolio would therefore reap the benefits of this growth, while if one country suffered, another would benefit: "the wider the distribution of one's capital in every respect … the less likelihood of becoming stranded financially, since only a worldwide catastrophe … could arise to affect adversely the whole of the world's securities at one time".[52] The attraction of global diversification was that it ensured that different types of risk were diversified away, improving the risk/return trade-off.

In terms of how much to invest in each security, the preferred number recommended for the private investors was ten securities, with equal amounts to be initially invested in each. This number tallied nicely with Lowenfeld's nine regions of the globe plus one "international" sector. However, some allowance was made for the amount of money to be invested: for example, Lowenfeld recommended holding five to six stocks for an investment of £500 to £1000 and eight to ten stocks for £5000 to £20,000.[53] There is also evidence that the Lowenfeld recommendations were put into practice. A firm founded by Lowenfeld in the late nineteenth century, the Investment Registry, both managed investor portfolios and offered advice to investors on how better to diversify internationally.[54]

There is thus ample evidence that shareholders were encouraged to include overseas companies in their portfolios, either as yield enhancers for a small proportion of their investment, or as part of a globally diversified portfolio where domestic and colonial stocks were in the minority. There was also specific support to invest in the "international" category, an early term for "multinationals".

Local stock exchanges flourished during the railway boom of the 1840s when the comprehensive geographic coverage of the railways attracted investors from all over the country. By 1885, the Phillips' Investors Manual was able to state that "the provincial stock exchanges are of almost greater importance in relation to home securities than London".[55] Many regional stock exchanges specialised in specific sectors—for example, Liverpool in insurance companies, and Manchester and Sheffield in iron and steel shares.[56] Chadwicks, the Manchester firm of accountants, actively promoted many of the larger iron and steel company flotations of the 1860s and 1870s, with a large number of Manchester people buying shares in the companies that Chadwicks promoted. Growth in the exchanges outside London was rapid. The number of commercial and industrial companies quoted on the Manchester Stock Exchange list more than tripled from 70 in 1885 to nearly 220 by 1906. The Newcastle Stock Exchange flourished in the 1890s with the flotation of shipbuilding companies such as Sir W. G. Armstrong Mitchell & Co.[57] New industries such as brewing, bicycles, cars, electricity, and gas all needed to raise new funds from whatever source they could, and the lower cost of raising money locally was attractive, in particular to relatively small companies.[58] In George Gissing's 1897 novel *The Whirlpool*, Harvey Rolfe, in order to pay for his wife's desire to be a concert violinist, sells his Consols and buys ordinary shares in a bicycle company, with disastrous results.[59]

Local investors played a crucial role in financing companies registered outside London and were involved in corporate governance, such as attending annual general meetings and voting on such issues as the annual dividend. For example, Jefferys has argued that local investors often knew the directors of the firms personally. This was particularly important in the early days of limited liability, when many shares were partly paid, with potential future calls; when high-nominal values prevented diversification across a number of shares; and when, as in the case of some bank shares, shareholders had unlimited liability.[60] Local investment was also encouraged when banks sold shares to potential clients and gas companies sold shares to customers.[61] One extreme example of such a local bias is the portfolio at death in 1902 of Susan Mullins, consisting entirely of shares with her native town in the title: Grantham Equitable Industrial Cooperative Society, Grantham Exchange Hall Company, Grantham Gas Company, Grantham Waterworks, Grantham Loan Company, Grantham Citadel Company, and Grantham Steam Laundry.

Rutterford et al. document this so-called local bias to investment, where investors preferred to buy securities of companies whose registered offices were close by. Such a local bias certainly existed. In a study of 223 share records of 47 companies registered in England and Wales for the period 1870 to 1935, they find that 40% of investors lived within 25 km of the company's registered office.[62] However, this local preference differed according to the type of security held: a higher proportion of ordinary shareholders preferred to live close to company HQ than did preference shareholders (34%), and this was also true for holders of private, unlisted company securities (49%).

One literary example of local bias is Arnold Bennett's *Anna of the Five Towns* published in 1902, which contains the following description of the portfolio of local securities that Anna's father had bought with his dead wife's inheritance, and which he was handing over to Anna on her twenty-first birthday:

> He was proud. They were the finest in the market, the aristocracy of investments, based on commercial enterprises of which every businessman in the Five Towns knew the entire soundness. They conferred

> distinction on the possessor, like a great picture or a rare volume. They stifled all questions and insinuations. Put before a jury of the Five Towns as evidence of character, they would almost have exculpated a murderer.[63]

This passage may capture the contemporary view of local investment. The father placed his trust in local firms for two separate reasons. First, he was as sure about their economic soundness as any other local businessman in the Five Towns (which were based on the pottery towns of the Midlands). This fits with the standard view in the economic history literature that investors tilted their portfolios towards local firms to protect themselves against significant market asymmetries and against related manipulation by insiders. At the same time, the passage reveals a possible second explanatory factor in local bias: local shares were also noteworthy assets. Their holders enjoyed social status and recognition in the context of shared norms and investment cultures.

Another reason for local bias may have been an element of local philanthropy. Out of a sample of 508 individual portfolios at death, we find 32 investors with 47 philanthropic corporate investments. These investments were in libraries, schools, university colleges, bowling clubs, and political clubs, as well as public meeting rooms. Fourteen investors—or just under one-third of those with philanthropic investments—held shares or debentures in Model Dwelling Companies, which built and managed homes for the working class and offered well-intentioned investors a slightly lower return than the market rate.[64] Overall, philanthropic investments had a market value of £17,000 compared to total portfolio wealth for the 508 investors in the sample of £1.4 million—a mere 1.2% of the total. One or two philanthropic investors in the sample stand out, with Edward James Herbert, Third Earl of Powis, previously MP for Shropshire, investing in six different charitable companies in his locality; but his average philanthropic investment was only £72 out of a portfolio worth more than £50,000. The wealthiest individual of all, Joshua Heap, worth over a quarter of a million pounds in shares alone, had only one charitable investment—a £10 joint-stock investment in his local bowling club. Two Church of England rectors invested philanthropically, one in St Leonards' Sussex School for Girls and the other holding £3500 or 7% of his portfolio in Model Dwelling Company securities. The most philanthropic investors, as a percentage of their investments, were Anne Morrison, worth £1200, of which £700 was in railway shares, £100 in an investment trust and fully one-third or £400 in a Model Dwelling Company; and Mary Main, whose only holding was £800 in Birkenhead School debenture stock. We know that George Eliot, who lived in London, invested £500 in Model Dwelling debenture stock in a portfolio worth over £27,000 in 1880, probably through her City-based adviser, John Walter Cross.[65] As Maltby and Rutterford argue, such philanthropy did not go unnoticed in the local community. Shareholder lists were often made public and philanthropists could advertise their generosity by attending annual general meetings and being involved in corporate governance.[66]

But there was a change over the period. Investors gradually began to live further and further from the companies in which they invested: the number living within 25 km of the company's registered office fell from 69% in the 1870s to just under 40% in the 1890s and 35% in the 1930s. This trend is particularly true for investors outside the London area. Non-Londoners had a high local bias initially—in the 1870s, 64.1% lived within 25 km, but this number fell to 38% by the 1910s and to only 16% by the 1930s. By contrast, Londoners exhibited a very high local bias that did not reduce over the period, ranging between 70% and 95% according to the decade. This data is based on a sample of over 33,000 investors listed in 261 different share records of forty-seven companies for the period 1870 through to 1935. The sample of forty-seven companies from seven different business sectors includes fifteen companies registered in London but with overseas operations, seven within the empire and eight in other countries. The remaining thirty-two companies had domestic operations.[67]

Investors living in provincial cities on the whole preferred domestic securities. Birmingham-, Liverpool- and London-based investors were the most outward-looking, with Londoners the most interested in empire stocks. Table 7.1 supports the anomaly pointed out in Davis and Huttenback that Lancashire investors, in this case Liverpool investors, had a relatively greater predilection for foreign securities than did, say, Manchester investors. The foreign companies in the sample are predominantly linked to Latin America, which had substantial shipping links with Liverpool. Also,

Table 7.1 Percentage of investors holding domestic, empire and foreign securities in selected cities

Company Type	Birmingham %	Bristol %	Glasgow %	Liverpool %	London %	Manchester %	Sheffield %
Domestic	84.2	91.6	26.5	76.2	58.6	87.3	96
Empire	4.4	2.5	10.6	7.1	23.6	4.4	1.4
Foreign	11.4	5.9	62.8	16.7	17.8	8.3	2.6
Total	100	100	100	100	100	100	100

Sample of 47 companies' shareholder records 1870 to 1935

more Scottish investors held foreign securities than those from any major city. This can partly be explained by the non-inclusion in our sample of Scottish-registered companies. Within London, there was also a geographic bias. Those based in London but not in the City (EC1) held almost 50% by value of the shares in colonial companies in the sample. For such investors, the north of England may have appeared more distant than the colonies.

Figure 7.1 shows the holdings in domestic, foreign, and empire shares in the sample, with London shareholders in two categories, EC1 and other. Figure 7.1 shows that non-Londoners in England represented 71% of shareholders for domestic companies, 48% for foreign companies, and 11% for empire stocks. The City concentrated on foreign and empire securities in almost equal numbers, but Londoners ex-City preferred empire to foreign shares. George Eliot is an example of an investor living in London but outside EC1. She conformed to the predilection for colonial securities. Her first security purchase was of £1900 nominal of Great Indian Peninsular Railway stock for £1825 which was guaranteed to pay 5% per annum dividend. From 1860, she took advantage of high-yielding colonial stocks, so that on her death in 1880, she had a portfolio with almost one-half invested in colonial securities, together with "international" stocks such as docks, and foreign investments in the USA and Brazil. Her only UK investments were Consols, shares in the Regent's Canal Company, some railway debentures, and Model Dwelling company debentures.[68]

Further evidence of overseas investment is provided by the investments of a sample of 508 individual portfolios at death for the period

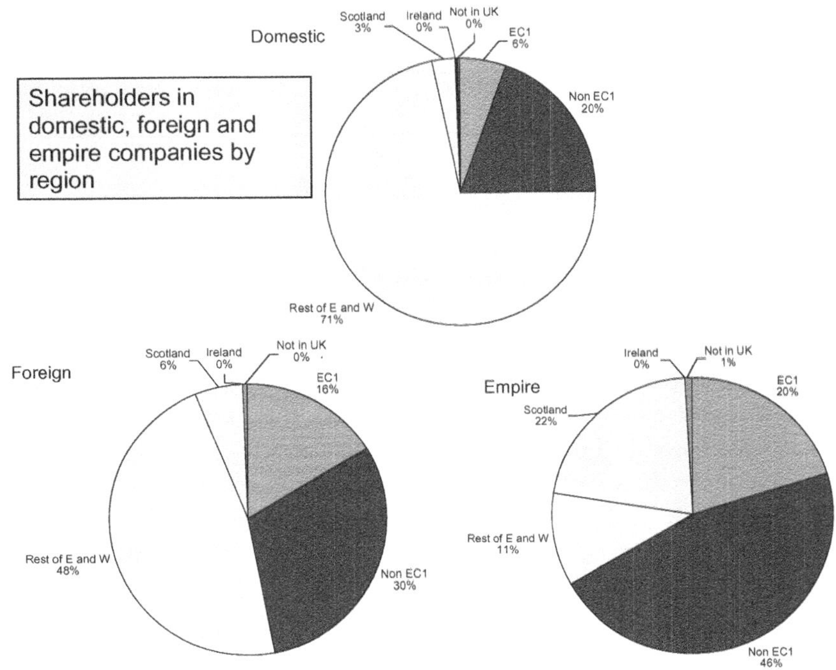

Fig. 7.1 Shareholders in domestic, foreign and empire companies by region
Source Sample of 47 companies' shareholder records 1870 to 1935

Table 7.2 International diversification by sub-period

	1870–1878	1879–1886	1887–1894	1895–1902	Total
No. of observations	155	115	121	117	508
Proportion of total financial portfolio wealth (%)					
UK government	32.2	24.1	11.6	27	22.1
UK corporate	40.1	50.4	62.4	41.5	50.5
UK securities	72.3	74.5	74	68.5	72.6
Colonial government	14.4	2.3	5.3	8.8	7.6
Colonial corporate	6.0	4.7	6.9	7.0	6.3
Colonial securities	20.4	7.0	12.2	15.8	13.9
Foreign government	4.3	10.0	3.2	3.4	4.8
Foreign corporate	3.0	8.0	10.6	12.0	8.5
Foreign securities	7.3	18.0	13.8	15.3	13.3

Sample of probate portfolios

1870 to 1902, as shown in Table 7.2.[69] For this sample, the level of overseas investment rose over time, from 21.2% to 27% in value terms over the period 1870–1902. In the final sub-period shown in Table 7.2, 1895–1902, UK investments amounted to 68.5% of the total by value, with foreign and colonial securities representing just over 15% each. Over the three decades to 1902, there was a decline in investment in Consols, as yields on Consols fell. At the same time, there was a fall in holdings of colonial and foreign government bonds and municipal stocks and a rise in foreign and colonial corporate securities, presumably yielding higher expected returns.

Over the period, there is clear evidence, as Audrey Jaffe has remarked, of "increasingly attenuated relationships between investors and the objects of their investments". From relatively large investments in companies close to home—with a typical portfolio including the local mill, railway, bank and factory—we find investor portfolios increasingly including more securities, held in smaller amounts, of companies that might be registered in the UK but whose activities were in far-off lands, where investors were unlikely to go. As a result, investors became dependent on the company directors and related experts to tell them what was going on.

Paul Delany also notes that there was a change in the type of rentier over this period. The first generation, discussed above, with local bias, was able to retire on money made from industry but still felt close enough to where the money had been made to be charitable, either buying not-for-profit securities or funding projects which they felt would increase social welfare, during their lifetime or on death. The second generation, Delany argues, had changed their views. Rentiers from birth, their preoccupation was not charity but culture. Henry James and Virginia Woolf epitomise this generation, but George Gissing in *The Odd Women* (1893) and *The Whirlpool* (1897), and E. M. Forster in *Howards End* (1910), expose its darker side. George Bernard Shaw, in his 1897 play *Widowers' Houses*, exposed the paradox of passive investment. The higher the return, <u>not</u> the higher the risk, then the more likely the activity was to be "immoral". In this play, the hero is faced with the dilemma of either living in poverty on £250 a year from—moral—British government bonds or being able to support a wife and children with £700 a year from an—immoral—investment based on extortionate rents on slum dwellings.

An alternative to investing in unethical local companies was to invest overseas, in colonial or foreign securities, which had a number of advantages. Investing in faraway places escaped the ethical dilemma highlighted in *Widowers' Houses*, achieved high returns, and enhanced social status. It also avoided increasing investment at home, which blighted the landscape and ruined the "rural idyll" promoted by artists such as William Morris. Delany argues that investing overseas reflected a "cultural aversion to the root and branch transformation of [domestic] society". Indeed, he argues that, for this second generation of investors, social status was "proportional to distance from reality".[70] Helen Schlegel in Forster's *Howards End*, and both Gissing and Forster in reality, were able to live cheaply on their unearned income in Italy for periods of time, with like-minded souls.

And money was paramount. Margaret Schlegel in *Howards End* sells her shares in Nottingham and Derby Railway, preferring to earn higher returns on "Foreign Things". Forster himself had shares in "Foreign Things", in his case, an Argentinian railway company, the British American Great Southern Railway. In *Howards End*, Margaret reflects on her finances: "You and I and the Wilcoxes stand upon money as upon islands. It is so firm beneath our feet that we forget its very existence".[71] She believed, as did Virginia Woolf, that "independent thoughts are in nine cases out of ten the result of independent means".[72] Henry Wilcox, though, gets his hands dirty, running the Imperial and West African Rubber Company, with his son, Paul, based in Nigeria, and feeling no qualms about cutting his overseas clerks' wages to improve the business's profitability.[73]

George Eliot's two stepsons went to Natal, where both died after failing to make a success of farming. For many young men, without social connections and unable to pass the Civil Service exams, the colonies appeared to be the only option and were considered to be "respectable". Trollope, who held South African bank shares which he bequeathed to his widow, had to provide financial assistance to his son, Fred, who got into financial difficulties farming sheep in Australia. Dickens urged his sons to emigrate.[74] These personal links made events in the colonies seem closer. And yet, the parents who sent their children abroad and invested in colonial stocks had little idea of the conditions their children would face.

There is some evidence that, despite these attenuated relationships, with investments in foreign and colonial ventures, investors did not completely disassociate themselves from the ethics of their investments. Forster admitted that he had been traumatised by Shaw's *Widowers'* Houses, feeling "hopeless" about investment thereafter.[75] After visiting South African mines in the early 1930s, he became an advocate for early ethical investing. Eliot commented after the second Afghan war of 1878–80 that it was a "black day for Indian finance, which means alas a great deal of hardship to poor Hindus". She had holdings in Indian securities but not in South Africa. After the death of her two stepsons, and of their father, and the forced return of a stepson's widow from Natal, she railed against the "wicked war" in South Africa and wrote, in correspondence with the editor of Blackwood's in relation to British losses against the Zulus, "we cannot afford either morally or physically to reform semi-civilized people at every point of the compass with blood and iron". Trollope also revised his earlier views on South Africa, critiquing in 1879 the perceived right of the British government to invade Zulu territory "because reforms have not been effected which we knew to have been impossible."[76]

As well as complaining privately and in print, investors could and did attend annual general meetings in large numbers, helped by accommodating boards of directors, who took note of where the shareholders lived when choosing the location of their meetings, and by the fact that most colonial and foreign companies listed on the London Stock Exchange held their meetings in London where the majority of their shareholders lived.

The British South Africa Company, chaired by Cecil Rhodes, held its meetings in London's Cannon Street Hotel, which held two thousand people, with hundreds more unable to gain access to its 1899 meeting. Indeed, Americans, in general, were impressed by British annual general meetings. In comparison, America's (and the world's) largest quoted corporation in 1899, Standard Oil, had fewer than 100 shareholders attending its annual general meetings.[77] The *Wall Street Journal* commented on the fact that British stockholders' meetings were often held in London, "in a hall that accommodates two thousand people and it is frequently crowded. There is always a good attendance. The questions are shrewd and searching, and woe betide the director who tries to evade them".[78]

Attendance at AGMs was helped by a substantial number of local investors for domestic industrials and by the dominance of London-based investors for foreign and empire companies with registered offices in London.[79] For those investors who lived relatively far away from the meetings, special transport could be laid on. For example, in the early twentieth century, the Midland Railway annual accounts included a list of special trains for shareholders from cities such as Manchester and London to Coventry, where the meetings were held. Free transport for railway shareholders was considered an early shareholder perk: one commentator suggested that investors in Irish railway stock did so in order to have a free annual trip to Dublin.[80]

Some meetings were so well attended that tickets had to be issued and police summoned to keep non-shareholders out. One example is that of the British South Africa Company at the Cannon Street Hotel in 1898, with Rhodes in attendance. Newspaper reports listed the presence of the wives and daughters of members of the board and how, after the meeting, Rhodes was cheered by those outside the meeting room who had not had a chance to show their approval in the meeting. With the British South Africa Company having 35,000 shareholders plus holders of share warrants to bearer, there were cries from the crowd suggesting only the Albert Hall would do for the next meeting.[81]

Records of annual general meetings show that the dialogue was not all one way. Although the chairman, usually chosen for his charm, held sway with the annual report, brave individuals dared to broach topics of social interest—either in writing before the meeting or verbally at the meeting. For overseas companies, particularly companies operating within the British Empire, these often related to employee conditions or, more generally, to "the native question".

For example, on the "native question", the chairman of Southern Mahratta, an Indian railway company, replied to shareholder concern expressed at the 1899 meeting about third-class overcrowding in trains by saying that he believed the company's treatment of third-class passengers was more considerate than that of any other company. A more extreme case was the British South Africa Company meeting of 1901 in which Rhodes referred to the:

> many letters from ladies and gentlemen who are deeply interested in the native question and the tone in them is that they have got the idea that I myself by the different positions I have held am extremely brutal towards the natives. It is one of those "good things" that have been started, and no one contradicts it. I am supposed to be a sort of "horror" in connection with the natives. To satisfy their minds I only say this—that the best judges are the natives themselves. I can put a record of the removal of the liquor from the natives of Pondoland, in the Kimberley compounds, and in the whole of Rhodesia.

The Rubber Shareholders' Association, formed in 1921, had a "crowded attendance" at its first AGM. The object of the Association was "to render the great body of shareholders articulate and to provide them, as it were, with a nerve centre".[82] One initiative was to attend the AGMs of all rubber companies listed on the LSE and ask the directors the same four questions relating to corporate governance and employee conditions. The chairman of KMS. (Malay States) Rubber Plantations, at the AGM of 27 November 1923, answered the questions before they were posed at the meeting. The first question was whether the company would be prepared to produce standardised accounts as recommended by the Rubber Shareholders' Association (RSA). The chairman of KMS refused. The second question was whether the company had any agency agreements and, if so, whether they would disclose details of them. The chairman of KMS said yes, they did have agreements, but details were confidential. The third and fourth questions related to remuneration, in particular whether manager and clerk remuneration had been reduced during the crisis, and whether directors had had their pay reduced or increased. The chairman complained that such questions implied that the board did not care about its staff. He then disclosed that all had had a reduction, directors as well as staff, and all had now returned to previous levels. The chairman also criticised the relevance of the RSA. With only 1910 members, he pointed out, how could the RSA represent the 223,000 individual investors in rubber companies of whom 193,000 lived in Britain and the remainder abroad. By 1927, the RSA had ceased to function. In the next year, a series of letters to the *Times* suggested the setting up of a general shareholders' association. A number of respondents criticised the suggestion, one arguing that it would be better to provide shareholder rights by company legislation, and another, an erstwhile member of the RSA, finding the "apathy of shareholders was absolutely heartbreaking".

This chapter has shown how both supply and demand for investment securities increased in the second half of the nineteenth century and the early decades of the twentieth century. In particular, there was increased demand for both foreign and colonial corporate securities. There is evidence of this in samples of shareholding records and probate files of estates at death within this period. However, the internationalisation of portfolios away from a bias towards local securities, some with a philanthropic role, meant a separation—both physical and mental—between the investors and the companies whose securities they held. As Jaffe and Delany have argued, and as Eliot, Forster and Gissing, among others, showed in their novels, by the twentieth-century rentiers preferred on the whole not to face awkward questions as to the ethics of their investments. However, there is evidence, in particular with respect to empire securities that some investors felt an emotional link as family members emigrated to make a new life. Investors also showed some concern for local employees and "the native question" at annual general meetings and in correspondence, but ethical investment as we understand it, although raised as an issue by GB Shaw as early as the 1890s, does not seem to have had a major impact on the search for higher yield through international investment.

Notes

1. John Galsworthy, *The Forsyte Saga, Volume I: The Man of Property* (Wordsworth Ware, 2001, first published 1906), 293.

2. George Robb, "Ladies of the Ticker: Women, Investment, and Fraud in England and America, 1850–1930", in *Victorian Investments: New Perspectives on Finance and Culture*, ed. Nancy Henry and Cannon Schmitt (Bloomington and Indianapolis: Indiana University Press, 2009).
3. IR19 Board of Stamps: Legacy Duty Office and successors: Specimens of Death Duty Account, 1796–1903, The National Archives, Kew, UK. The data were collected as part of ESRC research project RES-000-23-1435. The methodology behind the data collection and the characteristics of the data sample are more fully described in Janette Rutterford, Josephine Maltby, David R. Green, and Alastair Owens, "Researching shareholding and investment in England and Wales: approaches, sources and methods", *Accounting History* 14 (2009): 269–292. For further discussion and analysis of this data sample see: David R. Green, Alastair Owens, Claire Swan, and Carry van Lieshout, "*Assets of the Dead: Wealth, Investment, and Modernity in Nineteenth- and Early Twentieth-Century England and Wales*", in *Men, Women and Money*, ed. David R. Green et al. (Oxford: Oxford University Press, 2011), 54–80. See also David R. Green, Alastair Owens, Josephine Maltby, and Janette Rutterford, "Lives in the Balance? Gender, Age and Assets in Late-Nineteenth-Century England and Wales," *Continuity and Change* 24, no. 2 (2007): 307–35.
4. This figure reflects the total number of records preserved in the IR19 series which ends in 1902. This was a small proportion of the total actually submitted, the remainder having been destroyed. However, the sample itself appears to be representative of the broader population from which it was drawn.
5. This research was made possible by an Economic and Social Research Council Grant "Women Investors inEngland and Wales, 1870–1930", award no. RES-000-23-1435.We thank Steven Ainscough, Carry van Lieshout,Carien van Mourik, and Claire Swan for their first-rate research assistance and Marian Nicolson for her help withbuilding, maintaining, and querying the project's database.
6. However, the Inland Revenue statistics exclude freehold property not sold at death. The data are market values.
7. Ranald Michie, *The London Stock Exchange: A History* (Oxford: Oxford University Press, 1999), 71.
8. Michie, *The London Stock Exchange*, 71.

9. Cited in Ranald Michie, *The London and New York Stock Exchanges, 1850–1914* (Abingdon: Routledge, 2011), 118n67.
10. John Clapham, *An Economic History of Modern Britain, Machines and National Rivalries, 1887–1914* (Cambridge: Cambridge University Press, 1938).
11. *Economist*, June 4, 1888, 847.
12. Leslie Hannah, "The Divorce of Ownership from Control from 1900 onwards recalibrating imagined global trends", *Business History* 49 (2007): 412.
13. See Chris Cook and John Stevenson, *The Longman Handbook of Modern British History, 1714–1995* (London: Addison Wesley Longman, 1996), 187.
14. John Galsworthy, *Forsyte Saga*, 1922.
15. Hannah, "Divorce of Ownership", 414–16.
16. See Ranald Michie, "The London Stock Exchange and the British securities market, 1850–1914", *Economic History Review*, 38 (1985): 74.
17. Graeme Acheson and John Turner, "The death blow to limited liability in Victorian Britain: The City of Glasgow failure", *Explorations in Economic History*, 45 (2008): 235–53; John Turner, "Wider share ownership? Investors in English and Welsh bank shares in the nineteenth century", *Economic History Review*, 62 (2009): 176–77.
18. J. B. Jefferys, *Business organization in Great Britain 1856–1914* (New York, 1977), 161.
19. Ann Essex-Crosby, "Joint Stock Companies in Great Britain 1890–1930" (unpublished thesis, University of London, 1938), 31; see also Philip Cottrell, *Industrial Finance 1830–1914* (London and New York: Methuen, 1980), 86–88; Jefferys, *Business Organisation*, 458, Appendix E.
20. Jeffreys, *Business Organisation*, 458, Appendix E.
21. *Economist*, March 14, 1903, 477. The greater predilection by male investors compared to female investors to speculate still persists today. See, for example, Brad Barber and Terrance O'Dean, "Boys Will Be Boys: Gender, Overconfidence, and Common Stock Investment", *Quarterly Journal of Economics* 116, no. 1 (2001): 261–92.
22. See John Sears, *The New Place of the Stockholder* (New York: Harper & Brothers, 1929), 150; *Economist*, March 14, 1903; Louise Creighton, "Women and Finance", *Financial Review of Reviews* 59 (1910): 18–19. For a further discussion of annual general meetings in the USA and

the UK from 1890 to 1970, see Janette Rutterford, "The Shareholder Voice: British and American Accents 1890–1965", *Enterprise & Society* 13, no. 1 (2012): 120–53.

23. Barbara Bodichon, cited in Nancy Henry, *George Eliot and the British Empire* (Cambridge: Cambridge University Press, 2002).
24. Rutterford et al., "Who Comprised".
25. Anthony Trollope created a series of unmarried sisters and daughters in his novels. For example, the De Courcy sisters *in Framley Parsonage* and *The Small House at Allington*, Sir Marmaduke Rowley's eight daughters and Hugh Stanbury's two sisters in *He Knew He Was* Right, Lord Fawn's seven unmarried sisters in *The Eustace Diamonds*, and Frederic Aylmer's elder sister in *The Belton Estate* (Janette Rutterford and Josephine Maltby, "Frank Must Marry Money: Men, Women, and Property in Trollope's Novels", *Accounting Historians Journal* 33, no. 2 (2006): 169–99).
26. Creighton, "Women and Finance", 18–19.
27. The laws were complex but, in general terms, by 1884, they permitted investments only in safe British and colonial government stocks, in mortgages, and (for trusts subject to Scottish law only) in British and colonial municipal stocks, UK railway debentures and some safe preference shares (defined as those of railways whose ordinaries had paid a dividend for the last ten years). By 1914 the only permitted *company* investments were some (mainly colonial) businesses with state guarantees, and some debentures and preference shares of private sector *domestic* water and railway companies (again those defined as safe by having that 10-year track record of paying ordinary dividends). No full-fledged equities (that is no ordinary shares, save for the special cases of Bank of England and Bank of Ireland stocks) were permitted.
28. Alexander Cairncross, *Home and Foreign Investment, 1870–1930* (Cambridge: Cambridge University Press, 1953), 85.
29. Ellis Powell, *The Mechanism of the City* (London: P. S. King & Son, 1910), 127.
30. Ellis Powell, "The Democratisation of Investment", *Financial Review of Reviews* September 1919, 244.
31. See Dilwyn Porter, "'Trusted Guide of the Investing Public': Harry Marks and the *Financial News* 1884–1916", *Business History* 28 (1986): 1. These figures do not include the "bucket shop", which were

newspapers that had largely disappeared by the 1890s. See also Jefferys, *Business Organisation*, 355.

32. Applications for listing, Press Cuttings File, MS19096, Guildhall Library.
33. Janette Rutterford and Josephine Maltby, "'The Widow, the clergyman and the reckless': Women investors in England, 1830–1914", *Feminist Economics* 12, no. 1–2 (2006): 123–25.
34. Jefferys, *Business Organisation*, 318.
35. G. Smith Dalby-Welch Limited, *Finding the Buyers* (London Guildhall Library, Pamphlet 21957).
36. In Ellis Powell, *The Mechanism* (quoted in Porter, *Trusted Guide*, 1).
37. Victor Morgan and W. A. Thomas, *The Stock Exchange* (London: Elek Books, 1962), Appendix V.
38. Jan Tore Klovland, "Pitfalls in the estimation of the yield on British consols, 1850–1914", *Journal of Economic History* 54 (1994): 184–85; Richard Grossman, "New indices of British equity prices," *Journal of Economic History* 62 (2002): 136. For a discussion on the relative yields of domestic and overseas securities listed on the London Stock Exchange, see, for example, Michael Edelstein, *Overseas Investment in the Age of High Imperialism: The United Kingdom, 1850–1914* (New York: Columbia University Press, 1982), and Lance Davis and Robert Huttenback, "The political economy of British imperialism: measures of benefit and support", *Journal of Economic History* 42 (1982): 125.
39. *Chadwicks'* Investment Circular 1870, 52.
40. Henry, *George Eliot*, 78.
41. Daniel Thorner, cited in Henry, *George Eliot* [PAGE].
42. *Chadwicks'* Investment Circular 1871, 38.
43. On advice regarding home and foreign investment, see Desmond Platt, "British portfolio investment overseas before 1870: some doubts", *Economic History Review* 33 (1980): 8–9. See also William Goetzmann and Andrey Ukhov, "British investment overseas 1870–1913: a modern portfolio theory approach", *Review of Finance* 10 (2006): 261–300.
44. Essex-Crosby, *Joint stock Companies*. 35. See also Jean Jacques Van Helten, "Mining, Share Manias and Speculation: British Investment in Overseas Mining. 1880–1913", in *Capitalism in a Mature Economy: Financial Institutions, Capital Exports and British Industry 1870–1939*, ed. Jean Jacques Van Helten and Youssef Cassis (London: Aldershot, 1990), 159–85.

45. Michael Edelstein, "Realized rates of return of UK home and overseas portfolio investment in the age of high imperialism", *Explorations in Economic History* 13 (1976): 312.
46. Sidney Pollard, "Capital exports, 1870–1914: harmful or beneficial?", *Economic History Review* 38 (1985): 492.
47. Powell, "*The democratisation*", 251.
48. Henry Withers, "The best market for capital", *Financial Review of Reviews* 36(1908): 38.
49. *Chadwicks'* Investment Circular 1870, 30–1.
50. Samuel Beeton, *Beeton's Guide to the Stock Exchange and Money Market* (London, 1870), 26, 54.
51. J. B. Crozier, *Notes on the First Principles of Investment* (London: Financial Review of Reviews, 1910).
52. Stacey, *Stacey's Guide to Stock Exchange investment* (London, 1923), 38–39.
53. Henry Lowenfeld, *Investment: An Exact Science* (London: Financial Review of Reviews, 1907), 85. See James Foreman-Peck and Leslie Hannah, "Extreme divorce: The managerial revolution in UK companies before 1914", *Economic History Review* 65, no. 4 (2012): 1217–38.
54. Janette Rutterford and Dimitris P. Sotiropoulos, "Individual Investors and Portfolio Diversification in late Victorian Britain. How Influential Were Early Diversification Ideas?" *European Journal of the History of Economic Thought* 23, no. 6 (2016), 919–45.
55. Cited in William Thomas, *The Provincial Stock Exchanges* (London: Frank Cass, 1973), 114.
56. Thomas, *The Provincial*, 119, 123–24.
57. Thomas, *The Provincial*, 119, 123–24.
58. For example, see A. E. Harrison, "Joint-Stock Company Flotation in the Cycle, Motor-Vehicle and Related Industries, 1882–1914," *Business History* 23, no. 2 (1981): 165–90; and Katherine Watson, "The New Issue Market," *on the brewing industry.*
59. Paul Delany, *Literature, Money and the Market* (London: Palgrave Macmillan, 2002), 7, 127.
60. Jefferys, *Business Organisation*, 172–5. For a more detailed discussion of possible reasons for local bias, see Janette Rutterford, Dimitris P. Sotiropoulos, and Carry Van Lieshout, "Individual investors and local bias in the UK, 1870 to 1935", *Economic History Review*, forthcoming.

61. Lucy Newton and Philip Cottrell, "Joint-Stock Banking in the English Provinces 1826–1857: To branch of not to branch", *Business and Economic History* 27, no. 1 (1998): 117. For example, Dr Carpenter, Chairman of the South Metropolitan Gas Company, in evidence to the Committee on Profit-Sharing and Labour Co-Partnership in the UK, 1919, reported that they actively encouraged customers to buy shares in small amounts and had done so for all new issues during the last 25 or 30 years. Cited in Rutterford et al. "Who comprises", 10.
62. Rutterford et al., "Individual Investors".
63. Arnold Bennett, *Anna of the Five Towns* (London, 1902), 46.
64. For more information on model dwelling companies and local philanthropy, see Josephine Maltby and Janette Rutterford, "Investing in charities in the nineteenth century: The financialization of philanthropy", *Accounting History Review* 21 (2016): 263–80.
65. Henry, *George Eliot.*
66. Maltby and Rutterford, "Philanthropy".
67. For further information on the sample, see Appendix 2 of Janette Rutterford et al., "Who comprises". This sample was collected with the ESRC grant, RES-000-23-1435.
68. Henry, *George Eliot.*
69. For further information on the probate sample, see Rutterford et al., "Who comprises". For a more detailed analysis of the probate sample's international diversification, see Rutterford and Sotiropoulos, "Portfolio diversification".
70. Delany, *Literature*, 136.
71. E. M. Forster, *Howards End, 1910* (London: Edward Arnold, 1973), 11–12, 58.
72. Cited in Delany, *Literature*, 134.
73. Cited in Delany, *Literature*, 175.
74. Delany, *Literature*, 133
75. Henry, *George Eliot* [PAGE?].
76. Cited in Henry, *George Eliot*, 425.
77. Hannah, "Divorce of ownership", 418.
78. See Sears, *The New Place*, 150.
79. For further discussion of the location of shareholders in England and Wales, Rutterford et al. "Individual investors".
80. *The Economist*, 30 March 1929, 691.

81. In a separate paragraph, after the report on the British South Africa Company meeting, the management of the Cannon Street Hotel published an apology to those shareholders and directors due to meet in other rooms in the hotel and who had been unable to enter the building due to the crowds. *Times*, 28 April 1898, 13.
82. *Times*, 28 November 1923, 20.

References

Acheson, Graeme, and John Turner. "The Death Blow to Limited Liability in Victorian Britain: The City of Glasgow Failure." *Explorations in Economic History* 45 (2008): 235–53.

Barber, Brad, and Terrance O'Dean. "Boys Will Be Boys: Gender, Overconfidence, and Common Stock Investment." *Quarterly Journal of Economics* 116, no. 1 (2001): 261–92.

Beeton, Samuel. *Beeton's Guide to the Stock Exchange and Money Market.* London: Ward, Lock and Tyler, 1870.

Bennett, Arnold. *Anna of the Five Towns.* London: Chatto & Windus, 1902.

Cairncross, Alexander. *Home and Foreign Investment, 1870–1930.* Cambridge: Cambridge University Press, 1953.

Clapham, John. *An Economic History of Modern Britain, Machines and National Rivalries, 1887–1914.* Cambridge: Cambridge University Press, 1938.

Cook, Chris, and John Stevenson. *The Longman Handbook of Modern British History, 1714–1995.* London: Addison Wesley Longman, 1996.

Cottrell, Philip. *Industrial Finance 1830–1914.* London: Methuen, 1980.

Creighton, Louise. "Women and Finance." *Financial Review of Reviews* 59 (1910).

Crozier, J. B. *Notes on the First Principles of Investment.* London: Financial Review of Reviews, 1910.

Davis, Lance E., and Robert A. Huttenback. "The Political Economy of British Imperialism: Measures of Benefit and Support." *Journal of Economic History* 42 (1982): 119–30.

Delany, Paul. *Literature, Money and the Market.* London: Palgrave Macmillan, 2002.

Edelstein, Michael. "Realized Rates of Return of UK Home and Overseas Portfolio Investment in the Age of High Imperialism." *Explorations in Economic History* 13, no. 3 (1976): 283–330.

Edelstein, Michael. *Overseas Investment in the Age of High Imperialism: The United Kingdom, 1850–1914*. New York: Columbia University Press, 1982.

Essex-Crosby, Ann. "Joint Stock Companies in Great Britain 1890–1930." Unpublished thesis, University of London, 1938.

Foreman-Peck, James, and Leslie Hannah. "Extreme Divorce: The Managerial Revolution in UK Companies Before 1914." *Economic History Review* 65, no. 4 (2012): 1217–38.

Forster, E. M. *Howards End*. 1910. Reprint, London: Edward Arnold, 1973.

Galsworthy, John. *The Forsyte Saga, Volume I: The Man of Property*. 1906. Reprint, Ware: Wordsworth, 2001.

Goetzmann, William, and Andrey Ukhov. "British Investment Overseas 1870–1913: A Modern Portfolio Theory Approach." *Review of Finance* 10 (2006): 261–300.

Green, David R., Alastair Owens, Josephine Maltby, and Janette Rutterford. "Lives in the Balance? Gender, Age and Assets in Late-Nineteenth-Century England and Wales." *Continuity and Change* 24, no. 2 (2007): 307–35.

Green, David R., Alastair Owens, Claire Swan, and Carry van Lieshout. "Assets of the Dead: Wealth, Investment, and Modernity in Nineteenth- and Early Twentieth-Century England and Wales." In *Men, Women and Money*, edited by David R. Green, Janette Rutterford and Josephine Maltby, 54–80. Oxford: Oxford University Press, 2011.

Grossman, Richard. "New Indices of British Equity Prices, 1870–1913." *Journal of Economic History* 62, no. 1 (2002): 121–46.

Harrison, A. E. "Joint-Stock Company Flotation in the Cycle, Motor-Vehicle and Related Industries, 1882–1914." *Business History* 23, no. 2 (1981): 165–90.

Van Helten, Jean Jacques. "Mining, Share Manias and Speculation: British Investment in Overseas Mining, 1880–1913." In *Capitalism in a Mature Economy: Financial Institutions, Capital Exports and British Industry 1870–1939*, edited by Jean Jacques Van Helten and Youssef Cassis, 159–85. London: Aldershot, 1990.

Henry, Nancy. *George Eliot and the British Empire*. Cambridge: Cambridge University Press, 2002.

Jefferys, J. B. *Business Organization in Great Britain 1856–1914*. New York: Ayer, 1977.

Hannah, Leslie. "The 'Divorce' of Ownership from Control from 1900 Onwards: Recalibrating Imagined Global Trends." *Business History* 49, no. 4 (2007): 404–38.

Klovland, Jan Tore. "Pitfalls in the Estimation of the Yield on British Consols, 1850–1914." *Journal of Economic History* 54, no. 1 (1994): 164–87.

Lowenfeld, Henry. *Investment: An Exact Science*. London: Financial Review of Reviews, 1907.

Maltby, Josephine, and Janette Rutterford. "Investing in Charities in the Nineteenth Century: The Financialization of Philanthropy." *Accounting History Review* 21, no. 2–3 (2016): 263–80.

Michie, Ranald. "The London Stock Exchange and the British Securities Market, 1850–1914." *Economic History Review* 38 (1985): 61–82.

———. *The London Stock Exchange: A History*. Oxford: Oxford University Press, 1999.

———. *The London and New York Stock Exchanges, 1850 to 1914*. Abingdon: Routledge, 2011.

Morgan, Victor, and W. A. Thomas. *The Stock Exchange*. London: Elek Books, 1962.

Newton, Lucy, and Philip Cottrell. "Joint-Stock Banking in the English Provinces 1826–1857: To Branch or Not to Branch." *Business and Economic History* 27, no. 1 (1998): 115–28.

Platt, Desmond. "British Portfolio Investment Overseas Before 1870: Some Doubts." *Economic History Review* 33, no. 1 (1980): 1–16.

Pollard, Sidney. "Capital Exports, 1870–1914: Harmful or Beneficial?" *Economic History Review* 38, no. 4 (1985): 489–514.

Porter, Dilwyn. "'Trusted Guide of the Investing Public': Harry Marks and the *Financial News* 1884–1916." *Business History* 28, no. 1 (1986), 1–17.

Powell, Ellis. *The Mechanism of the City*. London: P. S. King & Son, 1910.

———. "The Democratisation of Investment." *Financial Review of Reviews*, September 1919.

Robb, George. "Ladies of the Ticker: Women, Investment, and Fraud in England and America, 1850–1930." In *Victorian Investments: New Perspectives on Finance and Culture*, edited by Nancy Henry and Cannon Schmitt, 120–40. Bloomington and Indianapolis: Indiana University Press, 2009.

Rutterford, Janette. "The Shareholder Voice: British and American Accents 1890–1965." *Enterprise & Society* 13, no. 1 (2012): 120–53.

Rutterford, Janette, and Josephine Maltby. "Frank Must Marry Money: Men, Women, and Property in Trollope's Novels." *Accounting Historians Journal* 33, no. 2 (2006): 169–99.

Rutterford, Janette, and Josephine Maltby. "'The Widow, the Clergyman and the Reckless': Women Investors in England, 1830–1914." *Feminist Economics* 12, no. 1–2 (2006): 111–38.

Rutterford, Janette, Josephine Maltby, David R. Green, and Alastair Owens. "Researching Shareholding and Investment in England and Wales: Approaches, Sources and Methods." *Accounting History* 14, no. 3 (2009): 269–92.

Rutterford, Janette, and Dimitris P. Sotiropoulos. "Individual Investors and Portfolio Diversification in Late Victorian Britain: How Influential Were Early Diversification Ideas?" *European Journal of the History of Economic Thought* 23, no. 6 (2016): 919–45.

Rutterford, Janette, Dimitris P. Sotiropoulos, and Carry Van Lieshout. "Individual Investors and Local Bias in the UK, 1870 to 1935." *Economic History Review* (forthcoming).

Sears, John. *The New Place of the Stockholder*. New York: Harper & Brothers, 1929.

Stacey, Herbert. *Stacey's Guide to Stock Exchange Investment*. London: The Basing Syndicate, 1923.

Thomas, William. *The Provincial Stock Exchanges*. London: Frank Cass, 1973.

Turner, John. "Wider Share Ownership? Investors in English and Welsh Bank Shares in the Nineteenth Century." *Economic History Review* 62, no. S1 (2009), 167–92.

Withers, Henry. "The Best Market for Capital." *Financial Review of Reviews* 36 (1908).

8

Canadian Regional and National Business Elites in 1912: Who Was Connected, Who Wasn't and Why?

Jon Mackay

Economic models often assume an individual's unfettered pursuit of private profit with a corresponding disregard for the public interest. Counter to this, economic sociologists have found that corporate leaders develop shared interests that often lead to the pursuit of their own class interests.[1] This implies that communities of businesspeople may, consciously or not, advocate and perpetuate conditions that ultimately affect a wider public's interests. One of the ways to understand these shared interests is to examine the networks linking corporate directors to one another. Earlier work has examined the demographic characteristics of Canadian business elites at the turn of the twentieth century, but there has been little focus on how their business ties spanned the nation and on the implications this network had for business development.

Using the *Directory of Directors in Canada* published in 1912, I recreate the national network of business elites and their ties to one another.

J. Mackay (✉)
Department of History, Wilfrid Laurier University, 75 University Avenue West, Waterloo N2L 3C5, Ontario, Canada
e-mail: jon.mackay@gmail.com

W.A. Pettigrew and D.C. Smith (eds.), *A History of Socially Responsible Business, c.1600–1950*, Palgrave Studies in the History of Finance,
DOI 10.1007/978-3-319-60146-5_8

I find that most growing urban centres throughout Canada generally maintained business connections with executives in Montreal or Toronto—the country's major financial and business centres. I also find an important exception to this pattern: the ethnically German city of Berlin in Waterloo County, Ontario, had few connections to the existing Anglo-Canadian business elites. This was true even though the city was a significant manufacturing centre in Canada located very close to Toronto. For the most part, it appears that the Berlin business community operated outside the dominant Anglo-Canadian business networks. Taken together, the Anglo-Canadian business community and the Berlin business community offer an instructive look at the social assumptions often underlying private business relationships and the ways in which the interests of different publics may or may not be served by these relationships.[2]

This paper develops the theme of connectedness between Canadian business elites. Based on the fact that the joint-stock company was the dominant form of successful business of the age, I examine how businesspeople are related to one another by the boards on which they serve. Early research concerned with these so-called corporate interlocks considered them to be indicators of potential collusion between corporations that planned to act against the public interest.[3] Modern management scholars often prefer to frame corporate interlocks mainly as sources of strategic information.[4] Concerns about interlocks as a means to facilitate collusion continue to be an important concern for researchers.[5] These concerns are not simply academic; some of the largest companies in America have recently been shown to have made collusive agreements, and their agreements appear to have been organized, at least in part, through common board appointments.[6] Corporate board interlocks have also been used to help determine the extent of ownership and control of corporate pyramids—groups of firms that are in effect controlled by a single person or family.[7]

The main purposes of this paper are as follows. First, I broadly outline the business relationships that existed between Canadian regions in 1912, paying close attention not only to the business ties between regions, but also to the ethnic composition of those regions. Second, I examine the board interlocks that exist between businesspeople and compare those that are prominent in their local business networks to those that are nationally prominent. I find evidence consistent with there being a hierarchical network built around the two major cities of Toronto and Montreal. Most urban regions maintain a series of business ties to one or both of these regions. The final section of the paper details a manufacturing city that was not part of this business hierarchy.

Waterloo County and its county seat of Berlin, Ontario, has few ties to either Toronto or Montreal despite its relative proximity to these regions. In fact, the region maintains a similar number of ties as cities that are over 3500 km away from Toronto, such as Calgary and Vancouver. To explain this result, I hypothesize that the regional elites of this region looked inward. They chose to work together and align the city of Berlin's public policies in ways to aid regional businesses, instead of accessing resources through the existing network of Anglo-Canadian business elites.

By looking inward, local business leaders forewent the advantages that presumably accrued to those with strong connections to the Anglo-Canadian business elites. Instead, local businesses relied on the goodwill of more established local businessmen to invest in new businesses. Over time, business elites and the city also invested in public goods in the form of public utilities. City policies to invest in businesses and offer tax breaks were also helpful. While these tax breaks were taken advantage of by local businessmen (who were also sometimes local politicians), these transgressions were not sufficient to deplete the city's resources. It appears that monitoring by the general public of peer businesspeople, and the knowledge that the region was at a relative disadvantage, ensured that no single individual took too much advantage of the regional common resources.

In summary, a variety of regional public policies (even though improperly administered), coupled with local businesses reinvesting in the area and in other businesses, helped local businesses to grow and thrive. This regional growth happened despite largely operating outside of the dominant Anglo-Canadian business hierarchy.

This research relies upon the *Directory of Directors in Canada* as a source for corporate elites. The *Directory* is an alphabetical list of the names of directors and managers followed by each individual's address as well as the companies they were currently serving with and their position in the firm.[8] This list was digitized, edited for typographic errors and parsed using a computer program to generate a network relating individuals and the firms with which they worked. Using this information, the 1912 network of business elites in Canada can be constructed in two ways. The first is to create a network of directors by relating individuals to one another based on whether they served with the same company. Individuals who sat on the same board together are nodes in the network and a line connecting them represents their relationship. The second network approach is to represent corporations as nodes in a network and then to relate these by the individuals that served with multiple corporations simultaneously.

The next step was to geolocate individuals and firms. The *Directory of Directors* gives the addresses of all the directors of companies. I resolved these locations using Open Street Map and Google's mapping API.[9] Careful attention was paid to ensure that locations were resolved properly, especially in cases where the names of locations have changed. (e.g. the city of Berlin was changed to Kitchener during World War II, so the lookups had to account for this.) I inferred the locations of company head offices using the common location of the majority of directors. This simple heuristic was successful in locating most companies properly. However, the locations of corporations were also manually reviewed in order to find incorrectly located firms. I paid special attention to cases where there was no clear majority of directors from a single region.

The result of the geolocation process was to search against a geographic place name and receive a latitude–longitude pair for each individual director/manager or a corporation's headquarters. To resolve this geographic point, an electronic map (GIS shapefile) available from the government of Canada's open data website was used to locate the point within the bounds of the surrounding 1911 census division.[10] The result is that firms are consistently gathered into the appropriate geographical region so that the regional characteristics of the population can be related to corporations from the period. In this study, when a city name is used, any results discussed refer to the census division from 1911 in which the city was located. Figure 8.1 shows a map of

Fig. 8.1 Map of the locations of individuals listed in the "Directory of Directors of Canada" from 1912. Nodes represent individuals and edges are boards of companies individuals sat on

North America and the locations of directors. Different colours represent Canadian provinces. All directors outside Canada are coloured grey.

Library and Archives Canada (LAC) made the 1911 census information available. LAC provided the raw census data that made it possible to determine the ethnic origin of the population in Canada at the census division level. However, the census data available from 1911 is limited. No information is available about the ethnic origin of people within different census divisions in Quebec. Information is nonetheless available for the rest of Canada.

Some note should also be made of the limitations and biases of the *Directory of Directors*. The *Directory of Directors* was compiled and published by W. R. Houston. Houston had a "close and complementary" relationship with the Toronto Stock Exchange.[11] He served as an assistant secretary of the exchange between the 1920s and 1930s.

His offices were located nearby and eventually were housed within the exchange building. Thus, it is not unreasonable to assume that Houston had detailed information about which firms were listed on the exchange as well as its then-larger rival exchange in Montreal. The lack of information on mining and resource firms in the *Directory* leads me to believe that Houston focused on firms listed in Montreal and Toronto. At that time, resource stocks would have been mainly listed on the Vancouver Exchange (and later the Alberta Exchange). Grains, produce and futures were listed on the Winnipeg Exchange. Although there does not appear to be a canonical listing of firms from that period or the exchanges to which they belonged, Houston's omissions imply that the exchanges in Montreal and Toronto are the focus of his *Directory*.[12] In total, the *Directory of Directors* lists 7017 individuals from 1593 corporations.

At the turn of the twentieth century, Toronto and Montreal remained the dominant financial and business centres in the young country of Canada. Throughout the country were a number of rapidly developing urban regions with their own local business communities. Outside Quebec, most of the population of the urban regions was ethnically British. The single exception to this was Waterloo County in Ontario, which began as a settlement of German-speaking Pennsylvania Dutch Mennonites. Because of the large number of German speakers, the region subsequently attracted German immigrants from Europe. It became the only urban region in Canada at the turn of the twentieth century where the majority of the population was German in ethnic origin and not Anglo-Saxon. Over time, it became known as a German region, and new immigrants were often directed there when they arrived in Canada.[13]

One of the most intuitive ways to examine corporate interlock networks involves using the "betweenness centrality". This measurement captures how well connected a node is to other nodes.[14] More specifically, it captures the degree to which a node lies in between other nodes. For example, a node would have a high betweenness centrality measurement if other nodes had to go through it in order to broadcast a message to all other nodes in the network. Similarly, a node would have a low betweenness score if other nodes generally did not have to

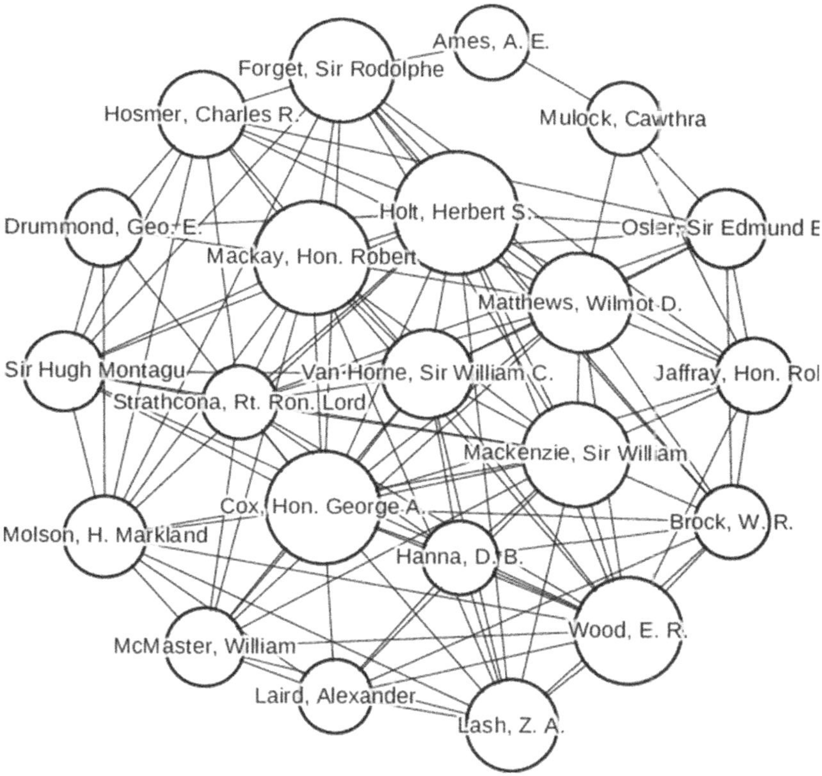

Fig. 8.2 Individuals with the highest betweenness centrality from the national corporate interlock network in Canada based on the Directory of Directors in Canada, 1912

pass a message through it in order to reach all other nodes efficiently. Figure 8.2 is a rendering of directors with the highest betweenness centrality measure in the interlock network. The lines between directors represent corporate boards where both directors served simultaneously. Table 8.1 is a listing of directors in the network with the highest betweenness centrality.

There are two revealing ways to use betweenness centrality when examining the corporate interlock network of Canadian industrial businesses in 1912. The first is to examine each urban region in isolation

Table 8.1 Most central director names, their home province and the urban locations of the boards they serve with

Director names	Director city	Canadian region director interlocked with									
		Major centers		East	Southern Ontario regions				Western Canada		
		Montreal	Toronto	Halifax	Ottawa	Hamilton	Brantford	London	Calgary	Winnipeg	Other city
Holt, Herbert S.	Montreal	x	x			x		x			Quebec
Forget, Sir Rodolphe	Montreal	x	x								Quebec
Mackay, Hon. Robert	Montreal	x	x								Quebec
Matthews, Wilmot D.	Toronto	x	x			x		x			
Murphy, Denis	Ottawa	x			x						
Cox, Hon. George A.	Toronto	x	x		x			x			Victoria
Strathcona and Mount Royal, Rt. Hon. Lord	Montreal/ Eng.	x	x					x			
Pitblado, John	Montreal	x									Vancouver
Molson, H. Markland	Montreal	x	x								St. Johns
Mackenzie, Sir William	Toronto	x	x						x	x	
Birge, Cyrus A.	Hamilton		x			x					
Wood, E. R.	Toronto	x	x								Victoria
Drummond, Geo. E.	Montreal	x					x				
Kingman, Abner	Montreal	x	x								
Curry, Nathaniel	Montreal	x	x	x							Amherst
Edwards, Hon. W. C.	Ottawa	x	x		x						
Richardson, H. W.	Kingston	x				x					Kingston
Van Horne, Sir William C.	Montreal	x	x	x						x	St John
Beck, H. H.	Toronto	x								x	
Allan, Sir Hugh Montagu	Montreal	x	x								Waterloo
Gibson, Hon. Wm.	Beamsville					x					
McDougall, Thomas	Montreal	x									Quebec
Mason, Colonel James	Toronto	x	x								
Strathy, H. S.	Toronto		x								
Laird, Alexander	Toronto		x								

and ask: Who are the most prominent individuals in this local region? The second approach expands on this but considers the country as a whole, asking: Who are the most prominent businesspeople in the country? It turns out that these measures are positively correlated in most regions. In other words, prominent individuals in a region also appear to have connections nationally. Whether individuals came to prominence nationally because they were already prominent in their community, or whether they gained prominence in their community because of their national connections, is an open question. Table 8.1 shows the individuals listed in the *Directory of Directors* that had the highest betweenness centrality, and the head office locations of the boards on which they sat.

Most of the growing urban regions of this period have public businesses that maintain some sort of corporate interlock tie with a director based in either Toronto or Montreal. In this study, I will briefly note the connections to the major centres from the following regions: Halifax, Ottawa, Hamilton, Brantford, Berlin, London, Winnipeg, Calgary and Vancouver.

Halifax, Nova Scotia, is the easternmost urban centre in this research. The business community in the Halifax region maintains most of its corporate interlocks to directors from Montreal, although some ties extend to Toronto as well. Within the region, all of the listed corporations in the city are interlocked to one another. One of the most central people in this local network is Robert Harris. Harris was a prominent businessman and Conservative politician who was eventually appointed to Nova Scotia's Supreme Court. Harris was well known in business circles and also maintained a friendship with Prime Minister Robert Borden, who appointed him to the Supreme Court in 1915. However, no single individual from the Halifax region was particularly prominent within the national business network.

Moving west to Ottawa, the single most central individual is Denis Murphy. Murphy was the best-connected corporate director and served as a central figure in Ottawa's business network. No other individual had a similar reach in the local business community. He also served as a Conservative member of provincial parliament. Nationally, he was also prominent. See Table 8.1 for an ordered ranking of directors with the highest betweenness centrality.

Hamilton was a major industrial centre of the age, especially well known for its steel. It is perhaps no surprise that the most central individual locally was also a key businessman in the industry. Cyrus Birge had a career spanning steel fasteners, blast furnaces and finally steel production itself. Given that the metal was used throughout manufacturing, and required large amounts of capital, power and raw resources to produce, it is not an understatement to say that this industry touched all others. In 1912, Birge was at the zenith of his career. Well respected and influential, he sat on the boards of industrial firms, a number of banks and the regional board of trade.

In Brantford, the network of corporate directors was somewhat smaller, comprised of just 62 individuals working at local firms. Unlike the previously discussed networks, the local business network in Brantford is split into two subnetworks. Although there are locally a number of more prominent businesspeople, none of them is particularly prominent on the national level.

In London, there are some disconnected business networks and some locally prominent individuals. The local network of business ties is not completely connected, but neither is it excessively fragmented, with the majority of the network being comprised of three well-connected networks. Because these networks are relatively well connected, there is not a single individual that acts to unite individual businesspeople together. This is also true nationally—no single individual from the London area of Ontario appears to be particularly prominent. The local network based on the *Directory of Directors* appears fragmented as well, suggesting that perhaps the regional network is denser and better connected than suggested by the *Directory of Directors*. Many of the key listed directors belong to prominent business families from the region. It seems likely that these well-known families had a number of local social connections not captured by the *Directory*.

Outside Toronto and Montreal, Winnipeg was the largest business centre in Canada around the beginning of the twentieth century. This region has over 350 directors listed in the *Directory of Directors*. Although generally well connected for a large business community, there were no prominent local individuals who were also nationally prominent. A similar story holds true for the other Western Canadian cities of Calgary and Vancouver. Both cities appear to have sparsely connected businesses. However, some caution with these results is necessary. As noted in the discussion of data and methodology above, the *Directory of Directors* is likely made up primarily of corporations that were listed in both Toronto and Montreal. Therefore, it is unlikely that the western cities have adequate coverage. At this point, Vancouver had its own exchange specializing in resource firms, and Calgary followed a year later in 1913 with its own exchange. Given the regional specialization in resources, it is unlikely that the manufacturing-heavy exchanges of Toronto and Montreal would have adequate coverage of these regions. It seems more reasonable to treat the networks resulting from these regions as incomplete samples of a larger regional network.

Waterloo County and its county seat of Berlin was the outlier. While most of the regional business networks are relatively well connected, this is not the case in the county of Waterloo; the corporate interlock network in this region is fractured into many smaller networks. However, other sources suggest that the local business network in Berlin was heavily interconnected. This suggests that the *Directory of Directors* does not adequately capture the actual business connections that existed in the region.[15] Sources indicate that many local business leaders had ties through common churches or the local board of trade. Many prominent businesspeople also served on city council.[16] The implications of this will be discussed in subsequent sections. While the largest urban centre in the region was Berlin, the nearby towns of Galt, Preston and Hespeler also had a significant number of manufacturers. Ties also existed between businesses operating in the countryside near Berlin, including the regional villages of Ayr and New Hamburg. There are no particularly prominent individuals locally or nationally based on the *Directory of Directors*.

In the major centres of Toronto and Montreal, the pattern of corporate interlocks is different from those generally displayed in smaller regions. There are almost 1200 directors listed in the Toronto region, more than any other region in Canada. Many of these directors tend to be extremely well connected. Over 200 directors in Toronto have more than twenty ties to other directors. Thus, within Toronto there appear to be a large number of well-connected individuals. However, when considering the national network of interlocks, a small group of directors appear to be very central. In other words, about one-sixth of all corporate members listed in the *Directory of Directors* are well connected locally in Toronto. However, only a small fraction of these well-connected elites maintain corporate ties outside Toronto. This small group of business elites includes some of the most central businesspeople in the nation.

The story is similar in Montreal. Herbert Holt is the businessman with the highest betweenness centrality in the entire Canadian business network in this period. However, considering the local Montreal network only, Holt is not significantly more connected within the city than a large proportion of elite businesspeople. Sir Rudolphe Forget appears to be the single most central individual in Montreal and the second most central man in the country after Holt. However, Holt has diverse ties to companies outside Toronto and Montreal, whereas Forget really has none outside these centres (See Table 8.1).

The national network exhibits a hierarchical structure, with Montreal and Toronto at the top and various regional cities across the country as subordinate. The majority of highly central directors tend to reside either in Montreal or Toronto. When considering just the local networks in those cities, no single director appears to be particularly well connected. Only when the entire national network is considered does it become clear that a few directors are central on a national scale. In part, this appears to be a result of the consolidation movement that was underway during the period. In order to gain economies of scale and market power, firms producing similar items were combined into larger entities across the country.[17]

Some note should be made of the local network structure in the smaller cities surrounding Toronto and Montreal. We can infer that regions which have one or two locally prominent directors have less developed local business networks. Examples of this are Ottawa and Halifax. In these regions, there were a few well-connected individuals. In contrast, in more developed business communities, there was not a handful of directors that acted as a single hub for information exchange.

Table 8.2 Percentage of corporate interlocks from each region (defined as 1911 census district) to firms in local area, Toronto and Montreal

City	Percentage of corporate interlocks to:			
	Own region	Toronto	Montreal	km to Toronto
Toronto	63.2		13.2	0
Montreal	58.1	21.9		541
Halifax	44.2	16.9	23.4	1795
Ottawa	48.3	33.7	4.5	449
Hamilton	35.9	29.6	14.1	69
Berlin	70	9.8	4.9	107
London	26.5	46.3	14.1	192
Winnipeg	50	25.9	12.4	2235
Calgary	63.9	11.1	0	3491
Vancouver	61.5	7.2	18	4386

Instead, there were a number of redundant connections, which ensured that information spread easily throughout the local business community. Examples of this include Winnipeg and London. Hamilton appears to have been a hybrid of the two. The region's steel industry made it an important manufacturing hub. Cyrus Birge, a businessman who spent his career involved with various aspects of the steel industry, was prominent. Birge had ties to finance and manufactures as well as raw resource suppliers that would be important for the steel industry. While Birge ranks high nationally in Table 8.1, his ties are geographically limited and extend only from Hamilton to Toronto.

Table 8.2 lists the major centres and notes the percentage of corporate interlock ties that reach to the major centres of Toronto and Montreal. An additional column includes the distance of each city from Toronto. The first column gives the percentage of corporate interlock ties that go to the local region. Approximately 60% of corporate interlock ties from Toronto and Montreal terminate locally. In Toronto, just over 13% of corporate ties extend to a director in Montreal. Similarly, almost 22% of Montreal corporate interlock ties are with individuals in Toronto. Many of the growing urban regions in Canada have a relatively high percentage of ties to one or both of these major cities. These regions also have a correspondingly lower percentage of corporate interlock ties to their own regions. As noted, this pattern does not represent the cities in Western Canada or the city of Berlin in Waterloo County.

The majority of corporate interlocks in Winnipeg, Calgary and Vancouver are within their local regions. However, Winnipeg maintains strong ties with Toronto (25%) and Montreal (12%). These percentages are unsurprising considering that Winnipeg was at the time a major centre in its own right. As previously noted, it is likely that the local network of Western Canadian cities is not accurately represented because Vancouver (followed soon after by Calgary) hosted its own resource-oriented stock exchange. However, the proportion of corporate interlock ties would give a reasonable indication of how connected the directors of firms listed in central Canada were to other businesspeople in either Toronto or Montreal.

Overall, the majority of corporate interlocks from businesses tend to tie back to Toronto, Montreal or both. Geographic proximity also seems to play an important role—the closer a city is to a major centre, the more likely there is to be a board connection to someone located in that major centre. The single exception seems to be in Waterloo County, with its German ethnic majority, which is virtually absent from the corporate interlock network. Approximately, 70% of corporate interlock ties from this region extend to other local companies. Almost 10% of corporate interlock ties are to Toronto and 5% to Montreal—some of the lowest percentages to these major centres of all of the cities. Berlin is located just over 100 km from Toronto. Closer inspection shows the manufactures from Waterloo County that do maintain corporate interlocks reaching into Toronto or Montreal are located in the nearby Anglo-majority town of Galt.

Waterloo County occupies some of the lands that were originally given as a reserve to the Six Nations in 1784. In land sales led by Joseph Brant, the Six Nations sold the largest portion of territory to United Empire Loyalist Colonel Richard Beasley. Beasley subdivided the land into homestead plots and set about selling it. Although the land was inland and away from the major centres of the time, it attracted a few Mennonite families from Pennsylvania who were in search of a peaceful life and cheaper land.[18] Waterloo County eventually became the home of a new Mennonite settlement in Canada.

Unlike other settled regions in Upper Canada, there was no Anglo-Saxon influence. There were no Crown reserves or reserves for clergy.

There was also no land granted to Loyalists to establish themselves as Anglo-Saxon elites in the region. Instead, the settlers often had family ties in common, sharing a common religion, language and the experience of journeying to Canada to start anew.[19] By the 1820s, the region saw an increase in German immigrants. Whereas the established Mennonites preferred to farm, the German immigrants attracted to the region were artisans who preferred village life. The village of Berlin was established on land sold by local Mennonites. Over the next decades, the German population continued to grow as Germans arrived in Canada fleeing the economic uncertainties caused by the Napoleonic wars. Many of these German immigrants were craftspeople and artisans seeking to contribute to village life—a useful complement to the Mennonites who preferred to farm.[20]

It is important that while the majority of inhabitants of Berlin were ethnically German, the region was not homogenous. Many of those who were ethnically German came from different regions of German-speaking countries. Berlin was the home to Evangelicals, Mennonites and Roman Catholics, and other Protestant strains. In fact, at the turn of the twentieth century, the Catholic-Protestant tensions that were common in the rest of English Canada were almost completely absent in Berlin.[21] The Canadian 1911 census lists almost 70% of the population as German in ethnic origin. Most of the remainder of the population had British origins. A similar proportion of the population were local industrialists.

As noted in the previous section, Berlin lacked the same kinds of director-level interlocks with other regions. Cultural differences appear to be one reason why there may have been a lack of business ties compared to other regions. However, this raises a more fundamental problem: How could businesses in Berlin and the surrounding region successfully grow without access to the same business ties that existed elsewhere? By 1912, Berlin was ranked fifth in terms of industrial output in Canada.[22]

Berlin and its surrounding region had very few natural advantages. There was no navigable waterway to reduce shipping costs. There were no natural resources that were particularly plentiful besides the outputs of the local farmers. However, it seems that these regional disadvantages contributed to a regional sense of identity. The Berlin Board of Trade tried to emphasize the common responsibility that citizens and businesses had to the town. For example, the Berlin Board of Trade report from 1907 proclaimed: "Towns do not just grow; they are built".[23] At a time when many regions were losing population to Toronto, the growth in manufacturing in Berlin did not go unnoticed.[24]

Manufacturing accounted for a sizable proportion of Berlin's regional employment. By some estimates, over 60% of the population was somehow employed in manufacturing. The advantages did not accrue only to those at the top. Approximately, 70% of the workers owned their own homes at a time when many workers in Ontario could hardly expect a decent living wage.[25] The rate of employment appears strong over this period, but not so strong as to inflate the prices of goods.[26]

This is perhaps one reason that residents developed a sense of common cause. German traditions that were kept alive in the area were another important factor for keeping businesses rooted in the region.[27] The region was home to German-language newspapers, musical societies, song festivals and a number of German-language churches of different denominations.[28] The unique culture available in the region stopped successful entrepreneurs from migrating to the larger centres of Toronto or Montreal as other successful families did. The fact that successful entrepreneurs stayed in the region has implications for local ownership. Near the turn of the twentieth century, none of the firms was owned outside the region. Even by 1910, the proportion of large companies owned outside the region was just over 10%.[29] While the inward focus of the region appears to have had significant advantages, it also encouraged local elites to enact policies to benefit themselves.

Berlin appears to have suffered less from labour unrest and price increases than nearby Hamilton and London.[30] For the most part, the business elites in Berlin had close ties with the city government. Not coincidentally, the city's major industries received generous (sometimes to the point of being illegal) tax breaks and bonuses. Similarly, the owners of enterprises received lower than market tax assessments on their private homes. This kind of arrangement was typical of Berlin, where the board of trade had significant overlap with the local city council.[31]

For a brief period, these close dealings came to a head with the election of Allen Huber to the mayor's office in 1908. Huber set about trying to dismantle the industrial "bonusing" scheme of the region and increase tax industrial assessments. Along the way, the democratic reformer removed the fences from around the public parks and made them free to all. However, Huber did not last for more than a single term and a somewhat more moderate, technocratic mayor replaced him. It would be another two years before the board of trade once again installed their chosen candidate for mayor.[32] Yet overall, despite these events, the city appears to have been better run than others during the period—for example, Halifax's regional government was fractured with infighting as reforms were introduced.[33]

Berlin's city council, which included prominent businesspeople, had a long history of investing in businesses that set up production in the region. Sought-after businesses could expect tax exemptions and other inducements.[34] Even though the city council and board of trade were careful in their investment decisions, there was also no lack of poor investments. One such failed venture was the construction of a sugar beet refining plant. Not only did the plant fail, but also the board of trade was given a $25,000 illegal grant by the city council to promote the venture to the public prior to a plebiscite on the issue. This mismanagement of public funds outraged Huber and launched the beginnings of his political career.[35] Despite this cronyism, the region appears to have been sufficiently well run to be a net benefit to the community.

Berlin was an early adopter of public commissions to run services. These included services that were critical to maintaining a stable operating environment for business. Such services included hydroelectric power, water and gas.[36] Local industrialists dominated the boards of the key utility commissions. However, once these boards were established, there was a corresponding decrease in the involvement of these industrialists in the city council. In other cases, where there were less direct benefits to local industry, such as sewer treatment, legal action had to be taken to spur the city to action. Eventually, however, all of these public utilities became a point of civic pride.[37]

Overall, Berlin made a series of investments that helped support regional businesses. Often these investments came in the form of inducements from the city council: lower than market property tax assessments, direct bonuses of cash or land to promising manufacturers and eventually the purchase of key public utilities. These decisions by the local government often benefited the business-owning elites. Other times, the elites pushed for these utilities, subsidized them and guaranteed profits to the city to gain its involvement.[38]

Successful businesspeople from the region tended to benefit from policies of the council and the various inducements council offered to businesses.[39] Many of these same local business leaders campaigned as local councillors and were elected and re-elected over time. To some degree, this speaks of the local population's satisfaction with the status quo.[40] At least during this period, it appears as though Berlin's citizens felt that supporting local businesses helped to ensure the continued prosperity of all citizens. The high rate of factory employment and home ownership among workers compared to other cities like London and Hamilton is one indication that they may have been right.

This paper has examined the corporate interlock business network that existed in Canada in 1912. Close attention was paid to the ethnic composition of regions in Canada that contained a large number of firms. Montreal and Toronto are clearly the major cities for business and finance of the age. Winnipeg appears as the third most prominent city in Canada, with a large number of directors located there. Across major manufacturing regions, there is a clear pattern of corporate interlocks from regional businesses to other directors located in Toronto and Montreal. The single exception to this pattern is the ethnically majority-German city of Berlin in Waterloo County.

Of all the growing cities in Canada, this region had the fewest corporate ties to either Toronto or Montreal. To explain this, I have argued that the cultural distinctiveness of the region allowed its population and local business leaders to develop a sense of common identity. This common identity helped the region invest in a series of common goods that helped local business grow despite the lack of connection to the Anglo-Canadian business elites operating in the rest of Canada. For the period under study, it is safe to say that the region experienced a degree of benign neglect by the rest of English Canada. However, in a few years, this situation would change significantly with the coming of World War I.[41]

The case of the city of Berlin, Ontario, has a number of implications for an understanding of the corporate interlock network that existed in Canada at the time. First, there was a clear hierarchical structure to business relationships throughout the country. These relationships were centred in the cities of Montreal and Toronto. This is consistent with broader analyses of the characteristics of influential elites in the Canadian economy 50 years later, which characterized Canada not as a classless society, but as a hierarchical one.[42]

More broadly, the case of Berlin, Ontario, contributes to a more nuanced understanding of the social role of corporations and how these corporations can act collectively to achieve certain outcomes. Berlin's corporate leaders were deeply involved in advocating for, and investing in, public goods that would benefit local businesses but also the population as a whole. The decisions to make regional private utilities (gas, water and sewer) into public utilities are examples of this pattern. It is important to note that these business leaders were also clearly not just interested in the public good—public funds were routinely misallocated and tax breaks for businesses were also abused. This is somewhat unsurprising given that the region's corporate leaders were also immersed in local politics. If one can take their continued re-election as evidence, business was generally seen as an important source of continued prosperity. With this in mind, the story that emerges is not that the public good was served out of pure altruism. Rather, it seems that a shared sense of being outsiders helped to ensure that the region was not critically mismanaged, at least by the period's standards. In other words, the existence of the Anglo-Canadian elites appears to have provided a credible threat to businesses in Berlin. This provided Berlin's business leaders with the incentive to develop various social goods in the region, while also taking advantage of inducements from city council, but not to the extent that the long-term viability of the region was threatened.

The network data for this research is available at http://jgmackay.com and will be forthcoming in *Connections* journal as a Data Exchange feature.

Notes

1. Michael Useem, *The Inner Circle: Large Corporations and the Rise of Business Political Activity in the U.S.A. and U.K.* (New York: Oxford University Press, 1986).
2. John Porter, *The Vertical Mosaic: An Analysis of Social Class and Power in Canada, 50th Anniversary Edition* (Toronto: University of Toronto Press, 2015).
3. Louis Dembitz Brandeis, *Other People's Money: And How the Bankers Use It* (New York: F.A. Stokes Company, 1914).
4. Gerald F. Davis, "Agents without Principles? The Spread of the Poison Pill through the Intercorporate Network", *Administrative Science Quarterly* 36:4 (1991): 583–613; Jeffrey Pfeffer and Gerald Salancik, *The External Control of Organizations: A Resource Dependence Perspective* (Stanford: Stanford Business Books, 1978).
5. Gerald F. Davis and Mark S. Mizruchi, "The Money Center Cannot Hold: Commercial Banks in the US System of Corporate Governance", *Administrative Science Quarterly* 44, no. 2 (1999), 215–39; Beth A. Mintz and Michael Schwartz, *The Power Structure of American Business* (Chicago: University of Chicago Press, 1985).
6. For academic analysis, see Jon Mackay and James D. Wilson, "The Silicon Valley Wage Cartel: How Cartel Membership Spreads and Its Impact on Management Job Transitions" (Sunbelt conference paper, Newport Beach, California, April 2016).
7. Randall K. Morck, David A. Stangeland and Bernard Yeung, "Inherited Wealth, Corporate Control and Economic Growth: The Canadian Disease", *Working Paper* (National Bureau of Economic Research, November 1998), http://www.nber.org/papers/w6814; R. Morck et al., "The Rise and Fall of the Widely Held Firm: A History of Corporate Ownership in Canada", in *A History of Corporate Governance Around the World: Family Business Groups to Professional Managers*, ed. R. Morck (Chicago: University of Chicago Press, 2005), 65–148; R. Morck, D. Strangland and Bernard Yin Yeung, "Inherited Wealth, Corporate Control and Economic Growth: The Canadian Disease", *SSRN eLibrary*, 1998, https://ssrn.com/abstract=141192; R. Morck and B. Yeung, *The Economic Determinants of Innovation*, Industry Canada Research Publications Program (Industry Canada, 2001).

8. The *Directory of Directors* is split into two sections. Both sections reflect the same information in different ways. The first section lists individual directors and the second section lists companies and then lists individuals that served with the company. In this research, the first portion of the *Directory of Directors* was digitized because the information was laid out so that it was conducive to automated optical character recognition and parsing.
9. http://www.openstreetmap.org/ and https://developers.google.com/maps/. Accessed April 2, 2016.
10. http://open.canada.ca/en/open-data. Accessed April 2, 2016.
11. George J. Murphy, "Early Canadian Financial Statement Disclosure Legislation", *Accounting Historians Journal* 11, no. 2 (1984): n40.
12. Thanks to Professor Leslie Hannah for a useful discussion of these issues.
13. John English and Ken McLaughlin, *Kitchener: An Illustrated History* (Toronto: Jaguar Book Group, 1996).
14. Martin Everett and Stephen P. Borgatti, "Ego Network Betweenness", *Social Networks* 27, no. 1 (2005): 31–38; Linton C. Freeman, "A Set of Measures of Centrality Based on Betweenness", *Sociometry* 40, no. 1 (1977): 35–41.
15. For more detail on local business ties, see Elizabeth Bloomfield, "Building Industrial Communities: Berlin and Waterloo to 1915", in *Manufacturing in Kitchener-Waterloo: A Long-Term Perspective*, ed. David Walker (Waterloo, Ontario: Department of Geography, University of Waterloo, 1987), 5–33 (23); English and McLaughlin, *Kitchener*.
16. Berlin Board of Trade, "Berlin Board of Trade Annual Report" (Berlin, Canada: Berlin Board of Trade, 1907); Bloomfield, "Building industrial communities"; Jack Lucas, "Berlin, Ontario, in the Age of the ABC", *Urban History Review/Revue D'histoire Urbaine* 41:2 (2013), 19–29.
17. T. W. Acheson, "Changing Social Origins of the Canadian Industrial Elite, 1880–1910", *Business History Review* 47:2 (1973), 189–217.
18. English and McLaughlin, *Kitchener*.
19. Ibid., 20–21.
20. Ibid.; for more on Mennonite attitudes towards business, see Janis Thiessen, "Work in Mennonite Theological Perspective", *Canadian Society of Church History Historical Papers* (2004), 5–14, http://historicalpapers.journals.yorku.ca/index.php/historicalpapers/article/view/39262. Accessed May 26, 2016.

21. English and McLaughlin, *Kitchener*, 74.
22. Bloomfield, "Building industrial communities", 9.
23. Berlin Board of Trade, "Berlin Board of Trade Annual Report"; Bloomfield, "Building industrial communities".
24. English and McLaughlin, *Kitchener*.
25. Bloomfield, "Building industrial communities".
26. See Canada. Dept. of Labour, *The Labour Gazette July 1909–June 1910* (Ottawa: Queen's Printer, 1910), http://archive.org/details/labourgazette1910cana.
27. Bloomfield, "Building industrial communities", 20.
28. English and McLaughlin, *Kitchener*.
29. Bloomfield, "Building industrial communities".
30. Department of Labour, Government of Canada, *The Labour Gazette July 1909–June 1910*.
31. English and McLaughlin, *Kitchener*.
32. Ibid.
33. Christopher Armstrong and H. V. Nelles, "Getting Your Way in Nova Scotia: Tweaking Halifax, 1909–1917", *Acadiensis* 5:2 (1976), 105; Henry Roper, "The Halifax Board of Control: The Failure of Municipal Reform, 1906–1919", *Acadiensis* 14:2 (1985): 46.
34. Elizabeth Bloomfield, "Boards of Trade and Canadian Urban Development", *Urban History Review/Revue D'histoire Urbaine* 12:2 (1983), 77–99; Bloomfield, "Building industrial communities"; City of Kitchener, "City of Kitchener Archives. Appendix A", By-Law (Kitchener: City of Kitchener, 1983), http://lf.kitchener.ca/.
35. English and McLaughlin, *Kitchener*, 105.
36. Lucas, "Berlin, Ontario, in the Age of the ABC".
37. English and McLaughlin, *Kitchener*.
38. Ibid.
39. City of Kitchener, "City of Kitchener Archives. Appendix A".
40. English and McLaughlin, *Kitchener*.
41. Mario Nathan Coschi, "'Be British or Be D–d': Primary Education in Berlin-Kitchener, Ontario, during the First World War", *Histoire Sociale/Social History* 47, no. 94 (2014), 311–32; English and McLaughlin, *Kitchener*.
42. Porter, *The Vertical Mosaic*.

References

Acheson, T. W., "Changing Social Origins of the Canadian Industrial Elite, 1880–1910," *Business History Review* 47:2 (1973), 189–217.

Armstrong, Christopher and H. V. Nelles, "Getting Your Way in Nova Scotia: Tweaking Halifax, 1909–1917," *Acadiensis* 5:2 (1976): 105–131.

Berlin Board of Trade, "Berlin Board of Trade Annual Report" (Berlin, Canada: Berlin Board of Trade, 1907).

Bloomfield, Elizabeth, "Boards of Trade and Canadian Urban Development," *Urban History Review/Revue D'histoire Urbaine* 12:2 (1983): 77–99.

Bloomfield, Elizabeth, "Building Industrial Communities: Berlin and Waterloo to 1915," in *Manufacturing in Kitchener-Waterloo: A Long-Term Perspective* ed. David Walker (Waterloo, Ontario: Department of Geography, University of Waterloo, 1987), 5–33.

Brandeis, Louis Dembitz, *Other People's Money: And How the Bankers Use It* (New York: F. A. Stokes Company, 1914).

Canada. Dept. of Labour, *The Labour Gazette July 1909–June 1910* (Ottawa: Queen's Printer, 1910).

Coschi, Mario Nathan, "'Be British or Be D–d': Primary Education in Berlin-Kitchener, Ontario, during the First World War," *Histoire Sociale/Social History* 47:94 (2014): 311–32.

Davis, Gerald F., and Mark S. Mizruchi, "The Money Center Cannot Hold: Commercial Banks in the US System of Corporate Governance," *Administrative Science Quarterly* 44:2 (1999), 215–239.

Davis, Gerald F., "Agents without Principles? The Spread of the Poison Pill through the Intercorporate Network," *Administrative Science Quarterly* 36:4 (1991): 583–613.

Department of Labour, Government of Canada, *The Labour Gazette July 1909–June 1910.*

English, John and Ken McLaughlin, *Kitchener: An Illustrated History.* Toronto: Jaguar Book Group, 1996.

Everett, Martin and Stephen P. Borgatti, "Ego Network Betweenness," *Social Networks* 27:1 (2005): 31–38.

Freeman, Linton, "A Set of Measures of Centrality Based on Betweenness," *Sociometry* 40:1 (1977): 35–41.

Lucas, Jack, "Berlin, Ontario, in the Age of the ABC," *Urban History Review/Revue D'histoire Urbaine* 41:2 (2013): 19–29.

Mackay, Jon and James D. Wilson, "The Silicon Valley Wage Cartel: How Cartel Membership Spreads and Its Impact on Management Job Transitions" (Sunbelt Conference 2016, California, USA, 2016).

Mintz, Beth and Michael Schwartz, *The Power Structure of American Business* (Chicago: University of Chicago Press, 1985).

Morck, R. et al., "The Rise and Fall of the Widely Held Firm—A History of Corporate Ownership in Canada," in *A History of Corporate Governance Around the World: Family Business Groups to Professional Managers*, ed. R. Morck (Chicago: University of Chicago Press, 2005), 65–148.

Morck, R., and B. Yeung, *The Economic Determinants of Innovation*, Industry Canada Research Publications Program (Industry Canada, 2001).

Morck, R., D. Strangland, and Bernard Yin Yeung, "Inherited Wealth, Corporate Control and Economic Growth: The Canadian Disease," *SSRN eLibrary*, 1998, https://ssrn.com/abstract=141192.

Morck, Randall, David A. Stangeland, and Bernard Yeung, "Inherited Wealth, Corporate Control and Economic Growth: The Canadian Disease," *Working Paper* (National Bureau of Economic Research, November 1998).

Murphy, George J., "Early Canadian Financial Statement Disclosure Legislation," *The Accounting Historians Journal* 11:2 (1984): 39–59.

Pfeffer, Jeffrey and Gerald Salancik, *The External Control of Organizations: A Resource Dependence Perspective* (Stanford: Stanford Business Books, 1978).

Porter, John, *The Vertical Mosaic: An Analysis of Social Class and Power in Canada, 50th Anniversary Edition* (Toronto: University of Toronto Press, 2015).

Roper, Henry, "The Halifax Board of Control: The Failure of Municipal Reform, 1906–1919," *Acadiensis* 14:2 (1985): 46.

Thiessen, Janis, "Work in Mennonite Theological Perspective," *Canadian Society of Church History Historical Papers* (2004): 5–14.

Useem, Michael, *The Inner Circle: Large Corporations and the Rise of Business Political Activity in the US and UK* (New York: Oxford University Press, 1986).

9

Trust, Reputation and Regulation: Securities Markets in Europe, the USA, and Japan Before 1914

Leslie Hannah

The reputation of capitalism before 1914 was mixed. On the one hand, many—at least in the rich world—believed that their living standards had generally been advanced by capitalist development. In countries as different as China and Turkey, republican revolutionaries overthrowing ancient dynasties—like many modernisers before and after them—appeared to want more of it. On the other hand, there were in many industrialised and developing countries socialist/labour movements, sometimes performing well in elections (Germany) or even participating in coalition governments (France). These questioned whether something more egalitarian and/or more efficient, probably involving more state intervention, could be devised. Against this backdrop, legislators sought to maximise the public and private benefits of their varied corporate systems by (variously) direct government management of businesses, public/private partnerships, antitrust interventions or regulatory controls (including new corporate laws and legislation for stock exchanges).

L. Hannah (✉)
London School of Economics, Tokyo, Japan
e-mail: lesliehannah@hotmail.com

W.A. Pettigrew and D.C. Smith (eds.), *A History of Socially Responsible Business, c.1600–1950*, Palgrave Studies in the History of Finance,
DOI 10.1007/978-3-319-60146-5_9

Individual corporations reacted to such legal nudges and sought to persuade both investors and the general public that their part of the market was working for broader societal concerns.[1]

This chapter focuses on a comparison of stock market size in the early twentieth century. It examines the competing corporate pressures to maximise shareholder returns, on the one hand, and to discipline managerial pursuit of conflicting objectives that were current at the time, on the other hand—including falling into line behind various regulations that were designed to protect investors and therefore uphold broader social obligations. This focus on shareholder value is now considered by the "varieties of capitalism" school to be more characteristic of "liberal market economies" (notably the USA, Canada and the UK) than of the "coordinated market economies" (notably France, Germany, Italy and Japan) that ostensibly put public and social concerns ahead of the interests of investors. This chapter suggests that such a division cannot be sustained historically.[2] This chapter also shows how local networks of trust between investors and enterprises often assisted stock market size as well as legal protections for investors and the state's attention to particular corporate governance provisions.

Why did securities markets grow? The argument that common law countries had an advantage over civil law countries in developing securities markets is now taken less seriously than it was.[3] After all, further back in history, pioneering exchanges only operated under civil law (in the sixteenth century no common law jurisdictions had formal stock exchanges) and among their modern descendants, two are known to have still had domestic corporate securities/GDP ratios higher than the USA early in the twentieth century.[4] Thus the tendency in recent work by legal historians is to go beyond the issue of legal origin, which was—with a few minor exceptions—unchanging, so cannot possibly explain the massive nineteenth-century rise, catastrophic interwar decline and post-1980 renaissance in global securities markets.[5] Recent work focuses instead on specific national statutes or private order institutions which encouraged stock market growth by providing shareholder protections.

It used to be thought that, unlike today, the early twentieth-century corporate law provided few shareholder rights, in contrast to later laws mandating access to good accounts and prospectuses or "anti-director" rights enabling investors to minimise agency problems. This view of Japan, France or the USA has not been persuasively challenged, at least as far as statutory enactments are concerned. The USA, for example, is reckoned to have had inferior accounting standards and permissive corporate laws driven by charter-mongering interstate competition.[6] By contrast, German and British scholars have recently taken a different view. Burhop et al. have suggested that the German legal changes of 1884 and 1896 created a strongly entrenched, bank-promoted shareholder value culture, later destroyed by Nazi legislation inimical to the publicly quoted firm.[7] Corporate governance standards promoting shareholder value in Germany and the USA before 1914 were thus the reverse of those ascribed to each country later in the century by the "varieties of capitalism" school. However, the UK appears to have been nearer to its modern characterisation in protecting shareholders: Foreman-Peck and Hannah have shown that UK statutory companies (which accounted for most quoted capital in the nineteenth century) had tough mandatory anti-director rights and other large quoted companies (which came to dominate by the turn of the twentieth century) generally adopted similar provisions voluntarily.[8] Acheson et al. have, more surprisingly, confirmed that this voluntarism was well under way in medium-sized as well as large quoted companies from the mid-nineteenth century.[9]

We might expect, then, to find that Germany and the UK had large securities markets before 1914, while those in the USA, Japan and France were constrained by their weak corporate laws. Table 9.1 confirms that this was not the case. However, it should be noted that the

Table 9.1 Market capitalisation of all quoted companies 1913/14

	UK	US	France	Germany	Japan
Bonds/GDP %	38	41	5	6	2
Equities/GDP %	151	50	51	42	53
All Corporate Securities/GDP %	189	91	56	48	55
Main Market Share (%) CHECK	67	51	83	82	60

Source L. Hannah, *Rethinking Corporate Finance Fables: did the US lag Europe before 1914*? CIRJE working paper, Tokyo University, F-994, October 2015, p. 31 (available online at https://ideas.repec.org/p/tky/fseres/2015cf994.html), except for Japan, which are the author's tentative estimates boundaries of markets were not then clearly defined, especially in common law countries, where exchanges were not then state-regulated, as they generally are everywhere today and were in many civil law countries (notably Germany) before 1914. There must therefore remain some uncertainty (apart from the clearly delineated boundaries in Germany) about historical estimates, relative to the clearly defined data produced by the World Federation of Stock Exchanges today. Table 9.1 also separates stocks from bonds, from which it emerges that before 1914 leverage was much higher in the Anglosphere (and particularly in the USA) than in civil law countries (again contrary to the usual view of bond markets post-World War II).[10] It should be noted that the five countries in Table 9.1 accounted for more than half of the world's quoted securities at this time.[11] Any theory of the determinants of market size needs to address this evidence.

If Table 9.1 is correct, then it provides no support for the conventional financial economics view (supported as it is by modern data) that legal protections for investors promote large stock exchanges, at least if one believes that Germany and the UK led in investor protections, because they stand at opposite ends of the spectrum of quoted corporate securities penetration for large industrial countries. Table 9.1 is also a useful corrective to other interesting hypotheses in the literature, which also explain outcomes that the table suggests did not happen. De Long argued that London had a small domestic equity market because German and American investment bankers engaged in information signalling for investors, while British bankers failed to do so. This founders on its mistaken explicandum, apart from other statistical problems.[12] Calomiris's hypothesis that universal banking enabled Germany to create a larger market for equities than the USA founders on the same basis.[13] Calomiris's reliance on the modern "pecking order" theory of debt finance is anachronistic historically, when many corporations were mainly equity-financed and bonds were sometimes a last resort,[14] though other aspects of his argument (e.g. American banks' weak lending capacity for large corporates, driven by government-imposed branching limits) may partly explain America's exceptionally high leverage.[15] Alternative political economy theories of today which relate small equity markets in coordinated market economies to social democratic reactions to the effects of world wars or the adoption of proportional representation in democratic elections also cannot have had much effect before 1914.[16] We must evidently look elsewhere to understand relative market sizes before 1914.

So what really determined stock market size? A case that both other political factors and private order institutions (stock exchanges, investment bankers) shaped stock markets can be made. Some stock markets—like the NYSE and LSE—were not functionally that different from the regulated markets of Berlin and Paris, because the natural monopoly features of centralised trading gave them the power to impose some minimal quality controls and liquidity requirements, and it has been argued that they did.[17] It is, however, not as clear as those advocating shareholder primacy today might argue that this increased overall market size by attracting investors on the "buy" side, for there was also a "sell" side.[18] While company promoters everywhere naturally considered investors' desiderata, directors in America strongly resisted policies like compulsory accounts publication (which European exchange-listed companies took in their stride).[19] In terms of maximising decisions to list, then, the existence in the USA (and UK) of a larger range of exchanges, several with formal listing standards or picky intermediaries not noticeably less restrictive than Germany's highly regulated exchanges, but many others more complacently willing to trade anything in which they could match bargains, may have extended markets, because some Anglosphere firms found these exchanges' permissiveness in corporate governance or publicity terms congenial (while IPOs and trading off official exchanges were banned in Germany). Local networks of trust, or confidence in one large block-holder with a track record, may—for better or worse (and maybe both)—have substituted for formal rules, especially in fringe markets. The reputations of ventures and the social networks of directors behind them may have had a greater influence on the size of securities markets than regulatory devices designed to protect investors. Such social and reputational mechanisms clearly existed, though there is a wide range of views on how effectively.[20]

Were fringe companies behind the Anglosphere's lead? There were about 1650 companies listed in Germany, 1182 in France, but around

10,000 companies featured in UK stock exchange directories and around 25,000 in American directories. The companies trading off major exchanges (and close companies with wider shareholdings only occasionally changing hands) came in many varieties and often had only a few dominant shareholders with voting control. Accounting information, corporate governance or managerial quality of the more marginal of these companies (especially unlisted ones, informally traded and with modestly dispersed holdings) often fell below LSE standards.[21] US entrepreneurs also found the low disclosure and liquidity requirements of some regional exchanges and OTC markets appealing.[22] The NYSE's economist sternly (and self-servingly) warned investors that pricing and trading of such smaller issues were more easily manipulated.[23] The "blue sky" laws adopted in most US states from 1911—though largely ineffective in protecting investors—reflected popular dissatisfaction with unscrupulous share pushers.[24] "Bucket-shops" even went as far as setting up fraudulent "stock exchanges" in their offices to dupe sucker investors.[25] Kennedy excoriates the waste involved in poorly vetted share issues in critical industries in the UK before 1914, and Chambers documents the poor returns of the late 1920s UK new issue bubble.[26] Seltzer suggests US issues were sometimes as bad in new industries.[27]

The world thus described is not one of corporate social responsibilities but of nakedly self-interested misrepresentations to defraud the investing public. Many insiders used the peripheral markets of the Anglosphere (which were much larger than the regulated regional exchanges of France and Germany) to unload on an ill-informed and over-optimistic public their least promising (not to speak of downright fraudulent) prospects, rather than—as in more positive accounts of financialisation—accelerating growth for star investments by relieving their financial constraints.[28] Yet clearly there were some successes even on these peripheral markets.

Networks of trust rather than formal government regulations or stock exchange listing rules seem to have, at least partly, protected shareholders in some well-known cases. For example, trusted Boston capitalists confidently operated—without the benefit of NYSE rules—initially in developing the telephone industry.[29] The case of the inventor, Alexander Graham Bell, is instructive. Bell formed partnerships for the first few years with a New England lawyer and a leather manufacturer that he knew professionally, but they had limited resources, even after the manufacturer sold his own business to fund the risky development, eventually committing $110,000. Uncertainty about patents, the form in which telephone usage would develop and predatory threats from Edison and Western Union put off other investors and operations were initially outsourced to multiple licensees with access to local capital. In July 1878, the $450,000 Bell Telephone Company was incorporated, bringing in eleven Boston angel investors (who insisted on voting control and the presidency, while accepting the prior profits claims of the three pioneers) and the independent £100,000 ($500,000) Telephone Company Ltd was floated in London at the same time.[30] It became easier to raise funds publicly with the settlement of patent litigation and a truce with Western Union. Shares in the new $10 m American Bell Telephone Company of 1880 changed hands, rising from $50 to $600 (increasing prices reflecting its perceived success), with 338 holders by the end of that year (though 56% of the shares remained with 12 core holders) and were traded by Boston brokers.[31] The company became more professionally managed and vertically integrated, issuing bonds and acquiring system operators and manufacturers. By 1886 there were 1860 stockholders,[32] but the Boston financial interests retained control: it was not until a generation after foundation—well after it had become one of the largest US corporations—that J.P. Morgan in 1901 introduced its securities to the NYSE and in 1904 to the LSE.

The Bell model of favouring local and trusted investors (who were granted significant powers of control over the ventures) prior to stock market flotation is representative of a broader trend. Lamoreaux et al. describe similarly informed, and productive, monitoring of early stage developments by long-term angel investors in Cleveland.[33] Several small banks and trust companies underwrote local securities and when the Cleveland Bourse (as it was commonly known) opened in 1900, medium-sized local enterprises such as National Carbon (batteries), American Multigraph (office machinery) and White Co (trucks) could broaden their local networks of investors. Even where local investors with power to choose and discipline managers did not retain control, extended liability rules encouraged some dispersed shareholders to monitor boards.[34]

Trust appears to have played a still greater role in encouraging large securities markets in the UK than it did in the USA. In the UK, there was a complex ecology of local promoters, proto-venture capitalists, investment trusts, managing agencies and financial groups playing information-sharing and monitoring roles.[35] The early exit route offered by junior market IPOs in London and the provinces clearly encouraged angel investors. It is possible that levels of trust in the business and financial communities were higher in the UK than USA. It was, after all, a more settled society with prosperous, long-established cities in which bourgeois elites had long experience of interaction, while the USA was a restless society in which foreign and internal migrants disrupted existing networks, while constantly introducing new elements with limited local social capital. That may be one reason why the UK's fringe markets (as well as its official exchange listings) were more developed than those in the USA.

However, a strong argument that a more restrictive approach would have usefully disciplined negligent profusion in the Anglosphere is made in Burhop et al's assessment of 1900-13 IPOs on the London junior market.[36] They experienced a high (19%) failure rate compared with IPOs on Berlin (9% in 1884–96, 1% in 1897–1914) or the London official list (2% in 1900–13). Contemporary investment advisers were aware of this, sagely advising their clients not to get involved in start-ups unless they had insider knowledge, but much opinion in the Anglosphere believed legal proscription would hamstring enterprise and therefore restrict market size.[37,38] Failure is not in itself problematic: on the contrary, tolerance of failure and an ability to terminate unpromising experiments swiftly are the essence of productive venture investing.[39] Yet, Burhop et al. conclude that investors would have benefitted from German-style legal restrictions closing down the junior market, testing the possibility that high returns by stars compensated for failures only to reject it.[40]

However, their assessment is both too short-term (between two and seven years) and based on low—and possibly biased—coverage (243 LSE junior market IPOs with adequate data, out of many thousands of firms traded but not officially listed).[41] Most of what we know about the differential growth of joint stock companies or the range of returns on patents suggests failure or modest returns are indeed the norms, but more salient compensating outliers are often found.[42] In any such highly skewed distribution, small samples might be dominated by particularly lucky or unlucky draws.[43] It was hard—even for market professionals—to evaluate an innovative project, since often the only way to learn about its potential was to invest in it and even then investors faced incalculable uncertainties, not diversifiable risks.[44] Today's IPO markets rely on investors' systematic over-optimism about the "next big thing,"[45] and long-run evidence suggests that a disproportionate share of new products, processes and services came from small firms (and really big innovations from very few of them).[46] The social benefits of innovation are considerably higher than the profits appropriated by investors in most industries,[47] so the social costs of restrictions might have been considerable. It is worth remembering that Massachusetts, to protect local investors from what the state (not unreasonably) judged an over-hyped scam, attempted (ineffectually) to ban investments in Apple's IPO in 1980; by 2015, Apple Inc. was the most valuable firm in the world.[48] Regulators therefore often acted over-cautiously in ways that might have hampered benefits for large populations of investors.

The LSE listing committee files include similar firms that Burhop et al's 1900–1913 sampling frame omitted: in the 1900 files alone two junior market approvals stand out to challenge Burhop et al's thesis that German-style protections for investors would have prevented widespread failure in the UK market and therefore suggest alternative explanations for market growth and success.[49] In that year, Shell Transport & Trading introduced £2m of its shares to the junior market, three years after Marcus Samuel—a London-based banker–underwriter and Asia merchant—founded the company to handle his petroleum interests (the family retained a controlling majority, so it could not be officially listed). Shell struggled to compete with Standard Oil, but Samuel pioneered tanker shipping between his oilfields and kerosene distribution chains, built a managerial and marketing hierarchy, refused an £8m buy-out offer from Rockefeller and sometimes sailed close to the wind by paying dividends out of capital. Temporarily weakened, Shell merged with Royal Dutch Petroleum in 1907 (as the 40% minority partner), started production in California, took over the Rothschilds' oil interests and in 1920 acquired the largest Mexican producer from British rival Pearson. Its shares then sold at 14.5 times the issue price, and some decades later Royal Dutch Shell became the world's largest corporation.

Also in 1900, Marconi's Wireless Telegraph Company first appeared on the junior market with only £137,083 capital, a more typical size.[50] Since 1897, when he was only 23, the eponymous Italian inventor's experiments had been financed by classic angel investors: family members with London financial connections and their wealthy acquaintances, mainly Irish flour millers, responding to a privately circulated typewritten prospectus. Distinguished scientists insisted that the upstart Marconi's signals would not be received in Newfoundland because of the curvature of the earth, but the patented radio technology the company owned seemed to have enough promise for the angels wanting quick payback to cash out their ordinary shares (there was no prospectus, just a "special settlement" introduction facilitating sales to more enthusiastic public investors). The LSE listing committee would not allow this on the main market, as Marconi and other insiders retained voting control, but junior market investors had no more inhibitions about that than investors today buying shares in Google or Amazon (also not—or at least not yet—put off by founders' autocratic control and weak corporate governance). Insiders do not always know best in uncertain technologies: outsiders who bought the impatient insiders' shares (and subsequent Marconi issues)—against professional advice[51]—had a roller coaster ride (and involvement in a notorious British political corruption scandal), but their ordinary shares were worth 9.8 times their issue price by 1912 and the longer-term outcomes were impressive. The company became one among several British electronics manufacturers (contributing to the development of gramophones, radios, radar, codebreaking equipment and television), and the subsidiaries that governments induced Marconi to spin-off spawned Radio Corporation of America (the leading US electronics manufacturer),[52] the British Broadcasting Corporation (the world's most trusted broadcaster) and Cable & Wireless (which dominated international telecoms from the 1930s). Such junior market stars compel at least the Scottish verdict "not proven" on Burhop et al's prosecution case for the death sentence, though their findings might support an argument for stronger broker vetting or a more structured venture capital sector (on modern lines). The cases of Shell and Marconi also imply that it was better to keep control in insider, trusted networks for longer and delay formal IPOs until performance and prospects were clearer.

Neither British investors—nor those in similarly unregulated US markets—always suffered from fringe financing, but did Germany's illiberalism on that boundary (the results evident in its relatively small market size in Table 9.1) stifle enterprise? Where financial repression caused problems, capital sometimes found alternative channels. Telefunken (rivalling Marconi) was founded in 1903, with firm Reich support for naval radio communications outside British control, as a joint subsidiary of AEG and Siemens. A year later, Deutsche Petroleum (rivalling Shell as an oil developer and distributor) was founded by Deutsche Bank. These pathways were presumably chosen because, as in most modern markets (but unlike the pre-1914 LSE), German exchanges (even regional ones) were barred from listing start-ups.[53] It is possible that Germany benefitted from having such established firms and banks (rather than a fickle public) nurturing ventures, but Deutsche Bank was itself sufficiently unconvinced of its own oil sector management skills to attempt (unsuccessfully) to sell Deutsche Petroleum to Shell.[54] Moreover, any benefit did not take the form of first mover advantage (both were founded later than their British rivals) or large scale (both were smaller in 1914). Contrariwise, in other areas of the same industries—notably fine chemicals and heavy electricals—German firms clearly performed more impressively than British; and there were yet others—like automobiles—in which both Germany and Britain lagged the USA and France. The problem with assessing the role of finance and corporate governance is that many other variables—tariffs, labour costs, market size, segmented procurement, industrial clusters, patents, technical and managerial skills, not to speak of luck—played a part in such outcomes. Even well-informed accounts depend as much as on their authors' priors on the evidence: note the widely differing assessments of finance versus other variables in the automobile, electricity and other industries by Kennedy and Michie.[55]

It is thus not easy to benchmark the Anglosphere's complex ecology of angel investor networks, financial trusts, investment groups and promiscuous start-ups against Germany's more ordered, slower-moving, less profuse but also sometimes successful universal banks and corporate bureaucracies, which appear to have encouraged pyramided ownership, often distrusted in the Anglosphere.[56] However, restrictions on diversity and experimentation by continental financial repression were not even admired by all participants in such regulated orders. The enthusiastic involvement of Deutsche Bank, Dresdner Bank, Crédit Lyonnais and Société Générale in the London and/or New York markets suggests an appreciation of the merits of deregulated, competitive markets was not confined to the Anglosphere.[57] There was convergence among advanced industrial countries on using more stock exchange finance, but the mixes chosen by investors, businesses and politicians—of government and corporate securities, of equities and bonds (and, among them, of "junk" and safe), of regulation and liberality, of accounting, anti-director rights or local trust—were in some sectors markedly differentiated nationally. Germany was most inclined to discipline financialisation by legal interventions and had an unusually small (if well-targeted) corporate sector for such an industrialised country.

The foisting of "lemons" on the investing public was easier outside the control of major exchanges, but was limited by their own shrewd caution. Those in the "top 1%", who owned most shares, were not all suckers, though some—including Rockefellers and Vanderbilts—were accused of suckering others.[58] Franks et al. argued that British investors were generally well informed about local businesses and that regional networks of trust operated to align the interest of shareholders and managers in many small provincially quoted companies.[59] It is evident that we need much more information on such mechanisms before we can confidently assess the reasons why shareholders were willing to trust firms on fringe markets with less clearly articulated corporate governance regimes than Germany's regulated exchanges or the LSE and NYSE official lists.

The difficulties of separating national investment cultures are also proven by an examination of international capital flows and investors. So far we have been considering national markets separately, but they were, of course, interconnected in the globalised world of pre-1914. Both corporations and investors had considerable leeway about where they could raise funds or invest, and there were enormous international flows of capital. Similar globalisation today has resulted in some capital markets setting global standards. Foreign firms listing on the NYSE in the 1990s, for example, generally had to substantially improve their reporting and governance standards to qualify.[60] The LSE—given its dominant scale and international role—might have played a similarly imperial card before 1914, but chose not to do so. It accepted a listing on major foreign exchanges (such as New York or Paris) as sufficient to qualify for a cross-listing on the LSE, thus listing some US and French companies which—if they had been British—would have been refused a listing because of their weak governance rules, poor accounting disclosure or inadequately dispersed shareholdings.

Interestingly, LSE investors seem not to have objected to this general principle, though occasionally the *Economist* warned against investing in undesirable US enterprises with poor governance and dubious financial structures.[61] Many companies operating overseas (e.g. in Australia, Brazil, Argentina and India) also chose not to issue first in their home market, but to register under European (especially British) law and raise capital from European investors. Such companies did typically need to meet London listing requirements and often used London intermediaries.[62] Of course, they—and American and other companies choosing to retain their own governance arrangements—had to pay higher dividends and interest to attract European capital (which in the event more than compensated them for the risk) so there was often no reason for Europeans to regret such investments, whatever the governance arrangements.[63] John Moody—who knew US markets as well as anyone—at the time remarked that it may have been such gung-ho enterprise that pulled finance in its wake rather than good finance/governance driving enterprise, and there were perhaps few places with more Keynesian "animal spirits" than the USA (and perhaps few with less than Old Europe).[64] However, Europeans typically did not have access to the local networks of trust, exemplified above in Boston or Cleveland, and they relied more on bond than equity contracts, because bonds offered the option of foreclosure if contracted cash flows were not delivered.[65] That was one reason why the US market was more leveraged than European markets (see Table 9.1)

Some two-thirds of global investment before 1914 was portfolio investment, but another third was foreign direct investment by multinationals, and in that case, it was managers, rather than investors, who (at least initially) made decisions on providing the funds.[66] Here too the British played a disproportionate role, with, in absolute terms more multinational investments than the USA, Germany and France combined. Measured in the same terms as Table 9.1, that is relative to GDP, British foreign direct investment in 1913/14 registered at 55%, France at 17%, the USA at 7% and Germany at 6% of their respective GDPs.[67] The multinational literature stresses that such investments are usually based on some advantage—for example of management or technology or branding skills—of the headquarters country that the host country did not have. It is possible that British management or technology was superior before 1914, or that Americans were too busy developing their own country to bother very much with implementing their own, high-quality management and technology abroad. However, perhaps one explanation that deserves more attention is that British finance and corporate governance were then qualitatively at the world frontier? One might expect that to result in larger British securities markets relative to GDP and more British multinational investment relative to GDP. That is precisely what the pre-1914 historical record reveals.

So the international picture augments my comparison of national investment cultures and regulations. While national investors were often attracted overseas by strong governance regimes, portfolio investors and multinationals were compelled to invest overseas because of the peculiarities of national outlook from the domicile countries rather than any particular governance controls in the markets they invested overseas. My analysis of the relative size of various securities markets in the early twentieth century complicates the view that differing regulatory arrangements explain diverges in size. Stock markets had long been understood as potentially socially pernicious institutions in various national cultures (with differing degrees) and states took action to rein in excesses that might have social repercussions. But the data I have marshalled clearly point to the significance of local networks of trust in building enterprises prior to and during successful stock market flotations that helped grow stock market size. Regulators may have hoped to discipline securities markets to broader social obligations, but organic social networks, yet again, often provided the means to satisfy these obligations without regulatory intervention.

Notes

1. For an authoritative, broad-ranging survey of methods of promoting corporate reputation, see Christopher Kobrak, "The Concept of Reputation in Business History", *Business History Review* 87 (Winter 2013): 763–86.
2. Peter A. Hall and David Soskice, *Varieties of Capitalism* (Oxford: Oxford University Press, 2001).
3. R. La Porta et al., "Law and Finance", *Journal of Political Economy* 106 (1998), 1113–1155; idem, "The Economic Consequences of Legal Origins", *Journal of Economic Literature*, 46, 2008, 285–332; and, for a critique, A. Musacchio and J. D. Turner, "Does the Law and Finance Hypothesis Pass the Test of History?" *Business History* 55 (2013), 524–42.
4. Brussels' alone was 120% of GDP (J. Annaert, F. Buelens and M. J. De Ceuster. "New Belgian stock market returns: 1832–1914", *Explorations in Economic History* 49 (2002), 189–204 at 192–4) and Amsterdam's 102% (Philip Fliers, email to the author, 20 December 2015). These figures are compiled on a basis comparable to those in Table 9.1 below.
5. For this characterisation, see especially R. G. Rajan and L. Zingales. "The Great Reversals: the Politics of Financial Development in the Twentieth Century". *Journal of Financial Economics*, 69, 2003, 5–50.
6. C. Grandy, "New Jersey Corporate Chartermongering, 1875–1929". *Journal of Economic History*, 49, 1989, 677–92; N. Lamoreaux, "Did Insecure Property Rights Slow Economic Development? Some Lessons from Economic History", *Journal of Policy History*, 18, 1, 2006, 146–164, at 151–6; J. R. Edwards, "Companies, Corporations and Accounting Change, 1835–1933: A Comparative Study". *Accounting and Business Research*, 23, No. 89 (1992): 59–73. State and federal regulators enforced some publicity and governance standards on US banks, insurers, utilities and railroads, but the NYSE struggled to persuade other listed company boards. K. A. Snowden ("American Stock Exchange Development and Performance, 1871–1929". *Explorations*

in Economic History, 24, 1987, 327–53 at 350) argues that federal ICC regulation improved informational efficiency in the railroad market (and that still accounted for most corporate securities on the NYSE until 1922). R. E. Wright (*Corporation Nation*, Philadelphia, 2014) argues for *deteriorating* US corporate governance around 1900 (when the market was rapidly growing). B. R. Cheffins, S. A. Bank and H. Wells ("Shareholder Protection across Time". *University of Florida Law Review*, 2016) suggest declining protection in state law from 1900 was mild and from the 1930s offset by federal protection (when the market was declining).

7. On more effective criminal prosecution of UK securities fraudsters, see Taylor, *Boardroom Scandals*.
8. "UK Corporate Law", see also Rutterford, "Shareholder Voice", and, on corporate accounting, Edwards, "Companies". Collins' and Margo's (*Enterprising*, p. 8) assertively pessimistic view is (irrelevantly for the study of stock exchanges) based on a study of UK *unlisted* company charters.
9. G. G. Acheson, G. Campbell and J. D. Turner, "Common Law and the Origin of Shareholder Protection", EABH papers, no 16–03, August 2016.
10. This table included only bonds of purely capitalist corporations. It thus excludes the bonds of the Prussian state railways (the largest corporation in the world by market value at this time, but entirely government-run) and of French state-guaranteed bonds (e.g. bonds of the *Crédit Foncier* or the six major railway networks (all with state-guaranteed stocks and bonds, one of which was state-run, though the other five were privately managed).
11. A. Neymarck, "La statistique internationale des valeurs mobilières", *Bulletin de l'Institut International de Statistique* (14, 1905), (19, 1911), 1–269; (20, 1915), 1296–1539.
12. J. B. De Long, "Did J.P. Morgan's Men Add Value? An Economist's Perspective on Financial Capitalism". In *Inside the Business Enterprise: Historical Perspectives on the Use of Information*, edited by Peter Temin (Chicago: Chicago University Press, 1991), 205–36; H. Bodenhorn, "Two Centuries of Finance and Growth in the United States, 1790–1980", NBER Working Paper 22652, 2016. De Long was misled by A. D. Chandler's recently published *Scale and Scope: The Dynamics of Industrial Capitalism* (Cambridge, MA: Harvard University Press, 1990)

whose conclusions on these matters are taken less seriously today (Jones, G, "Business Groups exist in developed markets also: Britain since 1850", Harvard Business School working paper 16-066, 2015, 4). J Fear and C. Kobrak ("Banks on Board: German and American Corporate Governance 1870–1914) *Business History Review* 84 (Winter 2010): 703–736) provide a more convincing account of the monitoring role of bankers. Hilt and Frydman ("Investment Banks") overcome survivor bias and other faults in De Long's analysis, though it remains a moot point whether the monitoring benefit was sufficient to outweigh high investment banker fees.

13. Calomiris, C. W. "The Costs of Rejecting Universal Banking: American Finance in the German Mirror, 1870–1914". in N. R. Lamoreaux and D. M.G. Raff, eds., *Coordination and Information: Historical Perspectives on the Organization of Enterprise* (Chicago: Chicago University Press, 1995), 257–322. Calomiris' supposedly larger German equity market derives from his doubling the Goldsmith/Sylla error, by including not only unquoted equity but also financial firm equity for Germany which are excluded from his US data.
14. G. H. Evans, *British Corporation Finance 1775–1850: a Study of Preference Shares* (Baltimore: Johns Hopkins Press, 1936); M. Freeman, R. Pearson and J. Taylor. *Shareholder Democracies? Corporate Governance in Britain and Ireland before 1850* (Chicago: University of Chicago Press, 2012); E. Hilt, "When Did Ownership Separate from Control? Corporate Governance in the Early-Nineteenth Century". *Journal of Economic History*, 68, 2008, 645–85.
15. See also Goldsmith, *Financial Intermediaries*, pp. 217–18. However, I suspect the major reasons for high US leverage were the unwillingness of distant European equity investors to trust US corporate governance (bonds offered a clearer power of intervention in easily defined circumstances) and the dearth of *government* bonds on the NYSE for domestic institutions and individuals, compared with major European exchanges. On this, see L. Hannah, "Leading Stock Exchanges before 1914: Equities, Bonds and the Neglected Role of the State", in K. Sogner, ed., *Entreprenørskap. Festskrift til ære for Even Lange* (Oslo: Novus Forlag, 2016), 13–28.
16. M. J. Roe, *Strong Managers, Weak Owners* (Princeton: Princeton University Press, 1992); E. Perotti, and E-L. von Thadden. "The Political Economy of Corporate Control and Labor Rents", *Journal of Political Economy*, 114, 2006, 145–75.

17. However, there is disagreement on whose rules were most stringent (Davis and Neal, "Evolution;" O'Sullivan, "Yankee Doodle;" Foreman-Peck and Hannah, "Corporate Law").
18. The intensification of NYSE efforts to enforce its disclosure rules around 1900, the abolition of its lax unlisted department in 1910 and serious external regulation by the SEC in 1934 were all followed by a decline in the securities/GDP-ratio. See also Cheffins et al., "Shareholder Protection".
19. F. A. Vanderlip, *From Farm Boy to Financier* (New York, D. Appleton-Century Company Inc, 1935); L. Hannah, "London as the Global Market for Corporate Securities before 1914". in L Quennouëlle-Corre and Y Cassis, eds. *Financial Centres and International Capital Flows* (Oxford: Oxford University Press, 2011): 126–60.
20. Lamoreaux et al., "Financing Innovation;" Franks et al., "Ownership;" Cull et al., "Historical financing;" Burhop et al., "Law;" Nye, "Company Promoter".
21. Steven Toms, "The Rise of Modern Accounting and the Fall of the Public Company: The Lancashire Cotton Mills, 1870–1914". *Accounting, Organizations and Society* 27, 1 (2002): 61–84; T. W. Guinnane,T. R. Harris, N. Lamoreaux and J-L. Rosenthal, "Contractual Freedom and the Evolution of Corporate Control in Britain, 1862 to 1929". *NBER Working Paper* 20481 (2014). F. Lavington (*English Capital Market*, London, 1921, 202–4) estimated that, in 1911–13, 2922 new UK companies registered as public raised a modest average of only £28,234 ($137,415) per company from investors, of which only one out of five applied for an initial LSE settlement (the LSE discouraged flotations of less than £100,000).
22. Eugene N. White, "Competition Among the Exchanges before the SEC: was the NYSE a natural hegemon?" *Financial History Review*, 20, 1 (2013): 29–48.
23. J.E. Meeker, *The Work of the Stock Exchange* (New York: Ronald Press, 1922).
24. J. Seligman, *The Transformation of Wall Street* (Boston: Northeastern University Press, 1995); P. G. Mahoney, "The Origins of the Blue-Sky Laws: A Test of Competing Hypotheses". *Journal of Law and Economics*, 46, 1 (April 2003): 229–251.
25. Harrison H. Brace, *The Value of Organized Speculation* (New York: Houghton Mifflin, 1913), 235–7.

26. W.P. Kennedy, *Industrial Structure, Capital Markets and the Origins of British Industrial Decline* (Cambridge: Cambridge University Press, 1987). D. Chambers, "Going Public in Interwar Britain", *Financial History Review* 17 (2010): 51–71.
27. Lawrence H. Seltzer, *A Financial History of the American Automobile Industry* (Boston: Houghton Mifflin, 1928), 24–6.
28. R. King and R. Levine. "Finance and Growth: Schumpeter Might be Right". *Quarterly Journal of Economics*, 103, 1993, 717–37.
29. J. W. Stehman, *The Financial History of the American Telephone and Telegraph Company* (Boston: Houghton Mifflin, 1925); R. J. Tosiello, *The Birth and Early Years of the Bell Telephone System 1876–1880* (New York: Arno Press, 1979); A. S. Pier, *Forbes: Telephone Pioneer* (New York: Dodds Mead, 1953).
30. In 1880, a maverick English judge determined that the Post Office had monopoly rights over the telephone, depressing that company's prospects; over the next three decades, the UK government asserted complete control and ownership.
31. It did not appear in the *New York Times* list of Boston Stocks until 21 February 1885, but was traded informally before that.
32. American Bell Telephone Company Limited. *Annual Report 1886/7*, Boston: Bell, 1887, 13.
33. N. Lamoreaux, M. Levenstein and K. Sokoloff. "Financing Innovation in the Second Industrial Revolution: Cleveland, Ohio, 1870–1920". in *Financing Innovation in the United States, 1870 to Present*, eds. Lamoreaux, K. Sokoloff, and W. H. Janeway (Cambridge, Mass.: MIT Press, 2007).
34. J. B. Jefferys, *Business Organisation in Great Britain 1856–1914* (New York: Garland, 1970); R. Grossman and M Imai. "Contingent Capital and Bank Risk-taking among British banks before the First World War", *Economic History Review* 66, no. 1 (2013): 132–55; G. G. Acheson, C. R. Hickson and J. D. Turner. "Does limited liability matter? Evidence from Nineteenth-century British banking". *Review of Law and Economics*, 6 (2011): 247–73.
35. Anon. *James Finlay & Co Ltd, 1750–1950* (Glasgow: Jackson, 1951), 75–84; Jefferys, *Business Organisation*; R. C. Michie, "Options, Concessions, Syndicates, and the Provision of Venture Capital,1881–1913" *Business History*, 25 (1981): 147–64 G. G. Jones, and A. M. Colpan, "Business Groups in Historical Perspective", in

Colpan, T. Hikino and J. R. Lincoln, eds., *Oxford Handbook of Business Groups*, 70–71 (Oxford: Oxford University Press, 2012): 67–92; Lucy Newton, "Capital Networks in the Sheffield region, 1850–1885". in J. F. Wilson and A. Popp, eds., *Industrial Clusters and Regional Business Networks in England, 1750–1970* (Aldershot: Ashgate, 2003): 130–154; Cochrane, Sarah. "Explaining London's Dominance in International Financial Services, 1870–1913". University of Oxford Department of Economics working paper 455 (October 2009; B. R. Cheffins, *Corporate Ownership and Control: British Business Transformed* (Oxford: Oxford University Press, 2008), 168–70; James G. D. Nye, "The Company Promoter in London 1877–1914". University of London PhD thesis, 2011; Janette Rutterford, "The Shareholder Voice: British and American Accents, 1890 to 1965". *Enterprise & Society*, 13, 1 (2012):120–3; M. Aldous, "Avoiding Negligence and Profusion: the Failure of the Joint-Stock Form in the Anglo-Indian Tea Trade, 1840–1870", *Enterprise and Society* 16, 3 (2015): 648–85.

36. C. Burhop, D. Chambers and B. Cheffins. "Regulating IPOs: Evidence from Going Public in London, 1900–1913". *Explorations in Economic History*, 51 (January 2014): 60–76.
37. Henry Lowenfeld, *Investment Practically Considered* (London: Financial Review of Reviews, 1909), 183–98.
38. Harrison H. Brace, *The Value of Organized Speculation* (New York: Houghton Mifflin, 1913); Rob McQueen, *A Social History of Company Law: Great Britain and the Australian Colonies 1854–1920* (London: Ashgate, 2009), 261–2.
39. Ramana Nanda and Matthew Rhodes-Kropf. "Financing Entrepreneurial Experimentation". NBER Working Paper 21278 (June 2015).
40. Unfortunately, they support that conclusion by evaluating the overall return by 1916 of a 1909–13 subset of their IPOs against Moore's LSE index, which is dominated by foreign (particularly American) shares effectively barred to British investors from August 1914 but performing better than permitted investments, many severely restricted or converted to armaments production (compare Dimson et al. 2015: 183; *Banker's Magazine* no. 779 August 1914, 183; and no. 869, August 1916, 15). Applying the same yardstick to officially listed domestic firms (which—by other yardsticks—Burhop et al. pronounce successful) would show that they, too, "failed".

41. A high proportion of their 1909–13 IPO sub-sample financed Malayan rubber plantations, whose business model involved planting new trees from which latex—much needed by the expanding automobile industry and the bulk exported to the USA—only began generating revenues after seven years, by which time wartime shipping shortages inhibited freight to its main market. Nonetheless, it is clear that this sector over-expanded in response to irrational investor exuberance.
42. F. M. Scherer and D. Harhoff, "Technology policy for a world of skew-distributed outcomes", *Research Policy*, 29 (2000): 559–66.
43. Shares in the household chemical manufacturer Reckitt & Son—thinly traded on the junior market by virtue of a provincial listing—registered higher capital gains *alone* than the best performer of their sample on capital gains *plus dividends*. By 1912, Reckitt was more than 60 times the mean size at IPO of their sample and the tenth largest British industrial by market capitalisation.
44. F. H. Knight, *Risk, Uncertainty, and Profit* (Boston: Houghton Mifflin, 1921).
45. T. Loughlan and J. Ritter. "The New Issues Puzzle". *Journal of Finance*, 50 (1995): 23–51.
46. Z. J. Acs and D. B. Audretsch, "An Empirical Examination of Small Firm Growth", *Economics Letters* 25 (1985): 363–66.
47. W. D. Nordhaus, "Schumpeterian Profits in the American Economy: Theory and Measurement". NBER Working Paper 10433 (2004).
48. *Economist*, 12 September 2015, 74 (Anon. "Vision and Reality").
49. London Guildhall Library, LSE Archives, MS 18000/1.The suggestion is not that these were typical, but they deserve consideration with those generated by Burhop et al's sampling frame (IPOs buying *Times* advertising, which offered no quality certification and attracted IPOs by known rogues). Introductions (such as the two noted here) were possibly a more common form of listing before 1914 everywhere and (having already developed broader shareholding by informed parties) may have been more successful than IPOs.
50. W. J. Baker, *A History of the Marconi Company* (London: Methuen, 1970).
51. Lowenfeld, *Investment*, 186.
52. US Navy suspicion of British control of warship communications induced the UK parent to divest American Marconi to form the core of RCA.

53. The NYSE, like German exchanges which required a three-year profit record, would also not fund start-ups (indeed, it insisted on a *five*-year accounting record), but the NYSE was accordingly a small player in rapidly growing sectors, compared with the curb and regional markets (or the LSE).
54. Chandler, *Scale and Scope*, 440.
55. W. P. Kennedy, *Industrial Structure, Capital Markets and the Origins of British Industrial Decline.* (Cambridge: Cambridge University Press, 1987); R. C. Michie, "Options" and "The Finance of innovation in Late Victorian and Edwardian Britain: Possibilities and Constraints". *Journal of European Economic History*, 17, 3 (Winter 1988): 491–530.
56. S. A. Bank and B. R. Cheffins, "The Corporate Pyramid Fable", *Business History Review* 84 (Autumn 2010): 435–458.
57. F. Gallice. "Une banque française dans la City: le Crédit Lyonnais à Londres (1870–1918)". Mémoire de DEA, Université de Paris X-Nanterre, 1994; C. Kobrak, *Banking on Global Markets: Deutsche Bank in the United States, 1870 to the Present* (Cambridge: Cambridge University Press, 2007); M. Pohl and K. Burk. *Deutsche Bank in London 1873–1998* (Munich: Piper, 1998); Hubert Bonin, Hubert, *Société Générale in the United Kingdom* (Paris: Société Générale, 1996).
58. Thomas W. Lawson, *Frenzied Finance* (New York: Ridgway-Thayer, 1905).
59. Franks J, C. Mayer and S. Rossi. "Ownership: Evolution and Regulation". *Review of Financial Studies*, 22 (10), 2009: 4009–4056. Janette Rutterford, Dimitris P. Sotiropoulos and Carry van Lieshout ("Individual investors and local bias in the UK: 1870–1935", Open University working paper 2015) confirm a strong (but declining) tendency for small local issues to be held by investors living within 25 km of the head office or place of listing, though find it was not associated with superior investment performance.
60. Recently, however, international cross-listings have declined, and the NYSE has lowered its standards, for example permitting dual class shares which it had earlier (beginning in the 1920s) attempted to outlaw. It is noteworthy that Hong Kong now stringently outlaws dual class shares that the NYSE tolerates: some Chinese firms with poor corporate governance have preferred an NYSE listing to an HKSE listing. There is no consensus even among today's most acute commentators on what is desirable: in one issue of the *Financial Times* (30 September 2015)

John Kay urged sympathetic consideration of the commitment potential of Amazon/Google unequal voting structures, while John Plender blamed the Volkswagen fraud on poor corporate governance driven by a similar structure. Hong Kong is one of the few exchanges sufficiently of the Plender persuasion to outlaw such share structures today, as Berlin did before 1914, the NYSE from the 1920s and LSE from the 1950s (though they began to abandon that principle soon after Hong Kong adopted it in 1987).

61. E.g the *Economist*'s prescient warning against investing in J.P. Morgan's International Mercantile Marine in 1902 (L. Hannah, "J.P. Morgan in London and New York before 1914", *Business History Review* 85 (2011), 113–150, at 132).
62. Latterly (in the wake of the Roosevelt corollary of the Monroe doctrine), some companies in Latin America and the Caribbean also adopted American standards and used New York capital markets.
63. M. Edelstein, *Overseas Investment in the Age of High Imperialism: The United Kingdom, 1850–1914* (London: Methuen, 1982); W. N. Goetzmann and A. D. Ukhov, "British Investment Overseas 1870–1913: A Modern Portfolio Theory Approach", *Review of Finance,* 10, 2006, pp. 261–300; B. R. Chabot, and C. J. Kurz. "That's Where the Money was: Foreign Bias and English Investment Abroad, 1866–1907". *Economic Journal,* 120, 2010, 1056–1079. Moreover, while some UK corporate bonds paid less than bank interest (reflecting their liquidity advantages over term loans), the reverse applied to many US corporate bonds, overpricing the default risk (Giesecke et al., "Corporate bonds").
64. N. Lamoreaux, "Did Insecure Property Rights Slow Economic Development? Some Lessons from Economic History", *Journal of Policy History*, 18, 1, 2006, 146–164; see also M. O'Sullivan, "The Expansion of the U.S. Stock Market, 1885–1930: Historical Facts and Theoretical Fashions", *Enterprise & Society*, 3, 2007, 489–542, at 534–7 and L. Davis. "The Capital Markets and Industrial Concentration". *Economic History Review*, 19, 1966, pp. 255–72. This literature is compatible with John Moody's view that finance expanded with trade, rather than fundamentally driving it (Friedman, *Fortune Tellers*, p. 89), the later position of some distinguished (and ideologically incompatible) economists from Joan Robinson to Robert Lucas.
65. E.g. D. R, Adler, *British Investment in American Railways 1834–1898* (Charlottesville VA: University Press of Virginia, 1970).

66. G. G. Jones, *The Evolution of International Business: an Introduction.* (London: Routledge, 1996).
67. Author's calculations from data in J. Dunning, *Explaining International Production* (New York, 1988), 74.

References

Archives

London Guildhall Library, LSE Archives, MS 18000/1.

Primary published material and calendars

American Bell Telephone Company Limited. *Annual Report 1886/7* (Boston: Bell, 1887).
Banker's Magazine, no 779, August 1914.
Banker's Magazine, no 869, August 1916.

Secondary Literature

Acheson, G. G., C. R. Hickson and J. D. Turner. 'Does limited liability matter? Evidence from nineteenth-century British banking', *Review of Law and Economics*, 6 (2011): 247–73.
Acheson, G. G, G. Campbell and J. D. Turner, "Common Law and the Origin of Shareholder Protection," EABH papers, no 16–03 (August 2016).
Acs, Z. J and D. B. Audretsch. 'An empirical examination of small firm growth', *Economics Letters*, 25 (1985): 363–366.
Adler, D. R, *British Investment in American Railways 1834–1898* (Charlottesville VA: University Press of Virginia, 1970).
Aldous, M. 'Avoiding Negligence and Profusion: the Failure of the Joint-Stock Form in the Anglo-Indian Tea Trade, 1840–1870', *Enterprise and Society* 16, 3 (2015): 648–85.
Annaert, J, F. Buelens and M. J. De Ceuster. 'New Belgian stock market returns: 1832–1914', *Explorations in Economic History*, 49 (2002): 189–204.
Anon. *James Finlay & Co Ltd, 1750–1950* (Glasgow: Jackson, 1951).

Anon, "Vision and Reality", *Economist* (12 September 2015).

Baker, W. J., *A History of the Marconi Company* (London: Methuen, 1970).

Bank, S. A., and B. R. Cheffins, 'The Corporate Pyramid Fable', *Business History Review* 84 (Autumn 2010): 435–458.

Bodenhorn, H, 'Two Centuries of Finance and Growth in the United States, 1790–1980', *NBER Working Paper* 22652 (2016).

Bonin, Hubert, *Société Générale in the United Kingdom* (Paris: Société Générale, 1996).

Brace, Harrison H. *The Value of Organized Speculation* (New York: Houghton Mifflin, 1913).

Burhop, Carsten, David Chambers and Brian Cheffins. 'Regulating IPOs: Evidence from Going Public in London, 1900–1913.' *Explorations in Economic History*, 51 (January 2014): 60–76.

Burhop, Carsten, David Chambers & Brian Cheffins, 'Law, Politics and the Rise and Fall of German Stock Market Development, 1870–1938', *European Corporate Governance Institute (ECGI)–Law Working Paper* No. 283 (2015).

Calomiris, C. W. "The Costs of Rejecting Universal Banking: American Finance in the German Mirror, 1870–1914," In *Coordination and Information: Historical Perspectives on the Organization of Enterprise*, edited by N. R. Lamoreaux and D. M. G. Raff, 257–322. Chicago: Chicago University Press, 1995.

Chabot, B. R., and C. J. Kurz. 'That's Where the Money was: Foreign Bias and English Investment Abroad, 1866–1907', *Economic Journal* 120 (2010), 1056–79.

Chambers, D. "Going public in interwar Britain." *Financial History Review* 17 (2010), 51–71.

Chandler, A. D. *Scale and Scope: The Dynamics of Industrial Capitalism*. Cambridge, MA: Harvard University Press, 1990.

Cheffins, Brian R. *Corporate Ownership and Control: British Business Transformed*. Oxford: Oxford University Press, 2008.

Cheffins, Brian R, S. A. Bank and H. Wells 'Shareholder Protection across Time' *University of Florida Law Review* (forthcoming, 2017).

Cochrane, Sarah. 'Explaining London's Dominance in International Financial Services, 1870–1913', *University of Oxford Department of Economics* working paper 455 (October 2009).

Cull, Robert, Lance Davis & Naomi Lamoreaux et al, 'Historical financing of small- and medium-size enterprises' *Journal of Banking and Finance*, Vol. 30, 11 (2006), 3017–3042.

Davis, L. 'The Capital Markets and Industrial Concentration' *Economic History Review*, 19, 1966, 255–72.
Davis, Lance and Larry Neal, 'The evolution of the rules and regulations of the first emerging markets: the London, New York and Paris stock exchanges, 1792–1914' *Quarterly Review of Economics and Finance*, Vol. 45 (2) (2005), 296–311.
De Long, J. B. 'Did J.P. Morgan's Men Add Value? An Economist's Perspective on Financial Capitalism' in *Inside the Business Enterprise: Historical Perspectives on the Use of Information*, edited by Peter Temin (Chicago: Chicago University Press, 1991), 205–36.
Dunning, John, *Explaining International Production* (New York: Routledge, 1988).
Edelstein, M. *Overseas Investment in the Age of High Imperialism: The United Kingdom, 1850–1914* (London: Methuen, 1982).
Edwards, J. R. 'Companies, Corporations and Accounting Change, 1835–1933: A Comparative Study' *Accounting and Business Research*, 23, No. 89 (1992): 59–73.
Evans, G. H. *British Corporation Finance 1775–1850: a study of preference shares* (Baltimore: John Hopkins Press, 1936).
Fear, J and C. Kobrak, 'Banks on Board: German and American Corporate Governance 1870–1914', *Business History Review* 84 (Winter 2010), 703–736.
Franks J, C. Mayer and S. Rossi. 'Ownership: Evolution and Regulation.' *Review of Financial Studies*, 22, 10 (2009), 4009–4056.
Freeman, M, R. Pearson, and J. Taylor. *Shareholder Democracies? Corporate Governance in Britain and Ireland before 1850* (Chicago: University of Chicago, 2012).
Friedman, Walter *Fortune Tellers: The Story of Americas First Economic Forecasters* (Princeton: Princeton University Press, 2015).
Foreman-Peck, James and Leslie Hannah, 'UK Corporate Law and Corporate Governance before 1914: a Re-interpretation', *EHES Working paper in Economic History*, no. 72 (2015).
Gallice, F., 'Une banque française dans la City: le Crédit Lyonnais à Londres (1870–1918)', Mémoire de DEA, Université de Paris X-Nanterre (1994).
Giesecke, Kay, Francis A. Longstaff, Stephen Schaefer, Ilya Strebulaev, 'Corporate Bond Default Risk: A 150-Year Perspective' *NBER Working Paper No. 15848* (2010).
Goetzmann, W. N., and A. D. Ukhov, 'British Investment Overseas 1870–1913: A Modern Portfolio Theory Approach', *Review of Finance*, 10 (2006) 261–300.

Goldsmith, Raymond, *Comparative national balance sheets: A study of twenty countries, 1688–1978* (Chicago: University of Chicago, 1985).

Goldsmith, *Financial intermediaries in the American economy since 1900* (Princeton: Princeton University Press, 1958).

Grandy, C. 'New Jersey Corporate Chartermongering, 1875–1929', *Journal of Economic History*, 49 (1989), 677–92.

Grossman, R. and M. Imai. 'Contingent capital and bank risk-taking among British banks before the First World War', *Economic History Review*, 66, 1 (2013), 132–55.

Guinnane, T. W. T., R. Harris, N. Lamoreaux and J-L Rosenthal, 'Contractual Freedom and the Evolution of Corporate Control in Britain, 1862 to 1929', *NBER Working Paper* 20481 (2014).

Hall, Peter A and David Soskice, *Varieties of Capitalism: The Institutional foundations of Comparative Advantage* (Oxford: Oxford University Press, 2001).

Hannah, L, 'London as the Global Market for Corporate Securities before 1914,' in L. Quennouëlle-Corre and Y. Cassis, eds. Financial Centres and International Capital Flows (Oxford: OUP, 2011), 126–60.

Hannah, L., 'J. P. Morgan in London and New York before 1914', *Business History Review* 85 (2011), 113–150.

Hannah, L, 'Leading Stock Exchanges before 1914: Equities, Bonds and the Neglected Role of the State', in K Sogner (ed.), *Entreprenørskap. Festskrift til ære for Even Lange* (Oslo: Novus Forlag, 2016), 13–28

Hilt, E. 'When Did Ownership Separate from Control? Corporate Governance in the Early-Nineteenth Century', *Journal of Economic History*, 58, 2008, 645–85.

Hilt, Eric and Carola Frydman 'Investment Banks as Corporate Monitors in the Early Twentieth Century United States', NBER Working Paper 20544 (2014).

Jefferys, J. B. *Business Organisation in Great Britain 1856–1914* (New York: Garland, 1970).

Jones, G. G. *The evolution of international business: an introduction* (London: Routledge, 1996).

———, and A. M. Colpan, 'Business Groups in Historical Perspective', in Colpan, T. Hikino and J. R. Lincoln, eds., *Oxford Handbook of Business Groups* (Oxford: Oxford University Press, 2012), 67–92.

Jones, G, '*Business Groups exist in developed markets also: Britain since 1850*', Harvard Business School working paper 16-066 (2015).

Kennedy, W.P. *Industrial Structure, Capital Markets and the Origins of British Industrial Decline* (Cambridge: Cambridge University Press, 1987).

King, R., and R. Levine. 'Finance and Growth: Schumpeter Might be Right', *Quarterly Journal of Economics*, 103 (1993), 717–37.
Knight, F. H. *Risk, Uncertainty, and Profit* (Boston MA: Houghton Mifflin, 1921)
Kobrak, C. *Banking on Global Markets: Deutsche Bank in the United States, 1870 to the present* (Cambridge: Cambridge University Press, 2007).
———, 'The Concept of Reputation in Business History', *Business History Review* 87 (Winter 2013), 763–786.
Lamoreaux, N, 'Did insecure property rights slow economic development? Some Lessons from Economic History', *Journal of Policy History*, 18, 1 (2006), 146–164.
Lamoreaux, N, M. Levenstein and K. Sokoloff. 'Financing Innovation in the Second Industrial Revolution: Cleveland, Ohio, 1870–1920' in *Financing Innovation in the United States, 1870 to Present*, Lamoreaux, K. Sokoloff, and W. H. Janeway, (eds.) (Cambridge MA: MIT Press, 2007).
La Porta, R. et al. 'Law and Finance', *Journal of Political Economy*, 106 (1998), 1113–55.
———, 'The Economic Consequences of Legal Origins', *Journal of Economic Literature*, 46, 2008, 285–332.
Lavington, F, *The English Capital Market* (London: Methuen, 1921).
Lawson, Thomas W. *Frenzied Finance* (New York: Ridgway-Thayer, 1905).
Loughlan, T and J Ritter, 'The New Issues Puzzle', *Journal of Finance*, 50 (1995): 23–51.
Lowenfeld, Henry. *Investment Practically Considered* (London: Financial Review of Reviews, 1909).
McQueen, Rob. *A Social History of Company Law: Great Britain and the Australian Colonies 1854–1920* (London: Ashgate, 2009).
Mahoney, P. G. 'The Origins of the Blue-Sky Laws: A Test of Competing Hypotheses', *Journal of Law and Economics*, 46, 1 (April 2003), 229–251.
Margo, Robert & William J. Collins, *Enterprising America: Business, Banks and Credit Markets in Historical Perspective* (Chicago: Chicago University Press, 2015).
Michie, R C., 'Options, Concessions, Syndicates, and the Provision of Venture Capital,1881–1913', *Business History*, 25 (1981): 147–64.
———, 'The Finance of innovation in Late Victorian and Edwardian Britain: Possibilities and Constraints', *Journal of European Economic History*, 17, 3 (Winter 1988), 491–530.
Meeker, J. E. *The Work of the Stock Exchange* (New York: Ronald Press, 1922).

Moore, Lynden 'World Financial Markets, 1900–1925', Working Paper.
Musacchio, A and J. D. Turner, 'Does the law and finance hypothesis pass the test of history?' *Business History* 55 (2013) 524–42.
Nanda, Ramana and Matthew Rhodes-Kropf. 'Financing Entrepreneurial Experimentation', *NBER Working Paper* 21278 (June 2015).
Newton, Lucy. 'Capital networks in the Sheffield region, 1850–1885', in J. F. Wilson and A. Popp, eds., *Industrial Clusters and Regional Business Networks in England, 1750–1970* (Aldershot: Ashgate, 2003), 130–154.
Neymarck, A, 'La statistique internationale des valeurs mobilières,' *Bulletin de l'Institut International de Statistique*, 14, (1905).
Nordhaus, W. D., 'Schumpeterian Profits in the American Economy: Theory and Measurement', *NBER Working Paper* 10433 (2004).
Nye, James G. D., 'The Company Promoter in London 1877–1914', University of London PhD thesis, 2011.
O'Sullivan, Mary A., 'Yankee Doodle went to London: Anglo-American breweries and the London securities market, 1888–92', *Economic History Review*, Vol.68 (4) (November 2015), 1365–1387.
———, "The Expansion of the U.S. Stock Market, 1885–1930: Historical Facts and Theoretical Fashions," *Enterprise & Society* 3 (2007): 489–542.
Perotti, E. and E-L von Thadden. 'The Political Economy of Corporate Control and Labor Rents,' *Journal of Political Economy*, 114 (2006), 145–75.
Pier, A. S., *Forbes: Telephone Pioneer* (New York: Dodds Mead, 1953).
Pohl M. and K. Burk. *Deutsche Bank in London 1873–1998* (Munich: Piper, 1998).
Powell, E. T, *The Evolution of the Money Market* (London: Cass, 1915).
Rajan, R. G. and L. Zingales. "The great reversals: the politics of financial development in the twentieth century." *Journal of Financial Economics* 69 (2003), 5–50.
Roe, M. J, *Strong Managers, Weak Owners* (Princeton: Princeton University Press, 1992).
Rutterford, Janette, 'The Shareholder Voice: British and American Accents, 1890 to 1965' *Enterprise & Society*, 13, 1 (2012): 120–3.
———, Dimitris P. Sotiropoulos and Carry van Lieshout, 'Individual investors and local bias in the UK: 1870–1935', Open University working paper 2015.
Scherer, F. M and D. Harhoff. 'Technology policy for a world of skew-distributed outcomes', *Research Policy*, 29 (2000): 559–566.

Seligman, J. *The Transformation of Wall Street* (Boston: Northeastern University Press, 1995).

Seltzer, Lawrence H. *A Financial History of the American Automobile Industry* (Boston: Houghton Mifflin, 1928).

Snowden, K. A. 'American Stock Exchange Development and Performance, 1871–1929' *Explorations in Economic History*, 24 (1987), 327–53.

Stehman, J. W. *The Financial History of the American Telephone and Telegraph Company* (Boston: Houghton Mifflin, 1925).

R. Sylla, 'Schumpeter Redux: A Review of Raghuram G. Rajan and Luigi Zingales's *Saving Capitalism from the Capitalists' Journal of Economic Literature,* 44 (2006) 391–404.

———, Wall Street Transitions, 1880–1920: from National to World Financial Centre," in L Quennouëlle-Corre and Y Cassis (eds.), *Financial Centres and International Capital Flows* (Oxford: Oxford University Press, 2011), 161–78.

Tosiello, R. J. *The Birth and Early Years of the Bell Telephone System 1876–1880* (New York: Arno Press, 1979).

Taylor, James, *Boardroom Scandal: The Criminalization of Company Fraud in Nineteenth-century Britain* (Oxford: Oxford University Press, 2013).

Toms, Steven. "The Rise of Modern Accounting and the Fall of the Public Company: The Lancashire Cotton Mills, 1870–1914." *Accounting, Organizations and Society* 27, 1 (2002): 61–84.

Vanderlip, F. A, *From Farm Boy to Financier* (New York: D. Appleton-Century Company Inc., 1935).

White, Eugene N. "Competition among the exchanges before the SEC: was the NYSE a natural hegemon?" *Financial History Review*, 20, 1 (2013): 29–48.

Wright, R. E, *Corporation Nation* (Philadelphia: University of Pennsylvania, 2014).

10

Adolf Berle's Critique of US Corporate Interests in the Caribbean Basin

Jason Russell, Andrew Smith and Kevin D. Tennent

The expansion of the USA into a global economic power began with the extension of its influence over the Caribbean and subsequently Latin America. This was not an accidental process and was instead the result of foreign policy decisions that led to USA's political and economic dominance in the western hemisphere. Adolph Berle, a key member of Franklin Roosevelt's Brain Trust, played an important part in this process. Berle has been somewhat lost to posterity, but he exerted considerable influence in the Roosevelt administration. He initially came to social and political prominence because, in the words of his biographer

J. Russell (✉)
Empire State College—State University of New York, Saratoga Springs, USA
e-mail: Jason.Russell@esc.edu

A. Smith
University of Liverpool Management School, Liverpool, UK
e-mail: A.D.Smith@liverpool.ac.uk

K.D. Tennent
University of York, York, UK
e-mail: kevin.tennent@york.ac.uk

W.A. Pettigrew and D.C. Smith (eds.), *A History of Socially Responsible Business, c.1600–1950*, Palgrave Studies in the History of Finance,
DOI 10.1007/978-3-319-60146-5_10

Jordan Schwarz, he wrote "that book".[1] The book in question was *The Modern Corporation and Private Property*, which called on the managers of US corporations to take the interests of a wide range of stakeholders, including workers and communities, into account when making a strategy. The impact of this controversial 1933 work, co-authored with Gardiner Means, generated extensive discussion in much the same fashion as Thomas Piketty's recent best-selling critique of inequality.[2] This discussion questioned the international, social responsibilities of US corporations as they began to flex their muscles in the western hemisphere.

This chapter relates the philosophical outlook presented in *The Modern Corporation and Private Property* to Berle's prior experience of living in the Caribbean basin and his subsequent efforts in the late 1930s to reshape US policy in that region. This chapter relates Berle to the existing business-historical literature on the relationship between American capital and the American state in the Caribbean basin and Latin America. This chapter draws extensively on Adolf Berle's personal papers, which are now located at the Franklin D. Roosevelt Presidential Library. This chapter argues that, while Berle was critical of the excesses of some US corporations in the region, he was neither anti-capitalist nor an opponent of US overseas economic expansion. In fact, the policies Berle promoted ultimately served to strengthen long-term well-being of US business interests overseas by reigning in the worst abuses of US business imperialism in the Latin America. Under previous Republican presidents from William McKinley onward, the US government had routinely backed up US companies by "sending in the Marines" whenever local political actors were standing in the way of profit. Berle believed that this policy was counter-productive to the long-term geopolitical and economic interests of the USA and its corporations. Berle's critique of US corporations was thus a fundamentally friendly one. Berle's belief that the long-term interests of US business in the western hemisphere could be served by sometimes siding with Latin American governments in disputes with particular US firms contributed to his strong support for Franklin Roosevelt's "Good Neighbor" policy. In the context of the US state's relations with American corporations, this policy represented an internationalization of socially responsible business practices. As Assistant Secretary of State for Latin American Affairs from 1938 to 1944, Berle influenced US policy during a crucial period in US–Latin American relations. During this period, the Roosevelt administration acquiesced when Mexico nationalized the holdings of US oil companies.[3] The decision of the Roosevelt administration not to give the US oil companies the unstinting support they had requested was fully in keeping with Berle's philosophy. By showing Berle's influence on Roosevelt's policy, this chapter thus offers a re-interpretation of the impact of that policy and its longer term implications for US multinational enterprise. In particular, it demonstrates how US foreign policy began to appreciate that prioritizing the overseas social basis for US corporate expansion offered a surer means to uphold the longer term interests of those corporations and their domicile nation.

The relationship between multinational enterprise and imperialism is a major research theme in business history. Business historians have published extensively on the chartered trading companies. The proto-multinationals of the early modern period were similar to, but nevertheless, conceptually distinct from the first true multinationals, which emerged in the nineteenth century. Robert Fitzgerald's recent account of the rise of the global company has underscored the difference between such chartered trading monopolies as the East India and Hudson's Bay Company and the multinationals that developed after about 1850.[4] A key distinction between the early modern proto-multinationals and the multinationals formed during the pre-1914 golden age of globalization is that while the latter were formed by states to mobilize mercantile wealth to advance public ends, multinationals were essentially private-sector creations that subsequently acquired political power to support their international strategies. Emerging scholarship on the transformation of capital during World War I—a period of enormous economic expansion in the USA—reveals interaction between governments and business that to an extent challenges the simple dichotomy of early modern corporations as public precursors to their modern descendants because it shows the clear public role and social obligations that modern private corporations were expected to honour.[5]

But the relationships between the state and private corporations were complex. Much of the secondary literature on the developments of the modern multinational focuses on the historical relationship between the emergence of the multinational firm and Britain's formal and informal empires, a theme that has been explored with great sensitivity by Geoffrey Jones, Howard Cox, Stephanie Decker and other business historians. As business historians have used corporate archives to explore the extent to which the interests of British multinationals were promoted by the British state, they have collectively painted a picture that forces us to reconsider the Cain-Hopkins thesis that the British Empire was run in the interests of gentlemanly capitalist firms located in the City of London.[6] The business-historical literature on the relationship between imperial power and the development of British multinationals shows that their relationship was complex: the projection of British military and political powerful overseas frequently assisted British multinationals, but the British state did not consistently defer to the policy preferences of Britain's multinationals.[7] Thanks to political historians such as Sarah Stockwell and Nicholas White, we now know that the British state maintained a degree of autonomy from British capital that is incompatible with a strong version of the Marxian account of the connection between imperialism and the multinational corporation.[8]

The literature on the relationship between US imperialism and the rise of US multinational corporations has also resulted in the development of a nuanced view that contrasts that of early authors such as Charles David Kepner and Jay Henry Soothill, who depicted US policy in Latin America as having been dictated by the interests of sinister US multinationals.[9] Kepner and Soothill focused on the political power in Washington of United Fruit, a firm known to generations of Latin American leftists as "El Pulpo". These authors suggested that United Fruit and other US multinationals active in the western hemisphere existed essentially because of US military imperialism in the region, a viewpoint that suggests that the international expansion of these firms occurred essentially at the point of a bayonet.

In sharp contrast, Mira Wilkins's discussion of the evolution of United Fruit de-emphasized the role of US political and military imperialism in her discussion of the development of US multinational firms in Latin America. Although Wilkins acknowledged that there was likely some truth in the left-wing criticisms of United Fruit as it existed in the early twentieth century, she suggested that the continued profitability of this firm was not due to US military power.[10] In her account of the rise of United Fruit, as in that of Robert Read, the formation of this vast vertically integrated enterprise with plantations in Latin America, railways and ships, and distribution facilities in the USA was simply a function of a shift towards vertical integration seen in all sectors of the US economy around the turn of the twentieth century.[11] These authors also explained the subsequent vertical disintegration of this company after 1945 with reference to non-political, technological factors that encouraged the firm to sell off its overseas banana plantations and rely instead on independent contract producers. In other words, the accounts of Wilkins and Reads implied that United Fruit pushed politics to the background, whereas those of the Kepner, Soothill and the *dependencia* theorists emphasized the political foundations of United Fruit and, by association, other US firms active in Latin America and the Caribbean.[12]

The most recent research on the history of US business in Latin America has staked out a middle ground between these two viewpoints that acknowledges the importance of US government political support to the profitability of these firms while also recognizing the relative autonomy of the US state and drawing on the insights to be derived from Wilkins's fundamentally Chandlerian perspective. For instance, Marcelo Bucheli's excellent study of United Fruit shows that while the non-political factors identified by Wilkins are certainly important in explaining the rise and fall of this vertically integrated firm, politics was also central to the strategies of this controversial firm.[13] Bucheli's accounts of ITT (International Telephone and Telegraph) in Chile and the oil industry in Colombia present similarly nuanced views of the relationship between US hard power and US business interests.[14]

This chapter builds on these earlier efforts to develop nuanced and balanced views of the relationships between the US state and US business interest in Latin America and the Caribbean by exploring Berle's evolving ideas about US business in the hemisphere and the impact of his ideas on the making of US policy. This chapter shows that while

Berle was certainly very critical of many of the actions of specific US corporations, his critique was ultimately intended to be a constructive one: by eliminating the worst abuses by particular US businesses in the region, the Good Neighbor policy supported by Berle was intended to make the region more hospitable for US capitalism as a whole. Berle's work in helping to create the Good Neighbor policy can, therefore, be seen as part of a broader policy of trying to save capitalism from itself. Our paper draws on the concept of "the relative autonomy" of the state, a theoretical perspective that has been used by political economists such as Leo Panitch and Sam Gindin[15] as well as by business historians such as Dimitry Anastakis.[16] Expressed in simple term, the relative autonomy perspective stresses that policymakers often defend the long-term interests of business as a whole by standing up to the demands of particular firms. The relative autonomy view thus contrasts with the classical Marxian view that business interests dictate policy to governments in capitalist societies. In our view, the relative autonomy theory corresponds with the archival research presented below.

The founders of the USA sometimes used the term "empire of liberty".[17] In the twentieth century, US policymakers eschewed the term "empire" when describing their country's role in the world because it was redolent of the overt colonialism of the European nations. Nonetheless, the idea that the USA has long functioned as a form of imperial power in the world has received considerable popular and scholarly attention. This is also true when considering the role of American business and capital in furthering the country's international influence. For example, Noel Maurer has recently described empire as a trap into which the USA frequently found itself ensnared from the late nineteenth century onward.[18] This interest in protecting US economic interests began with the Caribbean basin, extended to Latin America, then to regions around the world. A desire to keep European imperial powers away from American economic interests motivated the first clearly articulated American policy on interference in the western hemisphere with the introduction of the Monroe Doctrine in 1823. As Kyle Longley has noted, the need to ward off Russia from encroaching on the Pacific Northwest was the ostensible rationale for the Monroe Doctrine but the broader message to Europe was that further colonization in the western hemisphere would not be tolerated by the USA.[19]

American influence in the Caribbean region gradually increased through the nineteenth century as that of European powers waned, but markedly increased after the 1898 Spanish–American War. A victorious USA acquired former Spanish colonies in Cuba, the Philippines and other smaller territories but then did not call them colonies. Doing so would have made the USA equal to the country that it had just defeated. US policy was to instead implement legal frameworks and other infrastructure that was familiar to Americans and amendable to US business, then work to ensure that friendly governments ran the newly independent countries. As Panitch and Gindin have argued, the decision not to have extensive overseas territories and instead rely on capitalism laid the foundation for American global expansion.[20]

The second major turning point in US influence in the Caribbean, indeed across the western hemisphere, was the construction of the Panama Canal. Work on it began in 1901, and the canal opened in 1914. Julie Green has perceptively noted that the defeat of Spain marked America's emergence as a world power.[21] The construction of the canal was a remarkable engineering feat that demonstrated America's technological prowess. The colonization of the American West had been spurred by a belief in the country's manifest destiny to expand west across the North American continent, and Green argues that the extension of American influence into the Caribbean basin and beyond through the construction of the Panama Canal was a continuation of manifest destiny.[22] The canal was of such importance in the USA that Theodore Roosevelt's visit to the construction zone in 1906 was the first time that a sitting US president had left the country.[23]

In the early 1900s, Americans articulated a desire to expand influence abroad, particularly in the Caribbean. In 1929, for example, business-friendly journalist Samuel Crowther commented on how a "great American experiment" was being tried in the Caribbean.[24] Business was central to American expansion. Crowther argued that existing business practices in the region were corrupt, stating that "Very few of the entrenched Latin Americans can envisage absolute honesty—either morally or as a convenience".[25] In contrast, American firms were honest "and do not bribe".[26] Americans were not interested in becoming entrenched in Latin American countries because:

> The best citizens of the United States prefer to retain their citizenship and home ties. They also do not often care to become permanent residents of other countries. That is an attitude of strength and not of weakness.[27]

American companies such as United Fruit had made salutary contributions to the Caribbean basin countries in which they operated. Indeed, in Crowther's view, "the best proof, however, of the effect of American wages is that a labourer who has once worked for an American company will not thereafter work for anyone else".[28] Crowther's views, while aligned with American business interests, were surely not outside of mainstream public and policy-making discourse. The USA was developing the nations in the Caribbean in a "broad and scientific manner".[29]

The Panama Canal was a symbol of the most obvious example of what the US government and business interests thought that America should do in the Caribbean, but the same ethos was evident whenever an American company established operations in the region. The expansion of US power in the Caribbean was not without controversy. The use of force to expand US economic and foreign policy interests frequently involved using military force. The US army had been principally dedicated to fighting on the western frontier in the post-bellum period, but the navy had been gradually expanded although not yet equal in size to its European counterparts. The expansion into foreign operations began during and after the Spanish–American War, and was led by officers who had been schooled in manifest destiny while stationed in the American west. This included Leonard Wood, who served in both the Philippines and Cuba. His approach to America's role in the Caribbean was clear. For example, he stated that "Americanizing" the Cubans was an objective during the occupation of the island.[30] Wood further believed, when describing Cubans, that "the people here know that they aren't ready for self-government".[31] Americanizing the Cubans would solve that problem, along with other initiatives such as improving education and health care. This position also reflected a continuation of policies already pursued in the USA in the late nineteenth century.

Middle-class social reformers had long promoted the benefits of things like better education and health care to improve the lives of the working class. Wood was certainly reflecting those middle-class progressive policy positions during his time in Cuba. Progressives therefore stressed the importance of building a sympathetic constituency for American economic expansion into the region through social and educational programmes.

While the US military was broadly supportive of the agenda of extending US economic influence into the Caribbean, it would be a mistake to regard US military officers such as Wood as uncritical of US business imperialism in all respects. Wood, whose political sympathies were with Progressives who wanted to reform US capitalism through the imposition of regulations on Big Business, also believed that US business interests in the Caribbean needed to be reined in by the US government. His firm but fair attitude towards US business interests can be seen in the approach he took to Cuban and Filipino economic policy during the US occupation of those territories. Wood was supportive of the wider project of opening these territories up to US business; he did not support US business interests in all of their conflicts with locals. For instance, he argued that there should be full trade reciprocity between Cuba and the USA.[32] Not permitting Cubans to have access to the US market would have harmed Cuban planters and smaller commercial interests and probably, in Wood's view, the development of social institutions such as education and health care that he valued. In the policies of Leonard Wood, who served as military governor of Cuba and subsequently Governor-General of the Philippines, we can see the relative autonomy of the US state from US business interests and the importance the state attached to socially responsible American enterprise in international settings.[33] In this sense, Wood's ideas were a precursor of those of Berle.

Wood, as we have seen, was broadly supportive of US business imperialism although he occasionally supported policies that were opposed by some US business interests in the region. Not all American military officers were as convinced of the utility of supporting the expansion of American economic and political influence overseas. Marine officer Smedley Butler served under Wood during the Spanish–American War and was also later sent to Nicaragua and Haiti. He bitterly commented on an incident in Nicaragua in a 1912 letter saying "A victory gained for us by them at the expense of two good American lives, all because Brown Brothers Bankers have some money invested in this heathenish country".[34] Wood and Butler were part of the American military effort to expand American influence in the Caribbean, as was Jack Pershing. Pershing, also a subordinate of Wood's, led an American incursion into Mexico in 1914 and would subsequently command the American army that went to France in 1917. Wood, in particular, was involved in a war preparedness initiative that would directly influence Adolf Berle: the Plattsburg camps for junior officers. The camps were part of the pre-World War I preparedness movement that was opposed by President Woodrow Wilson. Plattsburg, located in upstate New York, was funded by the War Department but trainees were not compensated for their participation. These camps were modelled after training camps that Wood had created in 1913 for university students. The people who trained at Plattsburg were, in many cases, university educated and often had business or professional backgrounds. Adolf Berle and Gardiner Means were among the trainees.[35]

Adolf Berle's biographer argued that Berle wanted to lead a "causative life".[36] Berle was not a product of the American frontier, but his life was influenced by the experience of coming from an immigrant family. He was well educated, having graduated from Harvard Law School in 1916, and wanted to be influential.[37] Berle joined the army in 1917 despite having reservations about the US entering World War I. He recollected later in life:

> Most of all I didn't like this war. I didn't see any particular reason why the United States had to put all its energies into settling whether the Hohenzollerns dominated Europe or whether the French entrenched interests behind Clemenceau and so forth were to be the masters of Europe. This made me very unpopular in my undergraduate career.

He continued:

> They assumed (Harvard Law School) that as a matter of course that when a man's time came to go into the Army, he'd go into the Army.[38]

Berle's first major assignment, and first contact with the Caribbean, was in the Dominican Republic in 1917 following training at Plattsburg.[39] Service on the island as part of an American occupation force was highly formative for Berle. The US military was present in response to economic turmoil in the Dominican Republic that was adversely impacting American interests. Intervention was initiated by Woodrow Wilson, and Maurer has noted that it effectively led to an American military dictatorship.[40] From Berle's perspective, the American military was in the Dominican Republic because of sugar. This was at least partially true because, as Veeser has described, governments in the Dominican Republic began granting concessions to foreign companies in the late 1800s but the administration of them led to domestic disputes and disagreements with the USA.[41] His job, as an intelligence officer and trained lawyer, was to work on new laws that would change the terms of land ownership.[42] Berle would have fully agreed with Maurer's view that the USA was acting as a military dictator in the Dominican Republic. He remembered:

> At that time, the Dominican Republic was under occupation by the Navy and the Marines. A Navy admiral was governor, a Marine division was in control. I learned then what an intervention, military dictatorship, even by the United States, really meant. I didn't like the dictatorship very well, but couldn't do too much about it, but I did get something done and eventually, though much too late to be of any use to the war, the Dominican Land Act was duly passed and actually is in force still.[43]

Berle explained how his work on the Land Act was designed to facilitate an increased supply of sugar to the USA:

> In early 1917 I landed in Santo Domingo City and went to work clearing the land titles for South Puerto Rico Sugar Co. and incidentally for any other sugar company that would go to work to produce more sugar and export it to the United States.[44]

Siberia was meant to be Berle's next posting, but instead, he was appointed to be an aide to one of the American delegates to the

Versailles peace conference. Aged just 24, his duties included working on issues relating to the independence of the Baltic republics.[45] Berle learned a lot about relations between nation states during his time at Versailles:

> It was then I learnt the practice of foreign affairs was essentially a damnable profession. You may prevent it from being worse than it otherwise would be, but the amount of savage human misery that even a minor decision in foreign affairs can create may be infinitely grave.

Berle clearly had mixed feelings about his wartime experience and more broadly about how the USA should involve itself in foreign affairs. He did not see direct combat, but readily saw the challenges of direct military intervention and the seemingly intractable nature of relations between major powers. He was not bitter like Smedley Butler. He did believe, like Leonard Wood, that it was appropriate to organize matters such as land ownership laws so that they benefited American economic interests. The USA was a young, strong global power in 1919 while the major European countries were prostrate after the ordeal of total war. The European imperial model must have seemed bankrupt to Berle when he left Versailles. But it could not have escaped his attention that the USA was simply continuing manifest destiny into the Caribbean. The experiences that he had in the Dominican Republic and France from 1917 to 1919 would shape Berle's approach to the Caribbean in the tumultuous 1930s.

Adolf Berle continued with his mission to lead a life of consequence after World War I. He practised and taught law, and most importantly wrote *The Modern Corporation and Private Property.* Gardiner Means was listed as co-author on the front cover, but Berle was the principal author of the book. The book did not discuss foreign affairs and instead concentrated on the power wielded by American corporations. Berle was not opposed to capital and free markets. He instead believed that corporate power was a social and political issue, and that capital should be regulated. He was especially concerned with the concentration of power within the hands of corporate management. On the other hand, he believed that capital's interests should be protected, but within the framework of wider national domestic and foreign goals. The state should have primacy in policymaking.

Berle would become a strong advocate for the Good Neighbor policy and Franklin Roosevelt's approach to Latin American affairs. The roots of this policy can be found within the administration of Roosevelt's predecessor: Herbert Hoover. As Longley has noted, Hoover implemented changes in US policy towards Latin America. Direct intervention was no longer favoured. Hoover made a seven-day trip to key countries in the Caribbean and Latin America shortly after being elected in an effort to begin improving relations. Hoover differed from people like Leonard Wood because he was not a military man. He instead was a mining engineer and businessman. Hoover likely thought that achieving stability in the Caribbean and Latin America through commercial activity was a better use of American time and resources than dispatching armed force.[46]

Hoover's administration lasted just one term, but Franklin Roosevelt continued along the same path. A series of trade agreements were signed with Caribbean basin and Latin American countries between 1932 and 1941. An Import Export bank was created in 1934 to extend credit to Latin American countries in order for them to buy American goods. These policies were helpful for American domestic output, but they also drew Latin American closer to the USA. American military force was ready should intervention be absolutely necessary, but direct intervention did not occur during the Roosevelt years.[47]

Adolf Berle initially came to Roosevelt's attention while the latter man was still governor of New York State. Berle advised the new president on economic matters, and an often-lively correspondence took place between them. For example, Roosevelt once advised Berle that he did not mind being called "Caesar" but cautioned Berle about referring to him as "Napoleon".[48] The Brain Trust was comprised of thirteen people, and most of them had been educated at Harvard.[49] It included Dean Acheson, who would later become US Secretary of State. Berle was likely the member of this group who was most interested in the Caribbean and Latin America. At a time when the US would send diplomats who did not speak Spanish to Spanish-speaking countries, Berle could speak fluent Spanish. He was appointed Assistant Secretary of State in 1937. He publicly feigned indifference to the appointment, but privately recorded in his diary that his decision was based on political considerations rather than reluctance to actually join the State Department.[50]

The Good Neighbor Policy came to the forefront of US foreign policy during Berle's years at the State Department. It was, as Mary Stuckey suggested, a policy position that was part of a wider belief held by Roosevelt that the world was becoming like a neighbourhood.[51] This was a position articulated at a time of considerable domestic upheaval. Unemployment was high during the early Roosevelt years, the American economy was still weak, and the Democratic president faced often fierce criticism. One opposition group, the American Liberty League, had 124,000 members in 1936.[52] Roosevelt responded with the creation of a Good Neighbor League in the same year.[53] So, being neighbourly was a concept that was part of the Roosevelt administration's view of how Americans should operate both abroad and at home. Americans ought to be as socially aware, so the policy suggested, abroad as they should be at home.

As Scarfi has observed, a series of agreements concluded between 1933 and 1936 led to a final prohibition of hemispheric intervention in the Americas.[54] Roosevelt declared in 1933 that the USA would not engage in armed intervention in the affairs of neighbouring countries.[55] People in the Caribbean and Latin America were aware of the New Deal and approved of it.[56] There was also the pressing reality that fascist countries in Europe, especially Germany and Italy, were quite willing to interfere in the affairs of other countries. The Roosevelt administration was especially concerned about German efforts to promote fascism in Latin America from 1937 to 1938.[57] The 1938 Declaration of Lima saw countries in the Americas agree to convene yearly meetings of foreign ministers.[58] That was followed by a Declaration of Panama in 1939 that established a security perimeter around the Americas.[59] Aside from pro-Nazi sentiment in Argentina, there was not widespread interest in supporting the Axis cause in the Caribbean or Latin America.

The most compelling example of the way in which the Good Neighbor Policy encouraged the US state to act in the general and long-term interests of American business (rather than the short-term interests of particular companies) was the Roosevelt administration's decision to accept nationalization of the Mexican oil industry. This decision infuriated US oil companies. As Lorenzo Meyer has argued, American policymakers became gradually aware as World War II began that an agreement with Mexico over nationalization had to be reached. Doing so would demonstrate the viability of the Good Neighbor Policy to Mexico, but also across Latin America. The agreement that was finalized illustrated that being neighbourly was effective for overall US foreign policy, even if it upset certain US business interests.[60]

The minutiae of how relations between states actually operate can be found behind the treaties and declarations. It was in that realm that Berle brought his expertise to the fore. He was not parochial, and instead felt that interaction between the USA and countries in the Caribbean and Latin America should be reciprocal beyond trade. He was interested in exposing Americans to countries to the south. For instance, in 1939, he agreed to explore exchanges to Cuba for college and high school students. An organization called the American Peace Committee expressed interest in a congress of students that would "give democratic reality to the Good Neighbor Policy".[61]

Berle also responded to queries regarding domestic affairs in the Caribbean basin, and commercial interests were often central to discussions. For instance, a dispute arose in 1939 regarding two companies—All America Cables and Radio Corporation of America (RCA)—and their operations in Ecuador. Attorneys representing All America Cables wrote to Berle noting that the firms had operated in Latin America for some time. Indeed, in Ecuador, they had been able to take advantage of a "most favoured nation" designation. A new government came into power in Ecuador in 1938 and began to pressure All America Cables to accept a new and less favourable contract for communication services. The company's attorneys argued to Berle that the Ecuadorian government was confiscating contractual rights.[62] The position of the company was that the US government ought to provide it with uncritical support in its fight with the Ecuadorian government. Although it is likely that previous Republican administrations would have backed this US corporation, the Roosevelt administration took a very different approach.

This situation with All America Cables perhaps could have been easily resolved through diplomatic channels were it not complicated by the fact that the Ecuadorian government had, in addition to essentially voiding the initial contract, also contracted with RCA to provide communication technology. The agreement with RCA provided for joint operation of a communication network. Counsel for All America Cables did not question the right of the Ecuadorian government "to go into the radio business or the cable business in good faith on its own account" but they were clearly vexed that another competing American firm had entered the Ecuadorian market to conspire with the local government to displace their client. Counsel for All America Cables was especially aggrieved that RCA would be subject to a different rate of location taxation and other conditions than their client had previously faced. All America Cables' attorneys went on to cite sections of the agreement between the government of Ecuador and their client to further their contention that RCA was operating improperly.[63]

The All America Cables case is important because it illustrates some of the reasons why the Roosevelt administration pursued a policy of non-interventionism. For instance, against whom could force be used in the case of two American firms facing each other within the context of a legal dispute? This was a case that was also markedly different due to the nature of the firms involved. Both were providing advanced manufactured equipment and probably technical expertise to go with it. This was not an agricultural dispute or one pertaining to resource extraction. In fact, All America Cable would eventually become part of International Telephone and Telegraph (ITT). ITT was, as Marcelo Bucheli and Erica Salvaj have noted, a company that continued to expand in Latin America while also developing a difficult reputation.[64]

The All America Cables case is also a commentary on the Good Neighbor doctrine. The USA was attempting to negotiate a reciprocal trade agreement over a range of products with Ecuador when the dispute between All America Cables, the Ecuadorian government and RCA was taking place.[65] Suddenly intervening over one dispute could have damaged negotiations over a range of other products and industries. Being a good neighbor meant signing agreements and relying on formal dispute resolution mechanisms. Berle's thoughts on the All

America Cables and RCA dispute are not available, but he likely viewed it within the context of his training and experience as a corporate lawyer and saw it as an extension of what occurred in the USA. What he would not have perhaps noted was how greater trade integration between nations, and having American companies competing against each other abroad, would also eventually stimulate the emergence of global shareowners.[66]

Adolf Berle was willing to discuss detailed instances of international commercial disputes, but being involved in big initiatives provided more opportunity to really impact American policy. The USA began planning for the post-World War II world shortly after the conflict began and before the country entered it. In 1940, several subcommittees were established by the State Department to consider America's role in the coming years. Members of these committees included Sumner Welles, Dean Acheson, Green Hackworth, Leo Paslovsky and Adolf Berle.[67] Work on the agenda for the subcommittee that dealt with economic affairs actually began in 1939, and the topics on which it focused can be viewed as an expansion of policies that the USA was already pursuing in the western hemisphere including: the machinery of trade relations, tariff matters, governmental quantitative controls, "most-favoured nation" treatment, probable credit and investment needs of the post-war world, and types of monetary arrangements necessary for the promotion of trade, credit and investment relations.[68] The close, reciprocal link between political stability and economic stability was emphasized in these early planning documents.[69] A further assumption was that the post-war political arrangements would be regionally based, but economic relations would be universal (meaning open).[70] Regional economic formations would not be suitable. This was a clear call, at least, for a series of global trade agreements and even for free trade. What is most striking about the content of these planning documents is that, even before America had entered the war, there was a clear underlying assumption that it likely would emerge from the conflict in a position to shape the post-war economic order. These proposals would establish favourable conditions for the global expansion of capitalism, without necessarily doing so at the behest of capital. Panitch and Gindin have described how this process of relative autonomy led to the conclusion of international agreements such as Bretton Woods.[71] The road to agreements such as Bretton Woods at least partially originated in the committee work in which Berle participated in the early days of World War II.

The work of the post-war planning committees began to come to light once the USA entered the war and especially after the creation of the Atlantic Charter. Berle was an advocate of the charter, and it is a document that is also rooted in American policy in the Caribbean Basin and Latin America despite the popular perception that it was principally a trans-Atlantic initiative. Twenty-six countries signed the charter and eight of them—Costa Rica, Cuba, Dominican Republic, El Salvador, Guatemala, Haiti, Honduras, Nicaragua and Panama—were in the Caribbean Basin. This could be viewed as an American effort to further mitigate against Axis efforts to influence hemispheric affairs and consequently represented a continuation of the Monroe Doctrine. The USA was, however, also actively formulating and pursuing a foreign policy based on economic integration and that process had already been going on in the Caribbean for decades prior to World War II.[72]

Adolf was not the sole architect of the Good Neighbor Policy. Several influential policy-making figures contributed to it. His main contribution came through his belief that capital should be permitted to expand beyond the USA but should be regulated by the expectation that the long-term interests of US business would be best served by establishing economic relations overseas that furthered social cohesion. The USA indeed formed a post-war economic empire. This was achieved through the proliferation of American business and financial capital. Berle, looking back askance at what he experienced in the Dominican Republic and Versailles, rejected European forms of empire building. He stated during a 1948 speech to the Institute for Religious and Social Studies in New York City:

> The Good Neighbor Policy, though of world-wide application, received its principal effect in the western hemisphere, and is one of the ties by which the American family of nations are linked for their common welfare. Enunciation of the policy in 1933, and its prompt application by Secretary of State Cordell Hull at the Montevideo conference in that

> year revolutionized our relations with the other twenty republics of the Americas...If they cease to exist, the Pan-American treaties could become as empty as the endless series of temporary alliances, the scraps of whose paper clutter recent European history.

Berle even framed the ongoing success of Pan-American cooperation within the context of race relations:

> In blunt fact, the holding together of the American family of nations through the Good Neighbor Policy is difficult—perhaps impossible—if we continue the policy of race discrimination here. Since no American nation, including our own, can maintain itself effectively or defend itself successfully, except as a member of a group, the alternative is grim. The United States will be forced back into the old and discredited logic of empire—or will be left in dangerous isolation.

The Good Neighbor Policy was, in Berle's mind, an instrument of social cohesion and fairness as much as it was about foreign and economic policy.[73]

Adolf Berle lived during pivotal decades in the development of the USA. The country emerged as a global power then grew to be the dominant nation in the world. "Causative" individuals like Berle pursued deliberate policies to facilitate their country's advancement, and the first steps that they took happened close to home in the Caribbean. Berle further believed that the USA must pursue policies different from those that had been implemented by European powers. The emphasis that Berle placed on avoiding military intervention while pursuing ever-closer economic ties helped lay the foundation for the modern global economic order. Berle does not appear to have retained any papers pertaining to entities such as the International Monetary Fund, but he must have approved of them as they were an expansion of what the US began with the Import-Export Bank.

The Good Neighbor Policy had a lasting impact on the global economy. The USA still operates largely in sympathy with free trade, albeit with growing contemporary domestic resistance across from current political leadership and across the political spectrum. This approach has arguably allowed the country to maintain its global economic influence although perhaps at the expense of economic development in many American communities. Fascism was largely kept out of the western hemisphere—a key objective of the Good Neighbor Policy. Preventing the emergence of communist governments in Latin America was an American foreign policy objective during the post-war decades, and it was mainly successful with the major exception of Cuba. On the other hand, the USA tolerated decidedly undemocratic regimes in some countries in the western hemisphere.

There was continuity of thought in foreign policy from the time that the USA defeated Spain in 1898. Military intervention was discontinued, but the overall process of Americanization was constant. Building roads and hospitals, improving education and otherwise promoting American economic policies and practices were the main methods of trying to shape the Caribbean Basin and Latin America. As Robert Elias has shown, even baseball was a method of Americanization.[74] American business was often the vehicle through which these objectives were pursued. Berle was a major contributor to his country's policies in Latin America and the Caribbean, and those contributions were as significant as the book that he wrote on the power of corporations.

Berle's ideas about US business interests in the hemisphere need to be understood primarily in relation to his immediate context: like many New Dealers, Berle was far from hostile to capitalism and instead sought to save capitalism from itself. The domestic crisis of US capitalism in the early 1930s encouraged the paradigm shift in Washington that saw the US government adopts a very different stance towards US business interests in Latin America and the Caribbean. The legacy of the New Deal era is undergoing renewed scholarly scrutiny. This chapter forces us to rethink the makings of the Good Neighbor policy by linking it back to the domestic politics of the US in the New Deal era.[75] Like most historians, the authors of this paper are reluctant to make sweeping generalizations and to spell out lessons for the present based on historical case studies. However, we do think that the study of Berle and the making of the Good Neighbor policy could be instructive for present-day policymakers. Robert Reich, an author who sees himself as an intellectual descendant of Franklin Delano Roosevelt, has recently declared that it is necessary to emulate the New Deal of 1930 if we are to save capitalism from itself.[76] Those who agree with Reich's thesis may wish to study Berle's efforts in the 1930s to change the relationship between US-based multinationals and the US government.

Notes

1. Jordan A. Schwarz, *Liberal: Adolf A. Berle and the Vision of an American Era* (New York: Macmillan, 1987), viii.
2. See Thomas Piketty, *Capital in the Twenty-First Century* (New York: Belknap, 2014).
3. Daniel Yergin, *The Prize: the Epic Quest for Oil, Money, and Power* (New York: Free Press, 2003), 276.
4. Robert Fitzgerald, *The Rise of the Global Company: Multinationals and the Making of the Modern World* (Cambridge: Cambridge University Press, 2015), 34–37, 40, 45, 76.
5. Andrew Smith, Kevin D. Tennent, and Simon Mollan, eds, *The Impact of the First World War On International Business* (London: Routledge, 2016).
6. Peter J. Cain, and Anthony G. Hopkins, *British Imperialism: Innovation and Expansion, 1688–1914*. Vol. 1 (London: Addison-Wesley Longman Ltd, 1993).
7. Geoffrey Jones, "The Imperial Bank of Iran and Iranian Economic Development, 1890–1952", *Business and Economic History* (1987): 69–80; Geoffrey Jones, *Merchants to Multinationals: British Trading Companies in the Nineteenth and Twentieth centuries* (Oxford: Oxford University Press, 2000); Richard Peter Treadwell Davenport-Hine, and Geoffrey Jones, *British business in Asia since 1860* (Cambridge: Cambridge University Press, 2003); Howard Cox, Huang Biao and Stuart Metcalfe, "Compradors, Firm Architecture and the 'Reinvention' of British Trading Companies: John Swire & Sons' Operations in Early Twentieth-Century China", *Business History* 45, no. 2 (2003): 15–34; Stephanie Decker, "Corporate legitimacy and advertising: British companies and the rhetoric of development in West Africa, 1950–197.0" *Business History Review* 81, no. 01 (2007): 59–86.
8. Sarah E. Stockwell, *The Business of Decolonization: British Business Strategies in the Gold Coast* (Oxford University Press on Demand,

2000); Nicholas J. White, "The business and the politics of decolonization: the British experience in the twentieth century", *Economic History Review* (2000): 544–564.

9. Charles David Kepner and Jay Henry Soothill, *The Banana Empire; A Case Study of Economic Imperialism* (New York: Vanguard Press, 1935).
10. Mira Wilkins, *The Maturing of Multinational Enterprise: American Business Abroad from 1914 to 1970* (Cambridge, Mass: Harvard University Press, 1974), 515.
11. Robert Read, "The Growth and Structure of Multinationals in the Banana Export Trade" in *The Growth of International Business*, edited by Mark Casson (Boston: Allen and Unwin, 1983).
12. The relationship between dependency theory and other paradigms is discussed in Jean J. Boddewyn, "International business–government relations research 1945–2015: Concepts, typologies, theories and methodologies", *Journal of World Business* 51, no. 1 (2016), 11.
13. Marcelo Bucheli, "United Fruit Company in Latin America", in Steve Striffler and Mark Moberg (eds.), *Banana Wars: Power, Production, and History in the Americas* (Durham: Duke University Press, 2003): 80–100.
14. Marcelo Bucheli and Erica Salvaj, "Reputation and political legitimacy: ITT in Chile, 1927–1972", *Business History Review* 87, no. 04 (2013): 729–756; Marcelo Bucheli, "Multinational Corporations, Business Groups, and Economic Nationalism: Standard Oil (New Jersey), Royal Dutch-Shell, and Energy Politics in Chile 1913–2005", *Enterprise and Society* 11, no. 02 (2010): 350–399.
15. Leo Panitch and Sam Gindin, *The Making of Global Capitalism* (London: Verso Books, 2012), 79.
16. Dimitry Anastakis, *Autonomous State: The Struggle for a Canadian Car Industry from OPEC to Free Trade* (Toronto: University of Toronto Press, 2013), 5–12.
17. Gordon S. Wood, *Empire of Liberty: a History of the Early Republic, 1789–1815* (Oxford: Oxford University Press, 2009).
18. Noel Maurer, *Empire Trap: the Rise and Fall of US Intervention to Protect American Property Overseas, 1893 to 2013* (Princeton: Princeton University Press, 2013).
19. Kyle Longley, *In the Eagle's Shadow: the United States and Latin America* (Wheeling, Illinois: Harlan Davidson, 2002), 42.
20. Leo Panitch and Sam Gindin, *The Making of Global Capitalism: the Political Economy of American Empire* (London: Verso, 2012), 25.

21. Julie Green, *The Canal Builders: Making America's Empire at the Panama Canal* (New York: the Penguin Press, 2009), 5.
22. Green, *Canal Builders*, 12.
23. Green, *Canal Builders*, 16.
24. Samuel Crowther, *The Romance and Rise of the American Tropics* (New York: Doubleday, Heron, and Company, 1929), viii.
25. Crowther, *Romance and Rise*, 211.
26. Crowther, *Romance and Rise*, 212.
27. Crowther, *Romance and Rise*, 223.
28. Crowther, *Romance and Rise*, 248.
29. Crowther, *Romance and Rise*, viii.
30. Jack C. Lane, *Armed Progressive: General Leonard Wood* (San Rafael: Presidio Press, 1978), 69.
31. Lane, *Armed Progressive*, 103.
32. Lane, *Armed Progressive*, 109.
33. Lane, *Armed Progressive*, 257.
34. Ann Cipriano Venzon, ed, *General Smedley Darlington Butler: the Letters of a Leatherneck, 1898 to 1931* (New York: Praeger, 1992) 122.
35. Lane, *Armed Progressive*, 193.
36. Schwarz, *Liberal*, 1.
37. Schwarz, *Liberal*, 16.
38. Franklin Roosevelt Presidential Library, Adolf Berle Papers (hereafter ABP), Box 206, File: Columbia Oral History Transcript, 30.
39. ABP, Box 206, File: Columbia Oral History Transcript, 31.
40. Maurer, 102.
41. Cyrus Veeser, "Concessions as a Modernizing Strategy in the Dominican Republic", *Business History Review* 83 (Winter 2009): 731–758.
42. ABP, Box 206, File: Columbia Oral History Transcript, 31.
43. ABP, Box 206, File: Columbia Oral History Transcript, 31.
44. ABP, Box 206, File: Columbia Oral History Transcript, 34.
45. ABP, Box 206, File: Columbia Oral History Transcript, 38.
46. Longley, 164.
47. Longley, 170.
48. ABP, Box 10, File: Roosevelt, Franklin D., Roosevelt to Berle, 2 March 1934.
49. ABP, Box 16, File: Brain Trust.
50. Beatrice Bishop Berle, ed, *Navigating the Rapids: 1918–1971, from the Papers of Adolf A. Berle* (New York: Harcourt Brace, 1973), 126.

51. Mary Stuckey, *The Good Neighbor: Franklin D. Roosevelt and the Rhetoric of American Power* (East Lansing: Michigan State University Press, 2013), 62.
52. Stuckey, *Good Neighbor*, 12.
53. Stuckey, *Good Neighbor*, 16.
54. Juan Pablo Scarfi, "In the Name of the Americas: The Pan-American Redefinition of the Monroe Doctrine and the Emerging Language of American International Law in the Western Hemisphere, 1898–1933", *Diplomatic History* 41, no. 2 (2016): 216.
55. Stuckey, 173.
56. Longley, 168.
57. Longley, 175.
58. Longley, 175.
59. Longley, 176.
60. Lorenzo Meyer, *Mexico and the United States in the Oil Controversy* (Austin: University of Texas Press, 1977), 218.
61. ABP, Box 26, File: Berle, Assistant Secretary of State, 1938–1939, Frances M. Williams to Adolf A. Berle, February 23, 1939.
62. ABP, Box 27, File: Berle, Assistant Secretary of State, 1938–1939, Elihu Root Jr. to Adolf A. Berle, 26 January 1939.
63. ABP, Box 27, File: Berle, Assistant Secretary of State, 1938–1939, Elihu Root Jr. to Adolf A. Berle, 26 January 1939.
64. Marcelo Bucheli and Erica Salvaj, "Reputation and Political Legitimacy: ITT in Chile, 1927–1972", *Business History Review* 87 (Winter 2013): 729–55.
65. See Edward J. Sparks to Cordell Hull, December 30, 1936, in United States Department of State, *Foreign Relations of the United States Diplomatic Papers, 1937 Vol. 5 The American Republics* (1937), pp. 481–482, http://digicoll.library.wisc.edu/cgi-bin/FRUS/FRUS-idx?type=article&did=FRUS.FRUS1937v05.i0011&id=FRUS.FRUS1937v05&isize=M, accessed 24 April 2016.
66. Robert A. G. Monks, "Governing the Multi-National Enterprise: the Emergence of the Global Shareowner", Alfred D. Chandler Jr. and Bruce Mazlish, *Leviathans: Multinational Corporations and the New Global History* (Cambridge: Cambridge University Press, 2005): 189–202.
67. ABP, Box 54, File: Advisory Committees on Post-War Foreign Policy, Subcommittees.

68. ABP, Box 54, File: Advisory Committee on Problems of Foreign Relations, Economic Sub-Committee (April 1939 to December 1940).
69. ABP, Box 54, File: Advisory Committee on Problems of Foreign Relations, Economic Sub-Committee (April 1939 to December 1940).
70. ABP, Box 54, File: Advisory Committee on Problems of Foreign Relations, Economic Sub-Committee (April 1939 to December 1940).
71. Panitch and Gindin, 79.
72. ABP, Box 54, File: Atlantic Charter.
73. ABP, Box 147, File: Speeches—1948.
74. See Robert Elias, *The Empire Strikes Out: How Baseball Sold US Foreign Policy and Promoted the American Way Abroad* (New York: New Press, 2010).
75. For an example of new scholarship on the New Deal see Jefferson Cowie, *The Great Exception: The New Deal and the Limits of American Politics* (Princeton: Princeton University Press, 2016).
76. Robert B. Reich, *Saving Capitalism: For the Many, Not the Few* (New York: Knopf, 2015).

References

Archives

Franklin Roosevelt Presidential Library, Adolf Berle Papers (ABP): Box 10.
ABP: Box 16.
ABP: Box 26.
ABP: Box 27.
ABP: Box 54.
ABP: Box 147.
ABP: Box 206.

Primary Published Material and Calendars

United States Department of State, *Foreign Relations of the United States Diplomatic Papers, 1937, Vol. 5, The American Republics* (1937).

Secondary Literature

Anastakis, Dimitry, *Autonomous State: The Struggle for a Canadian Car Industry from OPEC to Free Trade* (Toronto: University of Toronto Press, 2013).
Berle, Beatrice Bishop, ed. *Navigating the Rapids: 1918–1971, from the Papers of Adolf A. Berle* (New York: Harcourt Brace, 1973).
Boddewyn, Jean J, "International Business–Government Relations Research 1945–2015: Concepts, Typologies, Theories and Methodologies." *Journal of World Business* 51, no. 1 (2016): 10–22.
Bucheli, Marcelo, "United Fruit Company in Latin America." In *Banana Wars: Power, Production, and History in the Americas*, edited by Steve Striffler and Mark Moberg, 80–100. Durham, NC: Duke University Press, 2003.
———. "Multinational Corporations, Business Groups, and Economic Nationalism: Standard Oil (New Jersey), Royal Dutch-Shell, and Energy Politics in Chile 1913–2005." *Enterprise and society* 11, no. 2 (2010): 350–99.
Bucheli, Marcelo, and Erica Salvaj, "Reputation and Political Legitimacy: ITT in Chile, 1927–1972." *Business History Review* 87, no. 4 (2013): 729–56.
Cain, Peter J. and Anthony G. Hopkins, *British Imperialism: Innovation and Expansion, 1688–1914*. Vol. 1 (London: Longman, 1993).
Cowie, Jefferson, *The Great Exception: The New Deal and the Limits of American Politics* (Princeton: Princeton University Press, 2016).
Cox, Howard, Huang Biao, and Stuart Metcalfe, "Compradors, Firm Architecture and the 'Reinvention' of British Trading Companies: John Swire & Sons' Operations in Early Twentieth-Century China," *Business History* 45, no. 2 (2003): 15–34.
Crowther, Samuel, *The Romance and Rise of the American Tropics* (New York: Doubleday, Heron, and Company, 1929).
Davenport-Hine, Richard Peter Treadwell and Geoffrey Jones, *British business in Asia since 1860* (Cambridge: Cambridge University Press, 2003).
Decker, Stephanie, "Corporate Legitimacy and Advertising: British Companies and the Rhetoric of Development in West Africa, 1950–197.0" *Business History Review* 81, no. 01 (2007): 59–86.
Elias, Robert, *The Empire Strikes Out: How Baseball Sold U.S. Foreign Policy and Promoted the American Way Abroad* (New York: The New Press, 2010).
Fitzgerald, Robert, *The Rise of the Global Company: Multinationals and the Making of the Modern World* (Cambridge: Cambridge University Press, 2015).

Green, Julie, *The Canal Builders: Making America's Empire at the Panama Canal* (New York: The Penguin Press, 2009).
Jones, Geoffrey, "The Imperial Bank of Iran and Iranian Economic Development, 1890–1952," *Business and Economic History* (1987): 69–80.
———, *Merchants to Multinationals: British Trading Companies in the Nineteenth and Twentieth Centuries* (Oxford: Oxford University Press, 2000).
Lane, Jack C., *Armed Progressive: General Leonard Wood* (San Rafael: Presidio Press, 1978).
Longley, Kyle, *In the Eagle's Shadow: The United States and Latin America* (Wheeling, IL: Harlan Davidson, 2002).
Maurer, Noel, *Empire Trap: The Rise and Fall of US Intervention to Protect American Property Overseas, 1893 to 2013* (Princeton: Princeton University Press, 2013).
Meyer, Lorenzo, *Mexico and the United States in the Oil Controversy* (Austin: University of Texas Press, 1977).
Monks, Robert A.G., "Governing the Multi-National Enterprise: The Emergence of the Global Shareowner", Alfred D. Chandler Jr. and Bruce Mazlish, *Leviathans: Multinational Corporations and the New Global History* (Cambridge: Cambridge University Press, 2005): 189–202.
Panitch, Leo and Sam Gindin, *The Making of Global Capitalism* (London: Verso Books, 2012).
Piketty, Thomas, *Capital in the Twenty-First Century* (New York: Belknap, 2014).
Read, Robert, "The Growth and Structure of Multinationals in the Banana Export Trade" in *The Growth of International Business*, edited by Mark Casson (Boston: Allen and Unwin, 1983).
Reich, Robert B., *Saving Capitalism: For the Many, Not the Few* (New York: Knopf, 2015).
Scarfi, Juan Pablo, "In the Name of the Americas: The Pan-American Redefinition of the Monroe Doctrine and the Emerging Language of American International Law in the Western Hemisphere, 1898–1933", *Diplomatic History* 41, no. 2 (2016): 189–218.
Schwarz, Jordan A., *Liberal: Adolf A. Berle and the Vision of an American Era* (New York: Macmillan, 1987).
Smith, Andrew, Kevin D. Tennent, and Simon Mollan, eds., *The Impact of the First World War On International Business* (London: Routledge, 2016).
Stockwell, Sarah E., *The Business of Decolonization: British Business Strategies in the Gold Coast* (Oxford University Press on Demand, 2000).

Stuckey, Mary, *The Good Neighbor: Franklin D. Roosevelt and the Rhetoric of American Power* (East Lansing: Michigan State University Press, 2013).

Veeser, Cyrus, "Concessions as a Modernizing Strategy in the Dominican Republic", *Business History Review* 83 (Winter 2009): 731–758.

Venzon, Ann Cipriano (ed.), *General Smedley Darlington Butler: The Letters of a Leatherneck, 1898 to 1931* (New York: Praeger, 1992).

White, Nicholas J., "The Business and the Politics of Decolonization: The British Experience in the Twentieth Century," *Economic History Review* (2000): 544–564.

Wilkins, Mira, *The Maturing of Multinational Enterprise: American Business Abroad from 1914 to 1970* (Cambridge, MA: Harvard University Press, 1974).

Wood, Gordon S., *Empire of Liberty: A History of the Early Republic, 1789–1815* (Oxford: Oxford University Press, 2009).

Yergin, Daniel, *The Prize: The Epic Quest for Oil, Money, and Power* (New York: Free Press, 2003).

11

Social(ist) Responsibility and Communist Management in Postwar Central Europe

Philip Scranton

In a socialist economy, enterprises were designed to be deeply socially responsible, far more so than under capitalism, because the public owned all firms, the people's tribunes (the Communist Party apparatus) supervised them, and their managers operated outside any nexus of markets for capital, materials, and clients. The primary purpose of communist enterprises was to deliver goods and services to citizens and agencies in the most socially efficient manner. Here, socially efficient meant more than technically effective or economically profitable. Being socially efficient entailed sustaining political commitments to full employment and low-cost, good-quality outputs amid rising living standards through comprehensive planning. However, in post-World War II Central Europe, the social, technical, and economic did not often harmonize readily, not least because political shifts and social upheavals altered the goals enterprise managers pursued. Still, in the absence of shareholders or bondholders, and given the non-market

P. Scranton (✉)
Rutgers University, Camden, NJ, USA
e-mail: scranton@rutgers.edu

W.A. Pettigrew and D.C. Smith (eds.), *A History of Socially Responsible Business, c.1600–1950*, Palgrave Studies in the History of Finance,
DOI 10.1007/978-3-319-60146-5_11

allocation of capital and the social ownership of assets, every enterprise was centrally and permanently responsible to society, in ways hardly imaginable to those running contemporary Western managerial corporations.[1]

Though efforts to achieve these goals proved erratic and often disappointing, communist enterprises' mandates and initiatives resonate intriguingly with those William Pettigrew and David Chan Smith have articulated for seventeenth-century British corporations, created by the monarchy to serve "national interests." Such early modern chartered corporations were expected to strive toward culturally approved goals to serve the national good. Among these were: transcending individual interests, promoting full employment, low prices and high wages, supporting the orphaned, indigent and widowed (and philanthropy more generally), and advancing state interests (not least through international trade), thus reinforcing political stability.[2] Seventeenth-century corporations existed for public purposes and could, in theory, be suspended or suppressed were they to fail in achieving them. The similarities with communist enterprises are extensive, though not comprehensive, as the latter were chartered or created by state authorities, tasked to subordinate private interests to serve the collective good, and charged with assuring full employment and providing inexpensive goods and services. Should they falter along the way, the state could (and did) shut firms down or oblige them to merge. Large enterprises delivered social services to workers and their families (e.g., healthcare and vacations), whereas the state assumed responsibilities for the widowed and orphaned (officially, no indigents existed). Furthermore, international trade anchored building both a stable state and a robust socialism, through exchanges within the Eastern Bloc and sales to/purchases from capitalist locales (more fraught, due to pricing and currency challenges). However, high wages for workers were in no way a priority, as central planners believed that constraining consumer demand, alongside restricting circulating currency, would carve out sufficient economic space for massive investments in heavy industrial capabilities (not least Cold War military goods), supply chain development for raw materials and power, and widespread infrastructure reconstruction and enhancement (railways, roads, canals, bridges, telecommunications, and their components).

Not for nothing did Central European jokes stress that the workers' state was being built on the backs of those who supposedly owned it.

Given the significance of Stalin's death in 1953 and his 1956 denunciation by Nikita Khrushchev, along with that year's Hungarian uprising/invasion, the ensuing discussion of postwar communist-era enterprises and their managerial challenges falls readily into two segments: from war's end to 1956 and from 1956 to 1970. This periodization derives from political events, yet in People's Democracies like Poland, Czechoslovakia, and Hungary, politics and the economy were so entwined that the two eras reflect enterprise dynamics as well. Hence, Hungarian economic reformer Bela Csikos-Nagy could stress that the wholly centralized "economic mechanism of the early fifties," installed "amidst attempts to overcome wartime damage, grew stronger [when reinforced by] the danger of an immediate war." Yet, by the mid-1960s, continuing, "relatively peaceful conditions" permitted reordering enterprise priorities to "ensure optimum efficiency."[3]

After 1956, Central European work on reconstruction and war readiness gave way gradually and unevenly to strive for social improvements (effective resource use, technical advances and improved standards of living), increased political independence (re the USSR),[4] and greater enterprise autonomy (re central planners and the Party). This transition did not go at all smoothly: Enterprise performances ranged from stellar to dreadful, waste and shortages proved endemic,[5] whereas problems of inter-firm, much less intra-bloc, coordination remained daunting. Exploring how management functioned amid such turmoil is the key purpose of this essay.[6] What follows sketches: (1) the postwar context for creating central planning and communist enterprises, plus the tasks and dilemmas their managers soon confronted; (2) fifties' crises and reform pressures; and (3) a brief review of Czech and Polish managerial initiatives or evasions through 1970. It poses a basic question: "What can business historians learn from Cold War communist firms and managers"? The conclusion will advance some very preliminary responses.

First, the postwar context. By summer 1945, Poland had been doubly wrecked, initially by the Nazis then by the Soviets; Hungary's largest city was a ruin, and western Czechoslovakia (the Sudetenland) was experiencing massive, forced emigration. Prague had been damaged, however, not destroyed.[7] Infrastructures everywhere were shattered—railways, bridges, telegraph/telephone systems, and electric power plants hammered to bits. Factories had been either flattened, or emptied of machinery, or left standing, windowless, holding only worn-out equipment. Retreating Germans had routinely dynamited what they could not load on trains and trucks; arriving Russians rapidly looted much of the remainder, filling railway cars with raw materials, machines, finished goods, and components for removal to the USSR, along with the trains themselves (and in Poland, the rails also).[8] Mass migrations, forced relocations, and border shifts as well brought what Ivan Berend termed "a social landslide at the end of the war."[9]

Creating economic plans for the three nations was an almost uniform process, drawing explicitly on Soviet practices, though the pace of industrial nationalizations, and especially of agricultural transformations, was quite uneven. Multi-year and annual plans emerged from central administrative units which set growth and output targets, allocated resources to monopoly sectors (construction, metalworking, and mining), decreed work rules, wage rates, bonuses and sanctions, and most crucially, devised literally thousands of indices to measure performance/outcomes at the product, factory, enterprise, and sectoral levels. "Fulfilling the plan," meeting or surpassing an index base (100% of the target), was everywhere the obligation of management, engineering, and labor. This was one key stimulus toward a communist version of "gaming the system."[10] There would be many others.

Three key levels of management emerged. The *central planning cadres* were an elite cluster of economists, engineers, and Party functionaries who devised "economic management," nationally and in relation to the outside world. They worked toward three, not-always-compatible goals: full employment, stable prices, and rapid growth (with rising productivity and living standards). Nationalizations at the firm level preceded amalgamations of enterprises, by sector, into state monopolies (food processing and railway supplies), supervised by Ministries (as for Heavy Industry), and administered by *directorate executives*. Here, the postwar problems of "missing" senior executives and novice top managers soon became severe, as the newly merged enterprises commonly employed

10–30,000 workers at multiple, scattered sites. Outside national railway systems, few Central European managers had ever faced so vast an array of coordination and control challenges.[11] Slovak economist Radoslav Selucký credited their persistent errors to "the inexperience of new people who fought doughtily for power but could not master the complex problems of running an advanced industrial society."[12] Third, at the factory, mine, or retail level, veteran *enterprise directors* and capitalist owners continued managing, many having returned from exile or prison camps to their former jobs. Their resumption of authority was frequently a source of contention from "liberated" workers, who rejected restoration of pre-war labor relations.[13]

Interactions among central planners, executives in the merged State Owned Enterprises (SOEs), and plant managers were at best cordial. As economist János Kornai explained, reviewing Hungary's 1950s textile, clothing, and shoemaking sectors: "the annual plans for enterprises carry no authority ... As soon as these plans are received, they are put away in a drawer." Their only utility was as prods "for mobilizing the workers" toward reaching targets. Equally problematic, the ministries and SOE leaders charged with delivering raw materials routinely failed to do so; deliveries were "halting, spasmodic," often because, in textiles, 80% of supplies were imported. Transport delays, currency issues, and within Comecon, shipment of materials not meeting specifications, made a shambles of plant-level planning in fabrics, apparel, and footwear, as did weak coordination between export trading agencies and producers concerning demand abroad.[14]

Worse, SOE bosses and economic ministries altered plan targets arbitrarily and sent out sheaves of "instructions," demanding reports and compliance with adjustments. In Hungary, in 1952, the then-current "five-year plan was changed 472 times, and the yearly plan ... 113 times." The Ujpest Leather Factory (near Budapest) received 102 "instructions" in the last four months of 1955, not counting plan modifications or ministry decrees, "each one of which contains further instructions." Ministry "inspectors" were another plague, arriving without notice to check on plan progress, absenteeism, or materials inventories.[15]

Such events reveal the designed powerlessness of managers in factories, cooperatives, or department stores, enmeshed in a system driven by *accountability without authority*. As *Selucký* detailed:

> The fusion of political and economic monopolies was theoretically defended by the principle of the unity of power and ownership. … The state runs the economy itself; it does not set up an independent organization for the purpose. Economics are entirely subordinated to politics and the state does not recognize economic management as an activity in itself… The individual enterprise, as the basic economic unit, is regarded at the same time as the lowest rung in the ladder of government.[16]

Hence, formally, enterprise managers were structural ciphers, destined to carry out orders from the center in a system that "may function downward well enough, but [in which] there will be no feedback, no flow of information from below."[17]

Elsewhere, meeting targets could be accomplished through ruses and manipulations, which provided opportunities for sometimes desperate creativity. One remarkable example must suffice here. In 1953, amid a severe shortage of iron and steel for reprocessing, Budapest's Iron and Metal Scrap Collection Enterprise received orders to increase output. With the collusion of management, its employees began systematically to defraud their ministry:

> The workers loaded a truck with 60 hundredweights [of scrap], passed the two weight controls [at their yard's gate], but at the railroad station unloaded 20 hundredweights only. They returned with the rest, added 20 hundredweights [again passed through the scales] and went back to the station, repeating this three times, and unloading the whole shipment at the last tour. They theoretically had delivered 180 hundredweights, while in fact only 100 hundredweights had been shipped. Next day, the names of the drivers were written on the production board, with the note that they had filled the norms to 130%. When the iron shortage became even greater, the workers loaded 20 hundredweights of stones at the bottom of the truck and heaped the scrap on top.[18]

The lack of coordination between reports *to* the Metals Ministry and reports *by* the Railway Directorate assured the scheme's invisibility.

Given that central planning was an allocative system and that all three countries faced major rebuilding challenges, construction tasks dominated immediate postwar initiatives, especially in creating heavy industry capabilities through state "investments." Yet construction work differed sharply from making steel rails, machinery, or traction equipment, given its project structure, constantly shifting work locations, unexpected obstacles, site-specific design changes and mobile, and temporary workforces. The vertical power relations governing production, transport, and distribution were inadequate, for construction proved to be regionally organized, locally networked, and effectively unmanageable from the center. Controlling budgets, workforces, and schedules was far harder than in factories, as was SOE or ministerial project oversight. For a sense of construction's scale, capital spending on public works, housing, industrial plants, and equipment alone "gobbled one quarter of all national income" during Poland's first Six Year Plan (1949–55).[19]

As with much else, investment flows were top-down; enterprises did not generate proposals to compete for funds, but did seek to increase their yearly allotments. Moreover, investment funds were "free money," granted without interest, required to be spent over a project's term, and loosely supervised.[20] Annually, state planners created a new pool; annually, thousands of new projects commenced. The positive side of this exercise was that reconstruction was everywhere rapid and construction employment soared, helping all three nations achieves full employment.[21] The problems, however, were many, including delays, fraud, waste, design errors, materials glitches, porous controls, poor results, and most painful, long lists of unfinished, and abandoned projects.[22] As one Polish commentator explained, capitalist building

> starts from the beginning, carefully examining the possibilities of the site, the needs of the client, the cost of every detail, etc.; while in socialist building the job really begins from the top. First, it is decreed that such and such a building has to be erected; then a plan is sent down, which is usually more or less unrealistic; a lump sum is appropriated for the cost, and the date is fixed on which the building should be ready. All the time, realities are significantly disregarded. The builders assigned to the job are in a grave quandary. They have to produce a building which is to suit its

> future purpose without deviating from the plan. Actually, they never are able to follow this plan exactly, and changes have to be carried out in the course of construction. At the end a building quite different from that originally planned is handed over.[23]

With acres of fresh projects budding every spring, construction managers walked away from incomplete jobs to start new ones, leaving "enormous resources of materials and human labor … frozen."[24] This opened the way for enterprise managers to improvise in getting the "finishing work" done, redirecting sums in construction budgets toward the informal or "second" economy. Company workers were paid to hang doors or connect electrical outlets in their spare time; quasi-legal outside contractors completed water piping and installed toilets. Comparable "arrangements" operated widely and quietly through the economy, as they were essential fixes for holes in the planning fabric.[25]

Central European communism indeed was, as Selucký noted, "a system that worked, more or less"[26]; but it needed to work more effectively to build socialism and sustain its social responsibilities. Thus, appropriately, a wave of reform initiatives emerged after Stalin's death, with differential effects across Poland, Hungary, and Czechoslovakia. Given space constraints, we must omit detailing the mid-1950s crisis, noting just that after Khrushchev's denunciations and the Hungarian crisis, the three countries followed different paths to managing socialist development. We can here only review the pattern created in Czechoslovakia, as well as one firm-level example in Poland, both drawn from a fuller version of this study.[27]

After years of steady growth, in 1963, Czechoslovak national income dropped, forcing recognition that growth was not automatic under socialism and that substantial economic restructuring had to be considered. Two related issues beckoned: first the necessity of installing "intensive" economic methods, underpinned by labor-saving technology (from turret lathes to adding machines), which would force socially unappealing layoffs and factory closures; and second the overhang of obsolete equipment, which would demand massive inputs of replacement capital. On the first count, during 1964, planners announced shutdowns for 2700 "production units," due to gross inefficiency and persistent losses. Their 83,000 workers would relocate to new, technology-intensive plants. Two years later, half of these factories were still operating (with 50,000 workers), as the question of where to redirect the labor force could not be solved.[28] The new plants had not been built, even as the machinery problem had become acute. Advanced equipment could readily be obtained from West Germany or France, but only if paid for in "hard money," as the koruna was not a convertible currency.[29] Moreover, a 1964 survey of Czechoslovak shoemaking showed that 40% of its machines "would need to be discarded by 1970, but authorities had no idea...how to replace them." In textiles, 7000 nineteenth-century looms were still running, whereas over 60% of food processing equipment was "worn out." Because of frequent breakdowns in manufacturing facilities, "maintenance alone claimed 300,000 of the not quite 1.9 million workers employed in industry." Capital spending had been heavily biased toward new construction, not machinery replacement, while machine repair was specifically excluded from investment expenditures.[30] So what were Czechoslovak enterprise managers doing, facing such situations?[31]

For the most part, they fought reforms that would add to their risks and responsibilities (such as undertaking market surveys and creating advertising) and plodded ahead to meet (or just barely exceed) plan targets, whether or not their firms' products were in demand.[32] Indeed, a Polish visitor noted that, though Czechoslovakia's "national income" rose by 15 billion crowns in 1967, of this gain, some 11 or 12 billion "were accounted for by production which remained unsold (increase in inventories)." Radio Free Europe analyst Harry Trend confirmed this, adding that "accumulated unsold inventories were valued at 200 billion crowns, a sum equivalent to the entire Czechoslovak national income in 1967!"[33] Meanwhile, construction companies continued to overbill, "lose track" of materials, and manipulate the system—collaborating with clients to generate invoices "for work not done," inflating materials, and overhead charges, a maneuver which helped "fulfill" the planned output targets.[34] Here, socialist responsibility dissolved before the imperatives of a careerism grounded in a studious indifference to enterprise outcomes.

But all was not grind and grab. Entrepreneurial semiconductor developers at CKD in Prague represent one example, among many. CKD was "the country's second largest industrial concern, after Škoda, building compressors, pumps, conveyors, electric and Diesel motors, and even streetcars," with 48,000 workers and five research institutes.[35] Jaroslav Kolar, deputy manager of CKD's electronics project, traced its origins to central planners' 1963 repurposing an old factory, formerly producing motorcycles.[36] Electronics specialists had realized that "without mass production of semi-conductive high-voltage parts, progress is simply not possible in our engineering fields." Hence, the CKD research team, which had been tracking the Western germanium-to-silicon transition, commenced prototyping semiconductors by 1964 and manufacturing in 1965. Staff retraining was fundamental. Motorcycle "craftsmen and workers used to a production line had to become toolmakers, since each piece produced was in fact a prototype. Completely new production lines had to be built almost from scratch. This we did all by ourselves."[37] By 1966, the semiconductor unit was running without state subsidies while cutting wholesale prices 15% a year, a rare thing in what we might call **managerial socialism**. As Kolar explained, the group leaders took chances, echoing Carnegie or Ford:

> I recall, for example, when in 1965 we deliberately took a calculated risk and permitted a single planned loss. We had to switch to a new technology if we did not want to assume a more dangerous risk, namely the risk of lagging behind world development. The profit which the new technology brought to us in 1965 exceeded by three times the loss caused by the rapid switch to new techniques.[38]

Responding to quickly changing demand was crucial. This necessitated achieving "flexibility, and pay[ing] more attention to merchandising, short-term market research, and long-term market estimates."[39] For Kolar, at base:

> ...the past system has not created proper conditions for prompt application of the latest technological achievements. Starting new production has often been difficult because of cumbersome regulations; production

> plans put emphasis on volume regardless of the optimum production structure... regardless of long-term prospects... [I]n the field of semiconductors, revolutionary discoveries of fundamental importance may literally be made overnight. [These] profoundly affect our estimates of future market capacities.[40]

CKD semiconductor managers inverted standard planning practice, designing, and producing for applications that did not yet exist, for "future market capacities." They could not do this by following the system's rules.

> [I]t is not overcautiousness and strict compliance with all existing usages and regulations, but a sound and well-calculated risk in our ventures that is the only guarantee of success. We have also found that to manufacture products to the highest technical standards to match those made abroad—and to manufacture them not in laboratories but on a mass production basis—was either utterly impossible, or possible only by disregarding a number of existing decrees and directives on technological discipline, permits normally required for starting new production, procedures for approving capital investment projects, minimum delivery periods set for the sub-suppliers, and by carrying out certain technological changes at breakneck speeds. Yet, we have deliberately assumed these risks. To be sure, a victor is never punished...[41]

Steve Jobs could hardly have said it better; after all, breaking the rules can also be a form of planning, in realizing otherwise-implausible outcomes.

CKD's brashness in "disregarding" ministerial rules and controls was hardly general, but enterprise managers' hostility to their overseers certainly increased. In 1969, post-invasion "normalizing" administrators introduced a system of ministry-enterprise agreements, "outlining the basic tasks and conditions [for] carrying out plan requirements." After "negotiations with the general managers in industry, the construction sector, and commerce," about 70 deals were finalized, but only when the GMs secured clauses promising "an increased commitment on the part of Party functionaries ... to fulfill the[ir] obligations." Previously, ministries had inserted "loopholes" in plan documents "which made it possible for [them] to shirk their responsibilities with regard to supplies, deliveries by cooperating enterprises, and imports necessary for production." This had to end. RFE's Trend summarized: "The distrust of ministries by enterprises has a long history: it is not the result of the short experience with 'agreements' since July 1969."[42] Ironically, in service of the social goods and their own careers, Czechoslovak managers had begun contesting the terms on which their firms would operate something novel and likely unsettling to directorates and central planners charged with promoting social advances and broadly ineffectual in securing them.

Moving the focus to Warsaw, we encounter the huge machinery-building enterprise, Ursus, which had constructed trucks and autos under a Fiat license in the interwar years and began developing a tractor line in 1939. After postwar rebuilding, tractors became its specialization, starting with the simplified C-45 (ca. 100,000 units, 1947–56). Larger, more powerful models multiplied after 1956, their success enabling Ursus to "give up" its annual state budget supplement in 1965, as declining production costs "guarantee that the factory makes a profit."[43] Ursus representatives regularly convened tractor-users' conferences, at which complaints about shortcomings (cracking of cylinder blocks) joined suggestions for improvements (closed, glassed-in cabs). Yet before the 200,000th Ursus rolled off the line in 1968, the proliferation of designs to meet internationally diversified needs had produced a nagging problem—shortages of spare parts. The parts situation had blown up in 1965, with national television news announcing that tractor repairs had stalled because of supply delays. The Ministry of Agriculture then aggravated the bottlenecks with "quite strange, incomprehensible" orders, for example routing some 600 tractors to a repair center which had expected twenty.[44]

The dilemma lay not just in weak planning for spares, nor in suppliers' "ugly habit of failing to discharge their obligations," but fully as much in the sheer complexity of the parts universe. Ursus machines together counted some "34,000 items of spare parts," adequate inventories of which would weigh 100,000 tons, needing annual replenishment by 300 parts-making firms so as to supply 4000 clients, chiefly distributors and repair units. Already in autumn 1964, over 4800 tractor parts were "reported to be in shortage"; 12,000 inter-regional inventory transfers only partly addressed the mess. Ursus had neither space nor sufficient underutilized tools to re-centralize parts manufacture, which is why Poland's Agricultural Equipment Sales Center had created a contracting network in the first place. Four years later, regional repair shop directors agreed that the famine persisted: "supply clerks ... are constantly traveling over the entire country for spare parts."[45]

In consequence, Ursus management recognized its practices were out of step with rising social expectations for efficiency, productivity, and profits. Thus, top executives undertook a wholesale restructuring in a truly rare communist-era maneuver: In 1967, they brought in the British consulting firm Urwick, Orr, and Partners to install a management-by-objectives operating framework for those occupying its 750 "management positions." In the prior setup, divisions reflected "technology rather than products," and "production managers did not have immediate control of materials or the allocation of tools." Ursus urgently sought to "introduce an equal distribution of competent personnel," thus eliminating "operational areas for which no one was responsible." During a three-year process, Urwick, Orr partnered with an Ursus team, working from "spacious" offices in the main administration building. In consequence, "many departments were found to be unnecessary," and others had to be created—especially in design and production. The process was a "battle with the establishment," especially with those threatened:

> The passive outlook of people occupying management positions has created an unending theme for satirists. Representatives of this outlook profess that it is unnecessary to undertake any decisions. After all, no-one will be criticized for evading a clear-cut position, but a mistakenly formulated decision can have fearful consequences. Until the present time, responsibility was accidental and was not a consistent policy. The main idea behind the ZBC [MBO] system incorporates interdependence of the subordinates and supervisors; the development of a passive outlook is practically impossible.

At the micro level, fear was widespread:

> A certain director of an assembly department, when asked to list all [his] functions, submitted several typewritten pages containing over 70 functions. He was apprehensive when asked to select several basic functions which were essential; he believed that such a limitation would lessen his importance in the plant and would result in the conviction that he was unnecessary.

And so it was: "The introduction of the ZPC caused numerous personnel reassignments, which uncovered the incompetence of certain directors and revealed the competence of others." Yet overall the reshuffling was far less drastic than the staff had anticipated.[46] By 1969, Ursus had formed its own team for continuing "the perfection of the plant organization." Trained by Urwick, Orr consultants (the last of whom left in 1969), the local "organizers are Poles who are presently called 'Englishmen' by the working forces." Word spread of this long-term restructuring effort and directors from other large firms arranged to visit. "They come, observe, and shake their heads in disapproval." Expecting a ready-to-install fix, "something that could be easily adopted," they found instead a program that had to be "adjusted to concrete conditions and continuously perfected" through organizational analysis and extensive training.[47] Such visitors departed and disappointed, and while Ursus prospered straight through the post-1989 transition, its managerial adaptations were rarely duplicated.

So, returning to our opening query, what can business historians learn from the practice of communist enterprise managements, at least tentatively, given the brevity of this encounter with their postwar histories? First, we might suggest that, on the social responsibility front, creating measures for achievement proved as tricky in the East as it has proven elusive in the West. Meeting planning goals indicated responsible social performance, yet operationally, so many obstacles confronted managers that they routinely closed their eyes to shoddy output or wasted resources and embraced schemes to game the ministries (and their indices). Building a better society ran a distant second to getting the goods out the door and the operation to the planning year's end. Resonances with capitalist enterprises could well be explored in this light. Second, just as business historians are urging that Western corporate triumphalism be tempered with a deeper investigation of failures,[48] conversely, unexamined assumptions that communist enterprises simply were failures merit reconsideration, through research into Central European firms and sectors registering durable successes, as noted above. Third, is it not conceivable that both historians and managers of sprawling global companies, durably focused on strategy and planning, might learn from encountering both the achievements and pitfalls of socialist planning, the costs and implications of each, and the multiple reform and reorganization efforts mounted in response to disappointing results from both centralization and decentralization? Last, it seems to me that contemplating the history of communist enterprises' social and political responsibilities can begin to frame *regulation* as a middle ground between the inadequacies of comprehensive planning, at one extreme, and societies whose firms are accountable only to shareholders and only for profits, at another. Libertarian fantasies resonate richly and ironically with the communist imaginary: Each took central stage in its own century, exhibited painful deficiencies, and gave way to regimes of calibrated reform and exploratory regulation. In sum, excising the "left option" from our business history memory bank leaves us with simplistic dichotomies about policy and process; restoring it can create a vital means for situating the historical dynamics of reform and regulation in between equally magnetic, yet equally faulty extremes, and in time, perhaps, defining a center that *will* hold.

Notes

1. Communist managers were also politically responsible to party cadres, present in every plant, mill, and mine, every department store, railway, and wholesale distribution unit, though not in the smallest of firms. We note this duality, which caused authority and responsibility problems, but cannot explore it further here.
2. See Pettigrew and Brock's essay in this volume. Another element of the national interest Pettigrew identified was environmental sustainability, not something communist planners considered before the 1970s. Notably many of these seventeenth-century corporations were

trading companies, whereas postwar communist firms were active as well in production, distribution, and infrastructural services (transport, power, etc.).

3. Bela Csikos-Nagy, "The 'Two Model' Theory of the Socialist Economy," *Közgazdasági Szemle*, 11 (September 1964), in *Translations on Economic Organization and Management in Eastern Europe* [TEOMEE], No. 393, JPRS 27070, 20 October 1964, 20–22. Stalin's postwar USSR policies assumed a Third World War would break out in the near term, a point perhaps remembered chiefly by specialists.
4. Assessments of Central European economic performance under socialism do take note of the persistent force military-oriented production exercised over access to and utilization of installed capacity. Just after the war, locomotives, rolling stock, trucks, and weaponry newly manufactured in Poland, Hungary, and Czechoslovakia (PHC) went directly to the USSR, some as 'reparations' (Hungary) and the rest at prices set by the Soviets. Later, the USSR concluded large contracts selling military goods (often used WWII materiel) to PCH to build armed forces, one-third of the price in goods returned to the Soviets, two-thirds in long-term loans at 2% interest. Sizable orders for Bloc-produced weapons followed in the early 1950s. Reducing these demands was essential to creating growth trajectories in all three states, but it was far from a simple matter, nor has documenting its extent been easy, given the secrecy about accounting for such work in national reports. See William Bomberger and Gail Makinen, "The Hungarian Hyperinflation and Stabilization of 1945–46," *Journal of Political Economy*, 91 (1983): 801–824, and Pal Germuska, *Unified Military Industries of the Soviet Bloc* (Lanham, MD: Lexington, 2015), esp. Chap. 1.
5. An early recognition of this appeared in János Kornai, *Overcentralization in economic administration: a critical analysis based on experience in Hungarian light industry* (Oxford: OUP, 1959). RFE undertook a partial translation and analysis of the Hungarian edition, published in January 1957, describing it as "sound ... and courageous criticism." See "Faults of Communist Planned Economy," HU OSA 300-8-3-3259, 23 October 1957. Kornai became a key socialist theorist of the 'shortage economy' in subsequent decades, before leaving Budapest for Harvard in 1986, then returning, after retirement in 2002, to the Collegium Budapest and the Central European University. He later described his

first book's foundation as "naïve reform-socialism." (K. Bossányi, "An Interview with János Kornai," *Acta Oeconomica* 48 (1990): 315–28, quote on 318.)

6. This is distinct from assessing how the economies worked, well or fitfully. Shelves of studies have taken up the aggregate questions (often having to rely on dubious data), but few investigators have explored enterprise operations at the ground level. The extensive translations of newspaper and journal articles, decrees and interviews, from PHC (and elsewhere) by the Joint Publications Research Service (ca. 1958–1992) and archived Radio Free Europe reports, interviews and analyzes make possible a more granular encounter with "doing business" under communism. Both collections are available online, JPRS by subscription and RFE free.
7. Keith Lowe points out that "[i]n Budapest, 84% of the buildings were damaged, and 30% of them so badly that they were entirely uninhabitable." *Savage Continent: Europe in the Aftermath of World War II* (New York: Picador, 2012), 6. US planes did bomb Prague in 1945, but the city did not suffer from ground warfare.
8. Poland lost ca. 10,000 miles of railway track and 85% of its rolling stock. (Ibid., 10.) See also Ian Buruma, *Year Zero: A History of 1945* (New York: Penguin, 2013). A Polish postwar report indicated agricultural depletions at 2.8 million horses (75%), 8.5 million cattle (60%) and 6.4 million pigs (80%). See Thad Paul Alton, *Polish Postwar Economy* (New York: Columbia UP, 1955), 32. A Radio Free Europe informant noted in spring 1951 that "Two large shipyards in Szczecin, which had been thoroughly destroyed by Russian dismantling, will be rebuilt." Both were once German-owned yards. See "Building Construction," RFE File HU OSA 300-1-2-1667, July 5, 1951, Open Society Archives at http://www.osaarchivum.org.
9. Ivan Berend (General Secretary of the Hungarian Academy of Sciences and team leader), "Hungary: 40 Years of Communism," *Társadalmi Szemle* (Social Review) February 1989, 5, JPRS East Europe (JPRS-EER-89-083), 26 July 1989. The CP Central Committee commissioned research on the "Historical Antecedents to the Current Situation," amid crumbling party authority and economic conditions.
10. At a Czech light bulb plant, planners scheduled production of "one million watts in bulbs" during 1951. Managers chose to meet the goal by making 10,000, 100-watt bulbs, rather than a much larger number of

25-, 50-, and 60-watt bulbs needed to reach the one million goal. The result was a shortage of lower wattage bulbs and a surplus of 100-watt ones. At a spare parts and metal fasteners factory, whose planning target demanded so-many thousands of kilograms of screws per year, managers, "in order to make things easier for themselves, design[ed] big screws which weight a lot, but can scarcely be used when small ones are wanted." See "Conditions in the Precision Machine Industry," RFE File HU OSA 300-1-2-19183, 8 May 1952. The same sort of "norm cheating" was practiced at Budapest's famed Ganz Electrical Works, where making "small screws, being unfavorable in terms of overall production norms, was entirely neglected." There, the supervisor was suspended in 1954 "and may go to jail." See '"Screw-Up" in Screw Factory,' RFE File HU OSA 300-1-2-44590, 11 March 1954.

11. Kornai, *Overcentralization*, 21–22.
12. *Radoslav* Selucký, *Czechoslovakia*: The Plan That Failed (London: Thomas Nelson, 1970), 53–54.
13. Workers would soon discover their power to influence either enterprises or the state was radically circumscribed. As Martin Myant noted: "To the majority of workers the labor process remained totally unchanged by the formal transfer of ownership to the state." Martin Myant, *The Czechoslovak Economy, 1948–1988: the Battle for Economic Reform* (Cambridge: Cambridge University Press, 1989), 45. However, their periodic outbursts in widespread walkouts and riots had substantial effects on political leaders, who frequently responded by trying to improve living standards and the availability of consumer goods. Labor relations issues are largely outside the scope of this essay, regrettably. For detail see Padraic Kenney, *Building Poland, Workers and Communists, 1945–1950* (Ithaca: Cornell University Press, 1997).
14. Kornai, *Overcentralization*, 10–13, 23. As a result, managers widely sought to hoard raw materials, to even out production swings, or over-ordered materials from suppliers, which led unsurprisingly to the latter's arbitrary reduction of deliveries, as it was usual for operating plants to request 150 or 200% of supply firms' output capacity. The Soviets were notorious for delivering shabby raw materials, low-grade cotton and low-BTU-yielding coal.
15. Nigel Swain, *Hungary: The Rise and Fall of Feasible Socialism* (London: Verso, 1992), 71.
16. *Selucký*, *Czechoslovakia*: Plan That Failed, 21 (emphasis in original). Selucký (1930–91), a Party propagandist in the 50s, moved on to

film-making and critiques of central planning in the 60s, becoming a professor of political economy at the Prague School of Politics and Economics, before exile after the 1968 invasion. He later joined the faculty at Carleton University, Ottawa, Canada.

17. Ibid., 23.
18. "Shortage of Iron and Metal Scrap in the Factories," RFE File HU OSA 300-1-2-56594, 25 March 1955. The report was by one of the drivers who traveled West to avoid arrest, though the ruse had not yet been uncovered when he departed Hungary in August 1954. Sixty hundredweights is six metric tons, 6000 kilos or 13,200 pounds.
19. Flora Lewis, *A Case History of Hope: The Story of Poland's Peaceful Revolutions* (Garden City, NY: Doubleday, 1958), 151–52.
20. Bela Czikos-Nagy explains: "[B]y eliminating the private ownership of capital and land, these production factors will be available to society at no cost. According to this concept, the use of collective capital, land, mining products, and other natural resources is free. New investments, too, are granted without the obligation of repayment." BC-N, "Certain Problems in Business Administration," *Pénzügyi szemle (Financial Review)*, 1 (January 1967): 1–14, in *TEOMEE*, No. 675, 28 March 1967, JPRS # 40438. For details on Czech investments in the 1950s, see Jan Michal, Central Planning In Czechoslovakia (Stanford: Stanford University Press, 1960), Chap. 8. Michal quotes the head of the State Planning Office: "We are building more, but the effect is less." (181).
21. See Domenico Mario Nuti, "The Contradictions of Socialist Economics: A Marxist Interpretation," *Socialist Register—1979* (London: The Merlin Press, 1979), 228–273.
22. Though much of the literature on socialist construction has focused on dreadful housing towers and shortages, we should remember that the vast majority of construction was industrial, commercial, and infrastructural. (Housing came last among state priorities.) Hungary had an extensive Ministry of Housing and Public Construction by the early 1950s, but it focused only on office and factory buildings. Other agencies sponsored construction in transportation (railways and bridges were crucial to the First Five-Year Plan), communications, agriculture, and extraction. Also, Budapest's MHPC coordinated with separate military construction units for everything from barracks to barriers. "Building Industry and Construction in Hungary Before the Revolution," RFE file HU OSA 300-8-3, 15 February 1957.

For Poland, see "Building and Construction Industry," RFE File HU OSA 300-1-2-15638, 18 January 1952.

23. "Building Construction," RFE File HU OSA 300-1-2-11807 28 November 1951. For additional site-specific reports on Poland, see "A Worker Looks at the Polish Building Industry, "RFE File HU OSA 300-1-2-44710, 18 March 1954, and "Jerry-Building in Gdansk," RFE File HU OSA 300-1-2-53197, 4 December 1954.
24. Ota Šik, *Czechoslovakia*: The Bureaucratic Economy (White Plains, NY: International Arts and Sciences Press, 1972), 51.
25. Maria Los, ed., *The Second Economy in Marxist States* (London: Macmillan, 1990).
26. *Selucký, Czechoslovakia*: The Plan That Failed, 10.
27. Philip Scranton, "Managing Communist Enterprises: Poland, Hungary and Czechoslovakia, 1945–1970," draft text available on request (scranton@rutgers.edu).
28. "The Threat of Unemployment in Czechoslovakia," RFE File OSA 300-8-3-1837, 10 May 1966.
29. Refusing convertibility was a strategy COMECON states used to insulate their economies from importing capitalist-world inflation. Keeping prices stable was a fetish for decades. For the USSR, it also structurally reinforced Central European dependencies on Soviet resources, along with military and commercial demand.
30. Jan Michal, *Central Planning in Czechoslovakia*, 173.
31. As for what planners were doing, see George Feiwel, *New Economic Patterns in Czechoslovakia*: Impact of Growth, Planning and the Market (New York: Praeger, 1968), an exhaustive study.
32. Josef Polacek, "How to Proceed with Our Advertising," *Podniková organizace* (Enterprise Organization), August 20, 1968, TEE-EIA, No. 46, JPRS 46768, October 29 1968. Polacek noted that since 1938, "our advertising stagnated and held itself merely on the sideline of business activity. The attempts to kill it alternated with the ones to revive it." Writing just before the invasion, he celebrated the "few veterans" and "new enthusiasts," but castigated "the mass of uncrystallized, often groping officials and artists who have gotten into advertising through various twists of fate, often against their will." See also Philip Hanson, *Advertising and Socialism* (White Plains, NY: IASP, 1974). On socialist foreign trade, see Marie Lavigne, *International Political Economy and Socialism* (Cambridge: Cambridge University Press, 1985).

Lavigne introduces the notion of "socialist multinationals" to conceptualize export relations with developing nations (170f).

33. K. Kraus, "Czechoslovak Economic Situation Analyzed," *Życie Gospodarcze* (Economic Life), May 19, 1968, in *Translations on Eastern Europe, Political, Sociological and Military Affairs*, No. 3, JPRS 45745, 20 June 1968; Harry Trend, "Pre-August Trends in Czechoslovak Economic Organization and Policy, Part III," RFE File 300-8-3-6022, 18 November 1968 (exclamation mark in original). Before joining RFE as an "advisor on economic affairs," Trend, a former head of the Ukrainian Congress Committee of America's Detroit branch, had taught economics at Wayne State University.
34. Ladislav Roubel, "Implementing the New System of Economic Incentives," *Finance a Uver* (Journal of Economics and Finance), November 1958, in *Selected Economic Translations on Eastern Europe* [SETEE], JPRS 1360-N, 16 March 1959. For similar problems a decade later, see Alexander Miartus, "Malingerers in Construction Industry Criticized," *Pravda* (Bratislava), 5 July 1969, in TEE-EIA, No. 155, JPRS 48504, 29 July 1969. For Poland, see Bolesław Kierski and Jerzy Withkowski, "Technical Problems in Construction—1959," *Inwestycje i Budownictwo* (Investment and Construction), February 1959, in *SETEE*, JRPS 1814-N, 31 July 1959 and Zenon Jakubowski, "Mismanagement, Theft at Industrial Sites," *Życie Gospodarcze* (Economic Life), 23 February 1969, in TEE-EIA, No. 107, JPRS 47766, 2 April 1969.
35. Ernő Fusi, "The Czechoslovak Machine Industry Through Hungarian Eyes," *Gépgyártás-Technológia* 7 (1967), No 10, 469–78, in *Translations on East European Machinery Industries*, No. 43, JPRS 43744, 18 December 1967, 7–21, quote at 14.
36. This was Jawa motorcycle, an internationally successful maker, whose bikes were exported to over 100 countries in the 1950s. Jawa relocated to a new facility at Týnec nad Sázavou, about 30 miles south of Prague, where it continues to make high-quality motorcycles. See https://en.wikipedia.org/wiki/Jawa_Moto.
37. Zdeněk Škoda, "Problems in Semi-Conductor Production in Czechoslovakia," *Hospodárske noviny* (Economic News) 20 January 1967, in *Translations on East European Electronic and Precision Equipment Industries*, No. 7, JPRS 40172, 8 March 1967, 1–15, quotes from 2 & 4. It should be understood that CKD was making electronic devices for machine controls and servos, not computer components.

38. Ibid., 4.
39. Idem.
40. Ibid., 8.
41. Ibid., 12. CKD Semiconductors continues manufacturing in Prague, since 2006 as a subsidiary of the Zurich-headquartered ABB Group, focused on robotics and automation technology. See https://library.e.abb.com/public/625b58f7a00325e3c12578780031 4d1e/CZSEM_General%20Presentation_FINALv5_Nov13.pdf.
42. Harry Trend, "The Return to Economic 'Normalcy' in Czechoslovakia, Part II," RFE File HU OSA 300-8-3, 22 June 1970, 5–8.
43. "100,000 Ursus Tractors," *Mechanizacja Rolnictwa* (Mechanized Agriculture), 16–31 January 1964, in *Translations on East European Agriculture, Forestry, and Food Industries*, No. 247, JPRS 24439, 1 May 1964. Note that declining production costs could not lead to declining product prices.
44. "Ursus Tractors and Farm Motors," *Mechanizacja Rolnictwa* (Mechanized Agriculture), 16–31 March 1966, in *Translations on East European Agriculture, Forestry, and Food Industries*, No. 441, 19 May 1966; "Planned Ursus Tractor Production Reported," Ibid., 15–31 July 1968, in *TEE-EIA*, No. 30, JPRS 46348, 4 September 1968; "Lack of Spare Parts is Synonymous with Building Socialism in Poland," RFE File HU OSA 300-8-3-44343, 30 January 1961. Spare parts were a universal trouble spot. For Polish railways, see "What are the Reasons for the Spare Parts Shortage?" *Sygnaly* (Signals) 25 October 1964, in *Translations on East European Service Industries*, No. 325, JPRS 27759, 9 December 1964.
45. Andrzej Pluciński, Discussion of the Problem of Spare Parts is Suspended," *Mechanizacja Rolnictwa* (Mechanized Agriculture), 1–15 March 1965, in *Translations on East European Agriculture, Forestry, and Food Industries*, No. 359, JPRS 29946, 5 May 1965; E. Fafara, "Spare Parts Shortage Hampers Farm Machine Repair," *Zielony Sztandar* (Green Banner), 11 March 1969, in *TEE-EIA*, No. 109, JPRS 47825 10 April 1969. Green Banner is a journal associated with rural issues, started by the Peasant Party in 1931. This, of course, is a core issue Janos Kornai identified in *The Economies of Shortage* (Amsterdam: North Holland, 1980).
46. Jakub Kopeć, "Recent Reorganization of Ursus Plant," *Przegląd Techniczny* (Technical Review) 9 March 1969, TEE-EIA, No. 110, 14 April 1969.

47. Ibid.
48. See Philip Scranton and Patrick Fridenson, *Reimagining Business History* (Baltimore, MD: The Johns Hopkins University Press, 2013).

References

"100,000 Ursus Tractors," *Mechanizacja Rolnictwa* (Mechanized Agriculture), 16–31 January 1964, in *Translations on East European Agriculture, Forestry, and Food Industries*, No. 247, JPRS 24439, 1 May 1964.

"Ursus Tractors and Farm Motors," *Mechanizacja Rolnictwa* (Mechanized Agriculture), 16–31 March 1966, in *Translations on East European Agriculture, Forestry, and Food Industries*, No. 441, 19 May 1966.

Alton, Thad Paul, *Polish Postwar Economy* (New York: Columbia UP, 1955).

BC-N, "Certain Problems in Business Administration," *Pénzügyi szemle* (*Financial Review*), 1 (January 1967): 1–14, in *TEOMEE*, No. 675, 28 March 1967, JPRS # 40438.

Berend, Ivan, "Hungary: 40 Years of Communism," *Társadalmi Szemle* (Social Review) February 1989, 5, JPRS East Europe (JPRS-EER-89-083), 26 July 1989.

Bomberger, William and Gail Makinen, "The Hungarian Hyperinflation and Stabilization of 1945–46, *Journal of Political Economy*, 91 (1983): 801–824.

Buruma, Ian, *Year Zero: A History of 1945* (New York: Penguin, 2013).

Csikos-Nagy, Bela, "The 'Two Model' Theory of the Socialist Economy," *Közgazdasági Szemle*, 11 (September 1964), in *Translations on Economic Organization and Management in Eastern Europe* [TEOMEE], No. 393, JPRS 27070, 20 October 1964, 20–22.

Fafara, E., "Spare Parts Shortage Hampers Farm Machine Repair," *Zielony Sztandar* (Green Banner), 11 March 1969, in *TEE-EIA*, No. 109, JPRS 47825 10 April 1969.

Feiwel, George, *New Economic Patterns in Czechoslovakia: Impact of Growth, Planning and the Market* (New York: Praeger, 1968).

Fusi, Ernő, "The Czechoslovak Machine Industry Through Hungarian Eyes," *Gépgyártás-Technológia* 7 (1967), No 10, 469–78, in *Translations on East European Machinery Industries*, No. 43, JPRS 43744, 18 December 1967, 7–21.

Germuska, Pal, *Unified Military Industries of the Soviet Bloc* (Lanham, MD: Lexington, 2015).

Hanson, Philip, *Advertising and Socialism* (White Plains, NY: IASP, 1974).
Jakubowski, Zenon, "Mismanagement, Theft at Industrial Sites," *Życie Gospodarcze* (Economic Life), 23 February 1969, in TEE-EIA, No. 107, JPRS 47766, 2 April 1969.
Kenney, Padraic, *Building Poland, Workers and Communists, 1945–1950* (Ithaca: Cornell University Press, 1997).
Kierski, Bolesław and Jerzy Withkowski, "Technical Problems in Construction—1959," *Inwestycje i Budownictwo* (Investment and Construction), February 1959, in SETEE, JRPS 1814-N, 31 July 1959.
Kopeć, Jakub, "Recent Reorganization of Ursus Plant," *Przegląd Techniczny* (Technical Review) 9 March 1969, TEE-EIA, No. 110, 14 April 1969.
Kornai, János, *Overcentralization in economic administration: a critical analysis based on experience in Hungarian light industry* (Oxford: Oxford University Press, 1959).
Kornai, János, *The Economies of Shortage* (Amsterdam: North Holland, 1980).
Kraus, K., "Czechoslovak Economic Situation Analyzed," *Życie Gospodarcze* (Economic Life), 19 May 1968, in *Translations on Eastern Europe, Political, Sociological and Military Affairs*, No. 3, JPRS 45745, 20 June 1968.
Lavigne, Marie, *International Political Economy and Socialism* (Cambridge: Cambridge University Press, 1985).
Lewis, Flora, *A Case History of Hope: The Story of Poland's Peaceful Revolutions* (Garden City, NY: Doubleday, 1958).
Los, Maria, ed., *The Second Economy in Marxist States* (London: Macmillan, 1990).
Lowe, Keith, *Savage Continent: Europe in the Aftermath of World War II* (New York: Picador, 2012).
Miartus, Alexander, "Malingerers in Construction Industry Criticized," *Pravda* (Bratislava), 5 July 1969, in TEE-EIA, No. 155, JPRS 48504, 29 July 1969.
Michal, Jan, *Central Planning In Czechoslovakia* (Stanford: Stanford University Press, 1960).
Myant, Martin, *The Czechoslovak Economy, 1948–1988: The Battle for Economic Reform* (Cambridge: Cambridge University Press, 1989).
Nuti, Domenico Mario, "The Contradictions of Socialist Economics: A Marxist Interpretation," *Socialist Register—1979* (London: The Merlin Press, 1979).
Pluciński, Andrzej, Discussion of the Problem of Spare Parts is Suspended," *Mechanizacja Rolnictwa* (Mechanized Agriculture), 1–15 March 1965, in *Translations on East European Agriculture, Forestry, and Food Industries*, No. 359, JPRS 29946, 5 May 1965.

Polacek, Josef, "How to Proceed with Our Advertising," *Podniková organizace* (Enterprise Organization), 20 August 1968, TEE-EIA, No. 46, JPRS 46768, 29 October 1968.

Roubel, Ladislav, "Implementing the New System of Economic Incentives," *Finance a Uver* (Journal of Economics and Finance), November 1958, in *Selected Economic Translations on Eastern Europe* [SETEE], JPRS 1360-N, 16 March 1959.

Scranton, Philip and Patrick Fridenson, *Reimagining Business History* (Baltimore: The Johns Hopkins University Press, 2013).

Selucký, Radoslav, *Czechoslovakia: The Plan That Failed* (London: Thomas Nelson, 1970).

Šik, Ota, *Czechoslovakia: The Bureaucratic Economy* (White Plains, NY: International Arts and Sciences Press, 1972).

Škoda, Zdeněk, "Problems in Semi-Conductor Production in Czechoslovakia," *Hospodárske noviny* (Economic News) 20 January 1967, in *Translations on East European Electronic and Precision Equipment Industries*, No. 7, JPRS 40172, 8 March 1967, 1–15.

Swain, Nigel, Hungary: *The Rise and Fall of Feasible Socialism* (London: Verso, 1992).

Trend, Harry, "The Return to Economic 'Normalcy' in Czechoslovakia, Part II," RFE File HU OSA 300-8-3, 22 June 1970, 5–8.

12

Afterword: The History (and Future History) of Socially Responsible Business

Rod Lohin

This book grew from the conference "From Public Interest to Private Profit: The Changing Political and Social Legitimacy of International Business", held at the Rotman School of Management, University of Toronto on 5–6 May 2016. It was jointly presented by the Centre for the Political Economies of International Commerce (PEIC), University of Kent, and the Business History Group at Rotman, with the involvement of the Canadian Business History Association. The principal sponsor for this conference—one of a series—was the Leverhulme Trust. I had the honour to work with Rotman organizers Joe Martin (Director of the Canadian Business and Financial History Program, Adjunct Professor of Strategy and Executive in Residence) and Christopher Kobrak (Wilson/Currie Chair of Canadian Business and Financial History and a professor of finance at ESCP Europe, Paris). Sadly, we lost Prof. Kobrak prior to the completion of this book, but it

R. Lohin (✉)
Michael Lee-Chin Family Institute for Corporate Citizenship,
Rotman School of Management, University of Toronto, Toronto, Canada
e-mail: RLohin@Rotman.Utoronto.Ca

W.A. Pettigrew and D.C. Smith (eds.), *A History of Socially Responsible Business, c.1600–1950*, Palgrave Studies in the History of Finance,
DOI 10.1007/978-3-319-60146-5_12

hopefully reflects his exceptional scholarship and personal enthusiasm and generosity.

I am the Executive Director of the Michael Lee-Chin Family Institute for Corporate Citizenship at Rotman. We sponsored and supported the organizers of the conference (with particular thanks to the tremendous work of Jennifer Puskar). The Lee-Chin Institute's purpose is to help current and future business leaders integrate sustainability into corporate strategy and practice. We do this by conducting academic and applied research, disseminating it to business leaders, and engaging students in both curricular and extra-curricular activities. Our research spans a range of issues, but tends to focus on corporate sustainability strategy, the emergence of social entrepreneurship, and the role of investment in creating positive social and environmental impact.

> If any one owe a debt for a loan, and a storm prostrates the grain, or the harvest fails, or the grain does not grow for lack of water; in that year he need not give his creditor any grain, he washes his debt-tablet in water and pays no rent for this year.
>
> Code of Hammurabi (First Babylonian Dynasty, about 1750 BCE), translated by Leonard William King, 1910).

However, like most business researchers, we build on a tradition of scholarship that developed fairly recently—arguably with the founding of the Harvard Business School in 1908. This partially explains why academic scholarship has tended to focus on the twentieth century (and now the twenty-first), particularly in the USA, the UK and other developed modern economies. We have fixated on examples in recent and contemporary business and have not fully explored the precedents of the past. For example, most management scholars would point to moments in the last few decades (or perhaps as far back as the 1950s or 1930s) as the point of origin of the debate about the role of business in society. This book shows that this debate is far older. The oldest writings of many cultures around the world, including the Code of Hammurabi quoted above, show that questions about business and society have been around as long as we have been producing and counting.

In this book, we examine the evolving relationship between business and society from 1450 to the mid-1900s with a range of cases. The scholars' work collected here explore an array of places and times involving different players. Nevertheless, the articles share a common theme: the constantly evolving interaction between business and society. The notion of business as we know it today formed over the course of this 500 year period—in political, legal, social, and even moral terms. Roles and expectations have continued to evolve and changed again and again. In this brief afterword, I place the essays in this book into the context of the ongoing work of the Lee-Chin Institute and other organizations interested in the relationships between business and society.

The most prominent early companies in Britain included the chartered trading companies such as the East India Company (EIC), the Hudson's Bay Company (HBC) and the like. Their charters outlined their relationship to the state as well as (in broad terms) their responsibilities to their society. For example, the EIC's charter declared its purpose is "For the Honour of this our Realm of England... for the Benefit of our Navigation, and Advancement of our Trade of Merchandize... for the Benefit of our Common Wealth."

David Chan Smith explores the importance of social networks in the early trading companies from the mid-15th century, in particular, how those networks were leveraged for broader social or charitable purposes. He presents the case of a company created specifically for Setting the Poor French Protestants to Work at Ipswich in the Linen Manufacture, resettling religious refugees in the wake of increasing intolerance in France (leading up to Louis XIV's revocation of the rights of Huguenots in 1685). This enterprise fulfilled a number of purposes: employment for a vulnerable group with unique skills, the potential for profit, the opportunity to build and leverage social connections between the governors, and a business-like approach to charity.

The situation is strikingly reminiscent to us today as we face waves of religious and political refugees and other immigrants. There remain varying opinions about the role that companies can play in employing them and otherwise advocating on their behalf; this example teaches us that there are precedents for doing so.

In their article, William Pettrigrew and Aske Laursen Brock explore the 17th century notion of leadership, in particular, how ensuing EIC Governors interpreted and enacted their office by engaging variously with the Board; the English court; with other trading companies (many of whom shared directors); with their ever-expanding overseas operations; with charities both individually and in cooperation with other companies; and even by leveraging their growing financial power "as state financiers."

The question of leadership remains active among business scholars and academics. However, a clear implication of this article is the degree to which leaders needed to interact with a wide range of societal stakeholders, an issue familiar to contemporary business scholars (notably in the work of R. Edward Freeman and Rotman's own Max Clarkson) and a prominent element of current corporate social responsibility research and practice.

Edmond Smith outlines the degree to which chartered companies in the seventeenth century in many ways had a stronger "social contract" with society than exists today, both in legal terms (specified in their charters) and in terms of social expectations. He states: "social responsibility in a seventeenth century business was far more responsive than initiatives in many companies today". He demonstrates this with reference to the prominent role of merchants and their trade associations (the "livery companies") in society, and in particular focuses on petitions, a mechanism for the EIC's governance to interact with their stakeholders in a fairly accessible and transparent manner. Over the course of the century, EIC leaders discussed and decided on thousands of petitions regarding wages, charity, employment, repatriation of goods and crime, which provide an interesting set of examples of how a company interpreted and enacted their responsibilities. Since that time, petitions have become associated more with political engagement than business. Nevertheless, contemporary companies are increasingly interested not only in research—and practical advice—on how to engage productively with their stakeholders, most notably with investor activists at their annual general meetings, but also in the increasing glare of activist campaigns, media (and social media) attention, boycotts and "buycotts," and other forms of consumer activism.

Mike Wagner specifically explores the changing relationship between the major British chartered companies and the state. He outlines examples of the reciprocal interest between the companies and the state in terms of both profit (revenues) and surety (other benefits). Initially, the state took the view that it should "incur minimal expense and should provide minimal assistance" while still gaining revenue and other benefits. This relationship evolved from sixteenth to the nineteenth centuries—at times, the state enjoyed benefits with little intervention. At other times, the state was forced to act to protect its interests by protecting and supporting companies. Examples include the expansion of the Royal Navy to protect trade from attack (during the ongoing conflicts with France during the eighteenth century), or diplomatic support to build trade opportunities (for the Russia Company in the early eighteenth century), or protective tariffs to fend off foreign competition (helping the Levant Company from French silk imports). He also notes the remarkable powers of the chartered companies, which vastly outstripped even those of the most powerful multinational today. The East India Company operated, he says, as a hybrid "company-state" (to borrow the phrase of Philip Stern). However, despite such power, the chartered trading companies eventually faded, giving way to other types of businesses more focused on specific goods (manufacturing) and services (finance) and agent-based networks.

Bob Wright describes the debate during the early history of the USA about of the objectives of business, the state and the non-profit organizations. "As the sole goal of business corporations became improvement of general welfare by means of private profit, non-profits took up the mantle of public service". This played out in practical, legal and regulatory forms throughout the period, and Wright notes the negative consequences of role confusion. He makes an argument for clarity that would apply equally well to a contemporary debate about the roles of business, government, and non-profits. With the advent of new organizational forms such as community interest companies (CICs) in the UK, BCorps in the USA, and the emergence of so-called social enterprises (which might be private or non-profit or even government organizations), clarity about objectives, roles and expectations are perhaps more difficult than ever.

Emily Buchnea shows the increasing concentration of trade and capital in companies based in New York and Liverpool, initially through agents and then through the development of companies with a clear multinational presence. She also outlines their engagement in some political (and social) issues, notably with their general opposition to the abolition of the slave trade. As well, mirroring another modern trend, she notes their tendency to participate in charity in the social context of their headquarters (such as Liverpool) rather than throughout their international operations.

Janette Rutterford describes the increasing number, diversity, and active engagement of public shareholders in the late nineteenth and early twentieth century UK in what has been called the "democratisation of investors". Shareholders increasingly included members of the middle and working classes. Of particular note was increase of women among shareholders, from "15% by number and 5% by value in the 1870s, rising to over 45% by number and over 33% by value by the 1930s". As well, she profiles the increasingly international nature of their investments given the potential for higher yields (with, of course, increased risk). She also notes the growing distance—literal and figurative—between investors and their investments outside of local markets, including the early movements for ethical investing, for example, relating to mining in South Africa. An unexpected bonus in Rutterford's paper is evidence of a number of "philanthropic investments" into libraries, schools, university colleges and, most notably, Model Dwelling Companies, which built and managed homes for workers and offered a competitive rate of return. This nineteenth-century financial innovation ultimately built tens of thousands of housing units in London and elsewhere in the UK. It is a remarkable early example of what has only recently been termed "impact investing": investments that generate returns and tangible social or environmental impact.

Jon Mackay gives a fascinating account of an unusual region of Canada in the early twentieth century. Berlin, Ontario (renamed Kitchener during World War I) flourished with few business, financial, or board ties to Canada's largest cities (Montreal and Toronto, among others). He attributes this to "a sense of common cause" given the region's concentration of German immigrants and its self-sufficiency and relative independence from other Canadian centres of political and business influence. He also notes their remarkable engagement in civic politics (sometimes to the point of cronyism and tax breaks for each other). Most relevantly, Mackay discusses the role of local business leaders in the development of shared community assets, notably public utilities for gas, water, and sanitation. While these were of interest to the business community, they benefitted the general population too—and provided value beyond economic growth and prosperity. This remains a familiar issue today, particularly in the rising expectation of companies to provide tangible benefits for communities when being granted rights to access local natural resources or markets.

Leslie Hannah explores the role of firms, the state and regulators in securities markets in Europe, the USA and Japan prior to World War I. He shows that each of these markets developed in their own ways but that the dominance of the largest market (in the UK) is not easily explainable by the "varieties of capital" argument. Again, the role of local networks and the trust that they generated may have played a role. Jason Russell, Andrew Smith, and Kevin D. Tennent provide an overview of the influence of US State Department official Adolf Berle in the stance of the USA in the Caribbean, and particularly relating to the role of business, in the 1930 to the 1960s. Previously, US intervention in the Caribbean had sometimes been direct and even brutal, and some have argued for the benefit of US companies (an interesting parallel to the case of UK support for its trade in earlier centuries noted above). Berle, a key advisor to Franklin Roosevelt, advocated for a policy of non-interventionism called the Good Neighbor doctrine. He encouraged "US corporations to take the interests of a wide range of stakeholders, including works and communities, into account when making strategy". This position is a remarkable echo of more recent ideas on corporate responsibility, in particular, stakeholder theory, with the additional layer of the role of the state in encouraging and supporting good behaviour.

Philip Scranton explores Central European companies during the Soviet era. In a system notionally devoted to ensuring political (and social) outcomes rather than profit, centralized plans and their execution rarely aligned. He outlines a range of performance among companies (from high to low) and some strange, unanticipated outcomes. He also describes a number of ways managers adapted, by gaming the system or even simply breaking the rules, such as the case of a semiconductor developer who simply worked around the plans—and succeeded. Nevertheless, he asserts that there may be more to learn from the experiences of companies in such a system than we might expect.

In sum, the articles in this book provide compelling evidence that the debate about business and society is nothing new. Some themes arise again and again across these places and periods, including the changing role of the state; the shifting nature, objectives, and expectations of business; implications for global and local markets; and the critical part played by social networks. Clearly, these are issues that we—as scholars, business leaders and critics, regulators, and members of our societies—continue to wrestle with today. This book has already contributed to the work of the Lee-Chin Institute, providing us with historical precedents on contemporary subjects we are researching. The behaviour of chartered companies, "interlock" or connections between boards, the shifting role of the state, the social role of livery companies (trade associations), and the financial innovation of model dwelling companies are just a few examples that relate directly to our present research program. Where once the chartered trading companies were given rights to explore new geographies with the promise of new goods, businesses today are laying claim to new domains—social and environmental. This holds great promise and a range of potential risks for businesses and our societies. It also presents us with rich ground for future research to better inform future action. Perhaps we will see this debate reprised in future management scholarship on the social responsibility of business in the twenty-first century—by then, hopefully better informed by what has come before.

Index

A

B

W.A. Pettigrew and D.C. Smith (eds.), *A History of Socially Responsible Business, c.1600–1950*, Palgrave Studies in the History of Finance,
DOI 10.1007/978-3-319-60146-5

The manufacturer's authorised representative in the EU is Springer Nature Customer Service Centre GmbH, Europaplatz 3, 69115 Heidelberg, Germany. If you have any concerns regarding our products, please contact ProductSafety@springernature.com

Printed and bound by CPI Group (UK) Ltd, Croydon, CR0 4YY
30/09/2026
02225216-0013